CULTURE SHOCK!

A Globe-Trotter's Guide

W9-DCE-611

Frederick Fisher

TIMES BOOKS INTERNATIONAL
Singapore • Kuala Lumpur

Illustrations by TRIGG

© 1995 Times Editions Pte Ltd

This book is published by
Times Books International,
an imprint of Times Editions Pte Ltd
Times Centre, 1 New Industrial Road
Singapore 1953

Times Subang
Lot 46, Subang Hi-Tech Industrial Park
Batu Tiga, 40000 Shah Alam
Selangor Darul Ehsan, Malaysia

All rights reserved. No part of this publication may be
reproduced, stored in a retrieval system, or transmitted,
in any form or by any means, electronic, mechanical,
photocopying, recording or otherwise, without the prior
permission of the copyright owner.

Printed in Singapore

ISBN 981 204 520 1

To 'Honey', Eileen, for a life together
of near fifty years that grows sweeter
with each new day of travel adventure

CONTENTS

INTRODUCTION

The *Culture Shock!* version of travel information bridges the gap between mere vacations, and adventures in far away places with strange sounding names. Fears, tremors and trepidations are relieved with common-sense knowledge of how to calm those apprehensions. *The Traveller's Guide* answers hundreds of questions about incidental but important facts. The answers cover how to travel extensively with peace of mind, to enjoy the most remarkable places, to have fun, and to relish the thrill of a high mountain or mighty sea.

How to be an Independent Traveller... tour packages... communications far from home... beat the shocking cost systems and save money... travel agent – friend or foe? These are some of the subjects discussed.

Novice travellers, and people who have undergone a dramatic change or tragedy in their lives, are encouraged to reinvigorate their lifestyles in ways they have probably not thought of. Would-be adventurers who have always bought – or had sold to them – package tours, because it was easier and cheaper that way: they can learn how much more fascinating it is to travel independently, unrestricted by a precise itinerary.

Culture Shock! A Traveller's Guide is for average adults, desiring to have fun and yet be comfortable, in interesting 'dreamabout' countries, within their time and budget limits.

Travel adventure is a rare spice for your life.

Chapter One

AND THE DREAMS COME TRUE

The essence is adventure, new horizons, cleansing of the mind, resurgence of health and interest, taste of different foods and regaining the vigour and curiosity of youth. Couples have seen their children grow up and leave home – creating a need to change lifestyle, live it up, see the world. Singles of 40 or over 70, retired, bored, or perhaps lonely from the loss of a mate, are looking for adventure before age cripples the interest – and the body. Rocking-chair blues are setting in as you see friends and neighbours vegetating. Younger folk, like Richard Bach's Jonathan Livingston Seagull, want to try their wings in the stratosphere of the outer world; or are entranced by *Lost Horizon*'s picture of a Shangri-la somewhere out there.

THE ITCH

Never mind why travel and adventure are on your mind; what you feel is like an itch – or like the breeze tickling your nose with an irresistible aroma. Now thoughts of *Where?* and *How?* begin. In the early 20th century, a trip to another continent was made by booking a passage on an ocean liner, crossing countries by train and touring by car in local areas. It was common to allow months or a year for such adventures. Now travellers can be on the other side of the world in under 24 hours from the time they rise in the morning. And at once they enter the ambience of 'Gay Paree', begin to climb the Himalayas in Nepal, take a boat down the Yangtze in China, or land in Singapore and – like that city's Lion – consider where the next thrill will come from.

For novices, whose only experience is a package tour to an island resort, the possibilities parade in the mind's eye. There are the eight wonders of the world to see. Notable destinations are continually being described in travel articles and documentary films. An esoteric whim may move you to the top of the world to climb the hundreds of steps of the Potala Palace in Lhasa, Tibet. Thoughts of plain fun-and-games tempt you to travel to a quiet relaxing beach resort and enjoy the sun and the water, good food and service. Perhaps you like it and want to stay a month. All right. With a deft change in plans, you may learn to snorkel, scuba dive or play tennis. Or more ambitious thoughts may lead you to trek over mild trails or seriously venture through jungles and up mountains. But perhaps what you most want is to soak yourself in a culture on the other side of the world.

SCRATCHING THE ITCH

Inexperienced and shy travellers need a jump-start to help them decide. Maybe the weather or chance dictates, or the mood hits at a decade-marking birthday. There comes a time when one's way of life changes; perhaps on retirement, or on being left at home without children – or a spouse. Single people become aware they are bored with their surroundings and need a new look at life from a different perspective. They hate to admit having been so absorbed in making a living – surviving if you like – that serious travelling is an unknown experience. There is a need for adventurous souls to discover the world outside and find out what is at the end of the Yellow Brick Road, 'Somewhere over the Rainbow'.

Prospective travellers dream and read about exotic, unpronounceable places. Literature abounds with tempting fictional history. Author-historian Michener tantalises with his versions of how our modern civilisation came about in Hawaii or Jerusalem. Wilbur Smith weaves endless tales of the African continent. Local newspapers produce travel columns about strange lands like Myanmar and Nepal. Colleen McCullough re-creates ancient Rome through the personalities of Julius Caesar and Gallus. These fictional history tales induce dreams of travelling to the far points of our world, where so many cultures and wonders of nature beckon.

Now is the time. Read on, let fantasy become dreams and dreams reality. The saying 'This is the first day of the rest of your life' has never been more to the point.

THE AGE OF MODERN TRAVEL

We of this expiring 20th century have a unique advantage over our parents. The age of air travel makes it possible for us to get to any land of our dreams within a day. The magic carpets of major airlines vie with each other to transport us in varying levels of comfort. A fast train in Japan moves at more than a hundred miles an hour. Slow trains in China cover thousands of miles of history. Modern cruise ships sail the mighty oceans and exotic rivers. Buses and mini vans take groups of travellers and their baggage from place to place in modest comfort with informative guides. Commercial coach lines crisscross territories in reasonable independent comfort. Hire cars are available in almost every part of the world, if you choose to drive yourself. Bicycles can be had for more esoteric touring – or for getting about the locality. Trekkers with or without much endurance or expertise can climb the lower slopes of a mountain or traverse the jungle on marked trails, and find hostels interspersing the routes.

DREAMS CAN COME TRUE

We are talking about you now – the average person turned adventurer, in almost any class of physical condition and most degrees of economic status.

Your dreams are your qualifications, and these can now become realities. Seek out the source of Darjeeling tea by visiting the delightful town of Darjeeling in the mountains of India. Fantasise yourself into the sensual life of Shah Jahan, who built the Taj Mahal in honour of the beloved wife who died in childbirth. Fly to New Delhi, and then on to Agra to stay for a day and a night in the aura of that ancient love. You can, with relative ease, gaze at the pyramids of Egypt or walk on the Great Wall of China – marvels of man's ingenuity.

After the first adrenalin-fed ambitious and adventurous odysseys, the novelty gives way to a wish to enjoy countries or scenes more thoroughly until they are impressed in the memory. Relaxed inveterate travellers, after sating themselves with the wonders of the world and its historic monuments, may elect to rent an apartment in a small town in Switzerland and explore Europe from that base. Britain, France, Italy and the Scandinavian countries are short flights away. For lovers of the sea and beaches, modest locales like the resort-worlds of Port Douglas or Broome, in Australia, offer pleasant havens in which to hunker down and go barefoot. Do for yourself, as the Aussies say, on the barbee, while enjoying an 80-mile beach and the offshore fascinations of the Great Barrier Reef. Go topless with a weird-looking open

Volkswagen Safari, and wander the hinterland at your leisure. Think of the pleasure of staying a month here and a month there, with a freedom so well deserved after a lifetime of work.

Some folk become specialist-venue junkies, desiring to enjoy music in each of the world's opera houses; or to play on every famous golf course, beginning with St Andrews in Scotland; or to follow a gourmet trail; or to stay in the ten best hotels around the globe. Travel magazines tout the newest and finest with hyped up wide-angle-lens pictures enhancing the tiniest of sandy cays. Robin Leach's television travel series depicts the aura of the exclusive, glamorous oases where the Rich and Famous play.

The urge to climb mountains fades as we get older, and we make no apologies for wanting to stay longer in one favourite place. There is comfort in unpacking in a commodious chalet at a pleasant beach resort. Ignore the ins and outs of tour groups, relax under the sun-screening palm trees on expansive lawns. Romantically walk the tidal beach far out into the bay at sunset's low tide. Your chalet becomes a vacation home away from home, complete with maid service and amenities. A choice of restaurants teases your palate and nightclubs your itch to dance. Side trips are enjoyed to a nearby city for shopping, or to the local waterfall or an offshore island to picnic for the day.

Dreams can come true, needing only desire and motivation. Make lists of the myriad wonders of the world to see, odd corners to visit and adventures to undertake – amounting, perhaps, to everything you want to do before your Final Journey. Let *Culture Shock! A Traveller's Guide* tell you how and when.

TIME

An important shock to your travel-culture is the discovery that you have always considered a holiday adventure in terms of two or three weeks. This is ingrained in our society by the international system of workers' holidays. After one year of employment, one week's paid vacation is allowed. Two years bring two weeks. Sometimes long-term employees are offered three weeks of paid holiday. Thus evolved a pattern of two-week trips plus sporting bonuses of stolen weekend days and free national holidays.

Now comes the transition, the real shocker. Suddenly you discover, between jobs, on retirement or with sabbatical leave, that you have months available. A habit of limited travel still brackets the mind. But the children are grown and have flown the nest, pets can be boarded and gardens farmed out. Surprisingly, there is even some extra money in the bank account because daily expenses are less when you are not working. All the old excuses for short-term travel are out of the window. The blinds are lifted, the door is open. Travel time now expands to six weeks or six months.

Excuses

The next thing that happens is the popping up of excuses. "I don't like to live out of a suitcase." "Daughter Sarah's graduation is right in the middle of the time we want to go." Fears, Tremors and Trepidations arise anew (see Chapter Three).

Fear not, excuse not; examine the negatives reasonably, or list them on a tablet. Compare, as with a ledger sheet of assets and liabilities, another column of all the fun places you might visit. List the anticipated joy of not having to cook, make beds or wash windows for a long time. If you find that delectable Shangri-la – a beach resort with everything you've ever wanted at a price you can afford – stay a month. Papa can snorkel to his heart's content, Mama can shop until the credit card overruns. Think about that – and all the negatives won't even tilt the balance sheet.

Beginning

The essence of re-orienting the mind to the new lifestyle is dreaming and planning. We suggest you buy a good world map and hang it near the breakfast table, for a visible and practical start. Begin the adventure. Stick pins in the places you have heard about and find interesting. Make research phone calls, visit the bookshop – and bring home the first instalment of your new life.

The scope is different; start thinking in terms of multiple trips for many years in the future. They take shape on a map, as destinations evolve into a pattern. Singapore, Malaysia and Thailand are together. Fiji and Tahiti are just two of the widely spread Pacific Islands. Hawaii, Alaska and the other United States are in a line if you live in Australia. India, Bhutan and Nepal could make a joint adventure, with Sri Lanka perhaps thrown in if the strife on that fascinating island subsides. Indonesia is a long 'L' from Sumatra to Irian Jaya. China looks like several trips. Make your world list in order of the probable importance of each region to your future plans.

What Time Will Mean

You allow a week for your first destination, and then new thoughts occur. "It would be nice to stay a month on the Costa Azul in Spain while we're on the continent. Portugal is so close, it would be a shame if we didn't drive along the coast and stay in Estoril for a week. Then there is the rest of the Mediterranean, including Corsica and Elba of Napoleonic fame. In Italy, with a day's drive between, are Florence, Rome and Naples. Across the channel is Palermo, in Sicily."

The discussion leads into the matter of how long you can be away. Between two average people this can take many nights of pillow talk and weeks of trying to decide. For extended adventures, no matter what the destination, there is never enough time once you get under way.

For those still committed to a career, on a mere three weeks holiday from work, be sure to stretch the time off to include a TGIF Friday, and talk the boss into your return on a Tuesday morning. That adds up to 24 days instead of 21 – neatly offsetting the days lost in international transit. Don't waste one of the extra days to pack your bags or close up the house. Plan ahead and do all the chores beforehand.

Book your travel tickets to leave as early as possible and return as late as possible.

In the following year, build up credits, angle for a four-week holiday by compromising on something during the year. Think aerobically, add a week each year by hook or crook. Soon you will be retired – and will already have accustomed yourself to lengthy travel.

TIMING

Proper timing is the key to successful and enjoyable travelling. Weather factors have to be included in the formula as you really won't like Melbourne in the southern winter of June, July and August. Beijing in January is miserable unless you love to wear thermal underwear and sniffle for days on end. Still in the work force? Dependent on scheduled holidays? Then pick the best destination for now and keep the others on a back burner for when you do have the privilege of selecting your own time.

School holidays or the annual *haj* of thousands to Mecca can suddenly upset a requested reservation on Malaysian Airlines. China's trade fairs in Guangzhou fill up Hong Kong's hotels in the spring and autumn. You don't want to be caught in the typhoon season in the middle of a Pacific cruise. These facts crop up when you begin talking to airlines and other travel people during the planning stage. Mark down any and all information regarding the right or wrong time to go, for future reference.

The space flight planners call this system 'Windows'. A window is the preferred or necessary space of time to take off and land. Create your own windows, when you list a destination, by marking a calendar with the ideal and near ideal times to travel there. Keep accumulating data to add to your Timing Calendar. A travel article may suggest the perfect occasion to visit because of a Mardi Gras festival or the Dragon Boat races or Chinese New Year. Once addicted to the thrill of travelling, you will have many years in which to visit the desired adventure spot at the optimum time.

Social Events

Family dates have to be added to your travel calendar as far in advance as possible: a wedding in the offing, a favourite niece's graduation from college or the bash of the year at your best friend's home. Knowledge in advance will allow you to work around those dates or find some way to weasel out of the obligation for a greater purpose. Somehow, being selfish in these matters has never been a negative word. It translates into personal happiness and comparing the joy of a wonderful adventure to missing a party.

Illness

Accidents and illness create the worst difficulties. If you or your travelling companion suddenly develop a problem that needs immediate attention, then you will have to change your plans. The serious illness of a close friend or relative poses a more awkward problem. Analyse it. You may conclude that, having made your splendid gesture, you could not do much that was helpful – and that all parties would be happier on your return if you went ahead with your plans.

Chapter Two

RETIRED AND ADVENTUROUS

TRIGG.

Newly-retired people are all for travel, now that they have the time. The desire is there; and then well-meaning friends and relatives become scoffers. They say, "You've worked hard all your life. You can rest now. Stay at home, enjoy your retirement and save your money for old age." The naysayers point out every article in the papers about plane crashes in China, tourists being killed in Miami, and Harrods being bombed in London – and then ask, "What if the arthritis acts up again?"

No cause for debate: it is your life and your decision. Enjoy the new chapter in your story. Do what you want. I equate the unfriendly word 'retire' with a new facet to my career – almost a reincarnation. You may choose to sit in your rocking chair, become an orchid fancier, grow peanuts ... *or* don wings and fly off into the wild blue yonder. Statistics show that occasional flying is a thousand times safer than driving to work every day; and a few days of beach and warm sun do wonders for aches and pains. Read the next chapter to rationalise all the worries. Look forward to the fun and adventure you'll have. Tell the friends and relatives, nicely, to buzz off and let you enjoy the rest of your life.

DO IT NOW

Retirement is a shifting-of-gears life change. Some indeed retire into the proverbial rocking chair, sit on the porch, worry about money and wait for the end to come. Others have planned and dreamed of what they want to do in the future. If you have travelled, on limited two- or three-week annual vacations, now is the moment to take a real trip. For the first time in your life, you can leave home for one or two months. Ask a neighbour to water the plants and feed the pets.

Explore the land of your dreams leisurely at its best time of year, avoiding bad weather and the edges of high seasons. Escape the crowds and miss the stiffer prices. Climb your desired mountain slowly, in physical comfort. Take a train across a continent, stopping en route for interesting interludes. Allow months, not weeks, to see in a relaxed manner the places you have dreamt about. Stay for a week at each ancient site instead of the meaningless one-night stand. Laze around in 'Deluxe Economy' comfort at an inexpensive resort, not worrying about cooking meals, doing the laundry or making the beds. It's nice being waited on for a few weeks, while indulging in the new sport of extended travelling. A fresh plateau of your life beckons, promising adventure and tingling the spine, like joining a Star Trek craft into outer space.

You will return home to the wonderment of family and friends, looking years younger, tanned, trim, dressed in bright

19

new clothes and minus facial pouches. Then show off the photos or video tapes of your escapades and adventures, and brag about planning an even longer trip next year.

The average person has spent 20 years maturing and 40 years working – and now deserves another 40-plus to travel around and have fun before counting as old.

NEW OUTLOOK

A residual advantage of travelling at this change-of-life stage is the proverbial new outlook, fresh start attitude. Yes, wandering does broaden the mind, extend horizons, re-generate ambitions and relax inhibitions. New careers are often conceived when visiting other parts of the world, meeting new people, developing ideas that may have lain dormant for many years.

Societies, nations, vehicles, and environments are changing rapidly. Closeted in our own country and home, we have hardly noticed these stepless changes. The age of electronics is a sleeping giant ready to engulf our lives. Easy air travel extends into the tiniest island and remotest area. When you get out of your own cocoon and travel with other people – adventurers like yourself – the exchange of ideas stimulates. You receive a stimulus to look around, obtain a new outlook and do something about it.

New horizons can take in another career. Assuming you have a retirement income, and some savings for security, you are not now trying to make a fortune. A fresh idea will be good in itself; and all the better if it adds to your income and so increases your opportunities to indulge in leisure and pleasure.

An interest in boats may develop into a cruise and holiday-fishing business in a beautiful harbour city, and produce enough revenue in three or four months of high-season work to pay for the upkeep of a magnificent sailing yacht – which will serve your own pleasure for the rest of the year. A cottage acquired by the seashore or up in a mountain resort area can be turned into a

Bed-and-Breakfast place, and provide a modest additional income. Your local newspaper may be keen to pay for personal interest travel articles: camera, laptop computer and baby-printer are all the equipment needed. Artistic hobbies, like painting or collecting antiques, develop into travel incentives and then perhaps begin to generate income. Such are the opportunities discovered while adventuring around the world.

DISAGREEMENT

Face it, put the facts on the table, and consider the downside. Two people, married happily for a quarter of a century, are suddenly confronted with freedom of choice – and become incompatible. Perhaps the man had a long and physically or mentally tiring career and wants to play golf or tennis, grow radishes and relax with cronies and a beer every afternoon. The lady of the house is looking forward to getting out of her home-workplace and away from the chores of making beds, cooking, washing windows and raising grandchildren.

Impasse? Travel can solve the problem if looked at in the light of a compromise solution. We suggest alternative ideas and open minds. A woman can travel safely and enjoyably in a small group or paired with a like-minded friend (see Chapters Nine and Ten), leaving the husband in his sedentary comfort with a fridge full of frozen dinners. It's not the end of their marriage or relationship, merely a new-found freedom to be enjoyed by both parties. In modern society there is every reason to change the tactics to prolong the game.

Another problem arises when the partners agree to travel but have different destinations in mind. Compromise is then in order. Let both lay their cards on the table and play the hand. Take a notebook and, under separate thee and me headings, list each other's ace destination idea – followed by a second and a third choice. Under each listed area, enter the probable activities there. A pattern develops, inevitably. Beach and sunshine pop up regularly on both sides of the page. Golf courses and fishing opportunities appear along with jungle treks and the viewing of ancient temples. Of 20 potential activities, 16 turn up under both parties' names. Not so bad, eh? Twenty per cent can easily be sorted out by common sense and compromise.

Plan several itineraries: the current trip and the next few years' adventures.

She will give up her night markets and beach hotel for two weeks, in favour of his yachting expedition. He will surrender golf in view of her yearning to see Nepal, where there are no golf courses. Surprisingly, human nature makes the yield better than expected. For many people find themselves disagreeing almost for the sake of doing so, in a spirit of stubborn refusal to see the other person's viewpoint. There is an old remedy: think of *how* you can do it and not *why* you can't.

Sometimes it dawns on people who have lived together all their adult lives that a couple of weeks away from each other will not cause disaster. It's a welcome change to have a wee bit of independence, a break from routine. He can go one way to play golf, take lunch and beer with the boys and maybe try a poker game. The telly can show sports broadcasts and rebroadcasts until he falls asleep in the chair. She at last can see the pyramids of Egypt, cruise down the Nile and shop in legendary bazaars. When the twain meet after a fortnight or two, romance buds anew, following the axiom 'Absence makes the heart grow fonder'.

"Go West young man," Horace Greely, an early American publisher and journalist, once advised. His meaning was: explore a new world, create a fresh start, opportunity is ripe on the tree. 'West' is symbolic of a new direction, and 'young' of your age as you see it. Thus explained, the advice is as good today as it was a hundred years ago.

The chapters that follow define in detail how to interpret that advice, and so create a wonderful future of travelling. Each section encourages you to research and find out for yourself the best way to enjoy your new lifestyle. Your destinations and activities change; hotels grow stale and you replace them with newer or older ones. The tourist's atlas is continually changing. Travel agents, airlines, modes of transport are in flux. We suggest how to travel confidently in our preferred status of 'Deluxe Economy' – which we define as the best possible accommodation at the best possible price.

It is never too late for adventure and pleasure.

Chapter Three

FEARS, TREMORS AND TREPIDATIONS

Fear of the unknown is typical amongst inexperienced travellers, especially in the case of a first adventure or a woman touring alone. Anticipated language barriers – plus world news of plane crashes, crime and riots – top the list. Next come worries about hygiene and personal health. Then concern about being away from family and home for extended periods. These mental aberrations eventually soften with experience, when the traveller realizes that the world of adventure is comfortable and home doesn't change much in a month or two.

Regardless of age, most people's ingrained desire for adventure is in conflict with those trepidations. The potential stalemate can be overcome by taking things slowly at first. Buy a well-run tour package that takes care of the travel details (see *Travel Agent – Friend or Foe?* in Chapter Four). You can then enjoy sightseeing, shopping, people and fellow-travellers without worrying about minor questions. On the next trip, spread the wings and soar out on your own – after which you will believe that luggage does not get lost most of the time, schedules are reasonably kept to, hotels honour reservations, and menus are in English.

My wife will often worry about enough hot water for her morning shower, while I fret over getting an extension of a few days at a particularly wonderful resort hotel we have stumbled upon. All such worries are trivial compared with the overall enjoyment of being in another part of the world, free as a seagull in the land of your dreams.

Well, here you are. The plane took off and landed on time, with your luggage. Hotel Super-Duper had your reservation and ensconced you in a beautiful room overlooking the ocean. A bowl of local fruit and a bottle of champagne are on the table, welcoming you to the Seventh Heaven. On the desk are brochures and information about all the remarkable things you can see and do during your stay. Thrills tingle the spine in anticipation of weeks of pleasure, adventure, interesting foods and the luxury of being taken care of.

FEAR OF FLYING

Fear of flying is the most common trembler, even for those who have flown dozens of times. The persistent and gruesome television coverage of some light plane that crashed in Timbuktu, with no survivors, dominates the evening news. The media choose to feature air crashes around the world as important information, even when they involve only a few people in a remote region on a small airline unfamiliar to the home audience. Not so with the half-dozen tragedies that occur on the roads of a nearby city every day, unless they involve a famous person.

Major air crashes, of the kind that happen once or twice a year, are heavily covered worldwide; the pictures made of them are shown again and again from the library of films.

Strangely (perhaps), only airline advertisements report the many safe flights completed each day to and from the destinations you have in mind. Can you imagine the news value of this television announcement: "Today's 72 flights between Tokyo and Los Angeles or Singapore all arrived safely and within time schedules. Some 21,600 passengers boarded, ate 64,200 meals and watched 144 films. Moreover, all 63,200 pieces of luggage were restored to their owners on arrival."? No news value there, but think about it.

The huge Boeing 747 you are booked on has a legendary record as the safest large plane in history. The chances of being injured or killed within a short radius of your own home, as against air travel of any kind, are millions to one. Think of every hour in the air as being safe from a local traffic accident.

Serious airsickness, though seldom occurring in large aircraft, is alleviated by doctor-advised pills or patches behind the ear. If you haven't been troubled by the problem before, don't worry about it.

First timers, and those who travel a lot and still tremble when strapped into the seat, can assuage their fear. Arrive early at the airport: at least an hour before the required time. This saves check-in queuing and gives time to have a post-check-in snack and watch the hundreds of other passengers, in peace. Actually being amid the excitement of other air travellers – business people, families, old or handicapped folk, and youthful backpackers – gives the assurance of safety in numbers. Major airports can be pleasant places with shops and restaurants, plus views of the landing field and aircraft taxiing. Arrive early, then, relax in a pub or cafeteria, change some money into the next country's currency. A good adventure novel or an intriguing crossword puzzle makes a soothing balm for pre-flight nerves.

Relieve yourself – ready or not – before boarding the plane. That means before entering your flight's numbered departure 'lounge'. To get up, stand in a queue when airborne, and use the tiny closet they call a toilet, is an unpleasant chore for a worried flyer. You feel and actually are safer, buckled into your armchair until you have landed – except for moments of leg-stretching.

In flight, read, watch the film, do another crossword puzzle or listen to programmes with the headphones. Snack but don't eat heavily. Liquor is far more upsetting than soothing in the oxygenated atmosphere at 35,000 feet above sea level. The odds are that the plane will bounce several times during a long flight. This is caused by air pockets.

Keep the seatbelt fastened at all times when you are seated. Never mind what the loudspeaker says about freedom to move about the cabin, or what your seat neighbour does.

Noises of the aircraft on take-off and landing are disturbing if you are not familiar with them. Engines are revved up or down, changing the drone of in-flight operation. Wheels and other gadgets go clunk and thump. This is the crew operating the machinery, not engines falling off. Settle down; the noises are comforting, evidence of someone flying the craft that is taking you to your destination.

Put the seat back, remove your shoes, tuck a pillow under your head or in the middle of your back; wrap a blanket round you if the air-conditioning is cold, taking special care of your feet. Try to nap, or daydream about the first full day after your arrival. It makes the time pass quickly and lulls the heartbeat.

Self-hypnosis
A family doctor once counselled me on how to take short naps when working hard or under stress. It is very effective on any long journey. Close your eyes and imagine yourself in peaceful familiar surroundings, whether of beach, woodland or neigh-bourhood. 'Walk' slowly, creating a mental image – in great

detail – with each step. Picture precisely each recollection: bush, tree, stone, bird, animal, wind-movement or wave. It's a form of self-hypnosis, and it can work wonders. Practise the identical scene, whether flying, trying to nap, or going to sleep at night. Repetition of this one sequence is the key to the door of relief. Even a brief ten minutes will slow down the whole spinning world to the speed of your idling body. You wake surprisingly refreshed. When it coincides with your normal time for sleeping, this 'hypnosis' should induce a longer natural sleep.

If you are reading a book, then to fall asleep, re-read the same page over and over and over again until the words blur and the eyes naturally close. Most passengers plug in the earphones to watch the movies or let music lull them. We prefer to dissociate ourselves from the in-house entertainment while flying. Trying to concentrate on the film while the person in front keeps moving is disconcerting. Speaker sound is notoriously poor in aircraft. If you enjoy good music while travelling, bring your own small battery-powered tape- or disc-player(s) with private earphones; you will enjoy them much more.

All of this advice is to transmute the fear of flying into a modicum of comfort by lulling the senses until the plane lands. In Chapter Eight, *Transport by Air* covers the jet-lag problem and endorses the theory of special exercises en route.

WHAT IF I FALL ILL OR HAVE AN ACCIDENT?

Chapters Thirteen and Fourteen give details, with specific instances and answers. For the moment we shall deal with the general question of illness while away, or being treated by an unknown foreign doctor. Your own physician knows your health background, your idiosyncrasies and what to do when your stomach acts up. "But what does this doctor know about me?"

I respond to such fears, and to the rest of the "what if's?" in the same lump-in-your-throat category, with a simplified answer: "Do the same as you would at home". If you get a cold, slurp bowls of noodle soup, drink pots of tea with lemon and honey, and sweat it out with bed rest. If the cold persists or serious dysentery takes over, see a local doctor; one is always, repeat always, available wherever you go. Except at the top of Mount Everest or the source of the Amazon, I assure you that medical facilities are accessible. The local doctor knows what flu bug is around, and the proper antibiotic to counteract it. If you are a real worrier there is nothing more I can say to help. A fatalist merely adds "*Que sera, sera*; whatever will be, will be."

Worrier or not, don't forget to read Chapters Thirteen and Fourteen, or to pack the information therein described, which would put a local doctor in touch with your records and – if need be – with your physician.

The key to calm and sensible travel is – be prepared.

PHOBIAS

A phobia is defined as an unnatural fear or great dislike of something. Mine is of heights, like climbing a ladder or getting into those glass elevators. My wife fears deep water and gets jumpy about strange noises. Phobias are easier to handle in a crowd – safety in numbers again. If it's hygiene and the table-ware, be continental and boldly wipe the things down with your napkin, and damn the snide look from the waiter. Consider any serious phobias before you leave, in the planning process.

People have phobias about small aeroplanes or boats, for example; and out of the way retreats often entail a feeder-airline and an hour-long boat ride in a choppy sea. Investigate, try to contact a traveller who has been there recently, to find out the exact situation. Selling agents obviously play down or ignore such problems.

A sudden confrontation with your worst fears can be very unsettling in a foreign country.

Pre-planning and information will ease matters. Admittedly, the problems will not disappear. But facing the anxiety head on, and discussing it with a friend or probable travelling companion, goes a long way towards alleviating the phobia or putting it in proper proportion.

Personal Experience
In New Zealand, we bought an air-travel pass with Mount Cook Airlines to tour the North and South Islands. Turbulent air and small planes are phobias of my wife and myself. The sales staff assured us that all flights in New Zealand were short and September weather was mild. After one particularly upsetting half-hour flight from Auckland to the Bay of Islands, we gave up the pass (no refund) and rented a car. The pilot couldn't understand our discomfort, as he flew the route every day with no qualms. Another facet of this experience was our discovery of the right way to travel in New Zealand. Except for moving between the two islands, driving is much the better way to enjoy the land of milk and honey and the Kiwi. Roads are pleasant, distances short and the small towns delightful.

☞ **Lesson Learned**
Don't stick with a bad situation because of pre-purchased tickets. Your comfort is more important.

TRUST THYSELF
Distrust is a phobia, often the result of a bad experience at some point in life. Money is one of the most vexing problems. It is human nature to wonder: "What if I lose my wallet? What if the taxi driver is going to take us the long way round and overcharge? What will happen if I don't tip the waiter or the porter? Am I getting the right exchange rate for my money?" My daugh-

ter used to ask, when we were travelling in Mexico, "How much is this in real money Dad?" Foreign currency often affects one as if it were Monopoly money.

Another common phobia is distrust that human beings will do what they said they would. Your guide arranged to pick you up at 9:00 and it's already 9:02 and she isn't there yet. "Oh my God, we'll miss the plane." Or, in the "what if?" category, suppose our neighbour forgets to water the petunias?

Control your fears as best you can by taking the specific precautions described elsewhere in this book. A general Pollyanna answer is "Relax and don't let paranoia overcome the enjoyment of your trip." Yes, there are people out to get the unwary; and an honest mistake can be made by others in charge of your adventure. A porter or waiter may sneer at you behind your back for not leaving a tip when they gave poor service. So what? Guides cause themselves all kinds of trouble by being too late, often after arranging an extra-early pick-up time for their own convenience.

The point is: trust thyself to know what to do in these instances. Worry, if you must, about anything and everything. But not to distraction. Life is too short.

LEAVING HOME

Three- to six-week adventures are not too severe on the routines of home life. Two- to six-month holidays require more sophisticated plans. The first time is the hardest because you remember all the things you should have done after you leave: too late. A written list prepared far in advance is important. Feed the pets... water the plants... cancel the monthly whist game or group social... clean out the perishables from the refrigerator... pay actual and foreseeable bills... stop the newspaper, the milk...

Leave Word of Where You'll Be

Travel agents provide the itinerary for the services you book.

Ask them to add addresses plus fax and telephone numbers of the major hotels, etc., as contact and mailing points for relations, friends and firms. Independent travellers will prepare their own itinerary and have these numbers readily available. Leave a copy of your intended route, dates and addresses with the family member or neighbour who will handle your mail and forward important items to you. Except in very remote places, airmail will take from four to ten days; it is generally reliable. For urgent matters, such international forwarders as Federal Express, United Parcel Service and DHL guarantee express delivery within 48 to 72 hours.

If you change your plans midway, do pass this news back.

FINANCIAL AFFAIRS

Your friendly bank manager can arrange to pay current bills, mortgages, utilities and even your credit card balance, from your basic account. Overdraft arrangements are quite common for known clients. It's best to leave the bank a copy of your itinerary, in case someone wants to deposit a million dollars in your account and the manager needs your investment advice.

WOOFers (Well Off Over Forties) with sophisticated financial affairs obviously have to make suitable arrangements with stockbrokers, bankers and legal advisors. It is common to give a *limited power of attorney* to a close member of the family, to be used in case of communication problems. Let me emphasise: with modern telephone, fax and air parcel facilities, most emergencies are easily handled.

Worry not, fret not, tremble not – enjoy, instead!

Chapter Four

CHOOSING A TOUR PACKAGE

You start your exciting adventure plans by choosing a tour package or selecting an independent holiday. The process absorbs your interest as you seek the location of your dreams. Finding the proper package of transport, accommodation and associated services is of key importance. The financial expenditure is significant; the time you invest may be more so – if it is the only chance to get away during a whole year. Anticipation of the fun and exhilaration of adventure is part of the planning process. A wonderful experience creates a desire to repeat it again and again. Poor episodes can easily sour the mood for extensive travelling in the future, reflected in the expression "what do I need this trouble for?"

It is very important therefore that you do considerable research into the intended travel area; carefully select the travel bureau and agent; compare tours and understand the system.

TOUR RESEARCH

Regardless of any friendship or supposed obligation to an agent, research the travel area yourself before visiting a professional. All major destination countries have friendly overseas offices, anxious to attract you, the money-spending tourist. Look in the *Yellow Pages* under 'Tourist information' or, if unsuccessful, try the listings under 'Embassies, Consulates and Legations'. People living far from an urban centre can call a city's Directory Enquiry service. A few coins spent on telephone calls at the outset can save you hundreds later. The immediate reward is the packets of data and brochures they cheerfully send you, to answer questions and stir up further excitement.

The first travel agency on record was established by Thomas Cook of Leicester in England in 1841, with branches gradually added around the world; now they are one of many chains. Personal visits and telephone enquiries to major international travel bureaux such as Thomas Cook and American Express will yield specific tour pamphlets before you feel committed to one of them. This first flood of information is only the beginning.

Travel Guides and Reference Books

Investigate bookshops that specialise in or at least have a full shelf of travel guides and related material such as the *Culture Shock!* series. A friendly salesperson can consult a computer for other items, available on order. You may have to look further than your favourite shopping complex. Do some more *Yellow Pages* phone reference work to find at least two shops that sound intelligent and knowledgeable. Those of us who left school many years ago tend to forget the public libraries. For instance, if you want to find out more about the animal kingdom in Africa to back up your intended tour, take time to research the library.

When you have acquired some background, the next step is to gather price information and draw up a budget. Consult the travel bureau that seems most considerate and relevant to your needs. If you detect misinformation or a pushy clod, take your leave and go to another.

TRAVEL AGENT – FRIEND OR FOE?

Of paramount importance is finding the right travel bureau and within it a specific agent or employee to *negotiate* your plans. A travel agency and its representatives are brokers between you and the providers of accommodation and long- and short-haul transport. The representative's job is to arrange a travel programme between you and those various vendors. The agent is supposedly representing your best interests, but commission agents earn their fees from their bookings. In legal parlance, this is a conflict of interest; therefore suspect the worst until proven otherwise.

Conscientious travel bureaux know that their best interests are served if you return year after year as a valued client. A positive approach sets the stage and states your new-found interest in travel. "We are looking for a good agency to help us arrange all of our travelling in the future. Please tell me something about your firm." The attitude and response will be very revealing, since the question is unexpected. If the response is "Where do you want to go?", you are not off to a good start. While most clients approach the firm with a request for specific travel arrangements, you are interested in the quality and methods of the agency first.

☛ **Travel Tip**
On entering a large travel office for the first time, look around, watch the traffic, observe the senior agents (often in glassed-in offices). It is usually possible to spot the

supervisors giving directions to others. Pick up a name from a desk plate, or ask directly for the senior agent. Offer a business card, introduce yourself as someone (perhaps important) seeking a reliable agency to arrange not just this one trip but years of future travel. You (as it happens) *are* important. Even if you are passed on to another agent, you are sure to get VIP attention instead of the treatment accorded to one who casually drops in.

The whole task is by no means easy. Singapore's *Yellow Pages*, for instance, prints 14 pages of Travel Bureaux. Phoenix, Arizona, has 10 pages, with over a hundred firms to choose from. You may have a friend or a friend's friend in the travel business. Take care; that happy chance could result in a spoiled trip and an ex-friend.

Choose wisely. Look for proficiency, demeanour and evidence of experience. The travel bureau and its staff are important factors in your proposed adventures. You desire the best value for your money and they are selling merchandise on a commission; different objectives. Even the celebrated Thomas Cook's and American Express employ personnel called agents to sell their products. The more the agents sell, the more their income: a lurking threat to your long-awaited adventure. Until you begin negotiating with them, you have no real idea of their expertise or their priorities.

The ideal agency is owner-operated, experienced in the business for many years, and the widely-travelled proprietor is there to supervise or handle your programme personally.

"Travel is cheaper by the dozen and with double occupancy." So saith the travel industry. Not always true – but 'Independent Travel' is the subject of the next chapter. Here we shall note the agencies' hype, and examine the where and how of the tour package. Asking the right questions to find out whether your agent is a friend or a foe is the key to enjoyable travelling.

Bypass the holiday weekend ads and look for the extended

tours. The standard brochure dealing with your destination will list package tours from 7 to 21 days. A map indicates the various routes from the arrival city. Your own research has given you an overview of the country, its size and principal points of interest.

Board Terms
American Plan means with a substantial breakfast. Half Board includes dinner also. Full Board means all meals included. If there is nowhere else to dine, you will probably get the best deal with Full Board. Lunch is immaterial but dinner at night is important. If there are alternative restaurants, it's more fun to go out on your own and enjoy a variety of dinners – and even snack lunches. Always ask how much it would be without the meals, to give you a comparison. If you are a coffee-and-toast breakfast eater, the morning buffet/American Breakfast is a waste of money. *A la carte* gives you full freedom of choice: whether to take (and pay for) the meal – and which items to take.

QUESTIONS TO TEST AGENCY'S COMPETENCE
- When were you last there?
- Is the flight non-stop, and how long does it take?
- What is the time change on arrival?
- If there is a choice of hotels, what are the differences?
- What do 'Superior', 'Deluxe' and 'Standard' mean there?
- Is the hotel in town or out of the way?
- Tell me about the side trips.
- Should we book them after arrival?
- Does the journey there involve small planes or boats?
- How much unescorted shopping time will we have?
- What is the weather like during the selected period?
- Specify the meals included.
- How many people will be on the same tour with us?
- Where do others in the group come from?
- Are children allowed?

- If coastal, is there beach swimming, snorkeling, etc.?
- When are the shark and stinger seasons?
- Is special equipment or clothing suggested?

Where and when to book side trips or day excursions is the sting question. Avaricious agents want to add everything they can to the itinerary. It is much better to arrange local tours on site.

☛ **Travel Tip**
Be efficient. Bring a note pad. Write the questions out beforehand; record the answers, and everything else including your opinion of the tour offered and the agent. Otherwise, after visiting three different travel bureaux, it would be impossible to remember which offered what.

Take the questions and answers seriously. A five-star hotel may be overwhelmed with problems, dulling its gleam. A reliable 50- or 100-room hotel in London will be far more personal than a 500-room one, if you are booked in for a week or more. Daily scenic side trips can be miserable if you are going to spend most of each day on a smelly bus or in a small boat in rough waters. Your previously-purchased guide book lists hotels and miscellaneous information (see Chapter Six). If you get answers that appear to contradict the guide book, ask specific questions such as "Why the Baywatch Hotel instead of the more important and newer Seaside Sheraton?" Package deals often have direct tie-ins with bargain based units, for the convenience and advantage of the packager; these units do not always give you your best value.

Shopping and Free Time
These are particularly important. Some tours are timed for the bus to stop for 15 minutes, and then the whistle blows to get back on board. Others are geared to prolong a tawdry shopping

opportunity beyond reason. The most desirable is an afternoon at leisure to browse through a market (or temple-cum-market) without guides or timetable.

Full Board
Having meals included (other than breakfast) is a deterrent to exploring unusual local restaurants. This becomes significant if you stay for more than a day or two in one place. The group gathers at breakfast and dinner every day of the trip because it is included, meaning you have already paid for it. But think: you have travelled thousands of miles to be here, investing a great deal of money in order to see, taste and have fun in a famous city or a picturesque town; and your guide book lists a particularly fine seafood restaurant on the wharf. Throw away your dinner coupon, separate from the travel group, get a taxi and take off by yourselves. This is the spirit of adventure travel, and it will leave in your memory the better taste.

Comments on Some of the Other Questions
Weather is unpredictable at best, but the general highs and lows for each month are available. Ask, even if you already know the answer, to see if the agent is alert. Major newspapers carry daily world-wide weather reports, but you have to monitor them for some time if you want useful information.

What companions to expect in your travel party? A mixed nationality group is very interesting to some travellers, but in-hibiting to others. Small children can be discomfiting to tourists looking for a change from such company.

Many beach resorts have magnificent ocean-front locations, but are impossible for swimming because of tides, rocks, sharks, unhealthy waters, or seasonally dangerous jellyfish. It is very disappointing to go there for sun, sea and surf, and find that only the sun can be enjoyed, or that you have arrived in the monsoon season when it is only the rain that you can soak in. Ask specifically, if you enjoy ocean swimming, about the beach and water conditions.

If, when you get there, you see a buoyed rope marking a safe-to-swim area, make sure that the net which the rope is supposed to support is there too.

The important key to the 'Friend or foe' question is: "Was the agent listening to and answering queries, or avoiding them?" An experienced agent is well travelled and well read. "I will find out for you, madam" is better than an intelligent guess.

COMPARING TOURS

To compare the value of various tours offered, use this simple formula. Count the days lost in transit from home to hotel, and from one area to another. Subtract these lost days from the total and divide the balance into the full cost of the trip. For example, a 21-day tour loses one day from home to Africa, and another on the return. The itinerary details one day each in changing from South Africa to Zimbabwe, thence to Kenya and so on, leaving 16 days available to enjoy the holiday areas of the tour. The value of your trip is 16, not 21, days.

Compare costs of different tours offered, by dividing the residual days into the package total. Well-planned tours have a minimum amount of wasted travel time. When you see the hype of 'Eight days and seven nights in tropical splendour', translate that as a six-day vacation. 'Three days and two nights' boils down to "How many hours will we actually have on the beach?"

Flight schedules are important. When you get to talking about the precise details of a particular tour, pay attention to the time of each flight and whether there is any choice. Late after-noon and evening flight departures incur a miserable lost day of waiting around with little to do. When there is no choice, at least you know what you are in for and you will look for something interesting to fill the void when you get there. Good planning will include places to see, or a local side trip to fill the lost hours.

Bad planning says queue up and wait. If there is no choice on your part, being forewarned gives the opportunity to select another tour.

☛ Travel Tip

Do read the contract, including the small print, thoroughly *before signing*. The if's, and's and but's are explicit about what contractual rights you have. Changes are never allowed, so don't accept an assurance from an aggressive agent that some item can be disregarded. Cancellation-and-money-back rules are the most important feature.

THE SYSTEM

The commercial system of the travel industry creates a wholesaler, and a retail travel bureau. Larger companies (wholesalers) organise specific tours, arrange for reduced fees from guaranteed space on airlines and hotels, and add a profit. Smaller agencies (retailers) pre-book packages to sell on. Though there is seldom a price difference, try to use the source (the wholesaler). Book with them direct because they will have the best up-to-date information. Originators are usually identified in the package pamphlet as (for example) Singapore Airlines' subsidiary Silk Air or the Qantas subsidiary, Jetabout. The originator will also have on hand plans for the next selling season, which may be when you are planning to go.

In summary, you wouldn't pay hundreds for new furnishings in the parlour without shopping around. Take time, use the same good judgement, and shop for your travel adventure. Find the right Friend and you won't have to fend off a Foe.

☛ Personal Experience

From New Delhi, the capital of India, our pre-booked itinerary included the customary day trip to Agra to visit the famous Taj Mahal. It consisted of three hours in an almost broken down bus, a miserable two-hour lunch stop, one hour at the Taj Mahal, another at the Red Fort, and three hours back in the heat, smog and slow traffic. In a 10-hour trip, our actual viewing time was no more than two hours. Caution: in any foreign country, don't take the travel desk's word for anything. Ask some returning tourists who took the same trip the previous day. Angry and disappointed customers are quick and frank to point out the problems and alternatives. In this case, we would have been better off discarding the pre-booked and prepaid side trip. We discovered later that the ideal way to see Agra is to fly in and stay overnight in the excellent hotel there. We could thus have enjoyed the Taj Mahal at and before sunset and sunrise for hours, when most of the tour buses and their thousands of people were absent.

Chapter Five

THE INDEPENDENT TRAVELLER

Dawn is breaking, your plane lands at the faraway airport. Chattering excitement builds around you as everyone gathers carry-on baggage. You leave the aircraft to arrive in a new world on the first day of your travel adventure. Formalities are completed in quick order and the luggage appears on the luggage belt. Thrilling sensations take over as the taxi takes you to the impressive five-star hotel in a strange city, or an arranged guide whisks you away to a thatched hut on a remote beach. Arrival is romantic, fascinating, pregnant with rare experiences and adventures. And... you did it all yourself.

There is an extra thrill in independent travelling. It is the freedom of arriving at your destination without a prescribed schedule. Time is your own. Tour the city, take a side trip, go shopping, stay a week or more if you like. Weary, now, from time and nervous energy expended during the last 24 hours of travelling? Take a day to relax by the pool, read the local brochures, talk to the nice people next to you about where they have been. No rush. You have plenty of time to soothe the frazzled nerves and plan the rest of your odyssey.

The Beginning
As with Chapter Four's tour package, decide on your area of destination: the Orient, Europe, Africa, the Middle East, South or North America, or the South Pacific. Follow the previous research suggestions: they are even more important if you are going to travel independently. Enquire for the air travel packages of the airlines which fly direct to your chosen destination. For really long air journeys, ask about Circle Pacific (CP) or Around the World Tickets (AWT) and similar combinations. When no airline covers your intended adventure completely, you might strike a bargain with two carriers in combination to give an all-encompassing fare. Increasingly, airlines are forming alliances which make bargains of this kind before you ask.

There is advanced planning to be done, with research; special air fares and travel packages will be discovered. This can be part of the fun for those adventurous self-confident souls who value the distinction of travelling at their own pace.

NON-SCHEDULED INDEPENDENCE
One method of Independent Travel is to select the destination area; and book the there-and-back flight and the first hotel, only. Then, free as air, you proceed to arrange the scenic strategy from day to day as the weather, local information and your moods suggest. To some, this may sound alarming or inhibiting. Others revel in the adventure of such freedom.

Time is important. On a three-day weekend you are more

likely to hunker down in the city, hotel or beach resort, see the local sights and relax by the pool. But on a three-week holiday, there is time enough to explore the country, take side trips to neighbouring scenic wonders, tour the museums or explode in a frenzy of shopping. Three months permit extensive travel over a range of territory – or a starfish pattern of intensive exploration from a central base.

The travel industry records a growing trend of people wanting to go out and see the world, *sans* schedule, and doing without greeters and meeters, precise reservations or pre-planned side tours. Until recently, this was mainly the device of back-packers, young independents travelling thither and yon for five dollars a day, hitching rides and bunking in hostels. At the other extreme were the wealthy, travelling first class, with entourage, by air and sea, being met by stretch limousines, and ending the day in presidential suites.

Now we, the great middle class and middle aged (from 40 to 80 plus), rise up to find our place in the sun, literally. The travel industry secretly calls us WOOFers (Well Off Old Folk, or Well Off Over Forties) in their plans to sell us tours. We, the Independent Woofers, have sufficient funds to travel in comfort and we shun the structured programme. I term the style of travel we like, Deluxe Economy.

We have a yen to rent a vehicle and self-drive around a country, stop at a series of interesting inns or stay put to visit the caves and waterfalls in some fascinating locale. Domestic airlines in most countries can shuffle us around with little advance notice. Many top-rated holiday areas have space available at the last minute, though not during a school holiday or when a convention has booked them solid for the weekend. However, we, the independent flexible travellers, can go on a Tuesday or a Thursday, take the morning or afternoon plane and adapt easily to whatever occurs.

The strategy is to book the overseas journey and the first

hotel. Research has netted a thick file of what to do and where to go during our stay. We have a tentative list of the more important scenic wonders and of nearby areas to visit; and we have practised how to say hello, goodbye and thank you in the local vernacular.

To set up our non-scheduled independent non-programme, we may elect to book the reservations directly or have a knowledgeable travel agency do the booking. I make the airline reservations myself, but ask the agency to write the tickets as a matter of convenience. Hotels are booked direct.

SCHEDULED INDEPENDENTS

On the other hand there is something to be said for a well-planned adventure, fitting into a general timetable with advance reservations. This is necessary when the allotted time is short. It is comforting to know that a guide or hotel car will meet you on arrival at each air- or seaport with satisfying efficiency. You have a pre-arranged schedule, theatre tickets have been booked, the side trip to the nearby mountain resort is confirmed – and will begin in the morning.

Travel agents advise that this will cost more than a packaged group tour. In practice they build a package with prices quoted by airline, hotel for room and meals, plus greeting and guide services. The total price, including commission/profit margin, is take-it-or-leave-it for the buyer. Our experience is that the hotel will give a discount (which may or may not be the same as the agent's commission), that only meals chosen and eaten have to be paid for, and that a guide is often not needed. There is seldom much difference between a package and the total of our independent costs.

You gain a great advantage in booking as an independent traveller. You don't have to share your dining tables, climb on and off buses in unison, queue to be counted for the morning adventure, or follow the lady waving the red parasol who is talking in an accent that you can't understand. For special tours you have the privacy of your own vehicle, and a personal guide with enough flexibility to make your day very special.

A combination of the scheduled dependent and a non-scheduled independent tour is an acceptable compromise. Arrange the overall travel in detail, with arrival accommodation confirmed in each of the places you intend to visit. Leave local tours and side trips to be booked on arrival. This will give you freedom in timing, to suit the weather and your inclinations. A one-day bus tour around the city with other travellers is endurable and cheap as a rule, and it is easy to organise day by day. It avoids being tied down by prepaid trips on your itinerary that don't seem very interesting now that you are about to go on them. Weather can interrupt; or a local dragon race festival be more appetising than the scheduled visit to the tombs of ancient rulers.

Most veteran Independents will pre-book favoured adventures on short holidays, and use the non-scheduled system for lengthy travel. Experience instils confidence. In our own case, we book the air travel and hotel ourselves by direct fax.

Accumulate all your information, ideas and tentative plans; then seek out a knowledgeable travel agency and let them make the basic reservations for you. *Avoid prepayment of hotels and side trips as much as possible.* The travel agent, in order to safeguard commissions, wants you to prepay everything. Insist that the hotel reservations be made with credit card guarantee, instead of paying in advance. The rub is, if you want to change after you arrive, prepaid vouchers are difficult to get refunds on. The agency's problem is that some hotels are awkward to collect commissions from after you have used their facilities. If the agent insists on payment in advance, then telephone until you find a company that will handle the trip the way you want; or make direct reservations yourself. Most foreign hotels will accept your written or faxed booking, and will be delighted to send a car to meet you at the airport for a nominal charge.

RESEARCH AND PLANNING

As we suggested in Chapter Four, you will want to do intensive research on your intended destinations. Bookshops and the libraries are useful, in particular the reference department. Don't be shy about asking the airlines' major sales arms for specific travel package information. You can use this to guide you, and adopt sections into your own final plans. Consulates or (better) Tourist Departments of foreign nations you plan to see, in or around your (nearest) city, will welcome visits. The advantage is their personnel are often natives of the country or have travelled extensively there. You can develop rapport and receive information with a more human touch than is available from a book.

The secret of Independent Travel is shockingly simple. Except as noted in the previous section, *do not make accommodation or local tour plans until you arrive.* Local travel offices and domestic airlines offer a host of one- to 21-day side trips at economical prices, easily purchased after arrival at any major destination.

Overseas Fly-and-Drive Plans

These usually offer special rates for a vehicle on arrival, and you may find it convenient to start then – especially if the car is delivered to your hotel. The United States, certain Asian countries, Australia and New Zealand are among many places where you will do well with only general advance plans, plus the first hotel – and a car in which to drive yourself at whim.

You can easily start a month in the United States by hiring a vehicle, in advance or on arrival, which you drive away and onto the extensive superhighway network. Inexpensive roadside motels are everywhere, as are meals at the tremendous variety of fast-food and cosy cafes. Disneyland requires no prior reservation, and the side roads off the main highways are well marked. Driving from north to south or coast to coast is simple; you can drop the rented car in almost any major city, and fly back to your departure point.

All of this can be done without pre-vacation bookings. While on the road, telephone ahead from one resting place to another, if you are concerned about an especially busy area. Road maps, travel guides and accommodation listings are readily available. Yes, you may find your first choice of a bed for the night fully booked, but rarely for more than a day or two (tour group or holiday weekend). Alter your plans on impulse, stay longer where you are or find a route round the problem area. Families can rent mini vans or motor-homes, giving a choice between camping grounds, motels or hotels proper – as the mood and pocketbook prompt.

SPECIAL AIR TRAVEL PACKAGES

A Circle Pacific (CP) ticket takes you around the Pacific Rim via any or all of the vast number of sea-cum-airports of the United States, Southeast Asia, Australia, New Zealand, Fiji and Hawaii. The price was US$2,500 per person in 1994, Economy, using selected pairs of airlines. They normally allow six months from gate to gate. You may stop at any destination, in a progressive circle, that one or other airline uses. Four stopovers are included. You pay US$50 more for each extra get-off-and-see

port-of-call. Around the World Tickets (AWT) are proportion-
ately more costly; they can involve a maximum of three airlines.
The criterion is to proceed always in a single direction, whether
easterly or westerly.

We start with CP and AWT information, as these provide
the best value for Independent Travellers who have the time and
enterprise to travel halfway or completely around the globe, but
who prefer a minimum of advance planning. Ask the airlines
concerned for the latest information; and then you can book the
tickets yourself, or ask your friendly travel agent to do the ticket
writing.

Circular route air tickets are the simplest mode of independent travel when you have the time and the wish for such a long
journey. Otherwise, round-trip fares to and from an explicit
destination are best – in the form of Fly or Fly-and-Drive packages sold by the airlines or their travel-agent subsidiaries.

A CP ticket can include a choice of the following: Los Angeles, San Francisco, Tokyo, Osaka, Beijing, Shanghai, Seoul,
Taipei, Hong Kong, Bangkok, Kuala Lumpur, Singapore, Jakarta, Darwin, Perth, Adelaide, Melbourne, Sydney, Brisbane,
Townsville, Cairns, Auckland, Christchurch, Nadi and Honolulu. Participating airlines have variants of the circular pattern.
They include Qantas, Japan, Singapore, United, Cathay Pacific,
British, Northwest, and New Zealand. Most of these also combine for AWT tickets as well.

The plan is flexible enough to allow you to change flight
dates during the trip, if space is available. Fares are payable 14
days before departure. An itinerary change en route costs an
extra US$100, for the service and the trouble of re-writing.
There is no charge for changing a flight date. Frequent-flier
mileage may have mounted up, but bear in mind that the 'freebie
flight coupons' can be used only for round-trip fares on a single
airline. Thus you cannot accumulate mileage towards a free
Circle Pacific ticket; but check for overlapping frequent-flier

plans. For instance, Qantas mileage accumulates on the American Airlines' 'Advantage' system. Many major airlines have combined their frequent-flier privileges with friendly non-competing lines.

Entry to the CP circuit is available at any of the Pacific Rim airports; AWT from those in Europe as well. Begin by seeking the advice of a convenient participating local airline on either of these marvellous all-encompassing travel systems.

SELF-BOOKING THE AIR TICKET

You are ready. Dates are firm. Destinations and general time limits for each stopover have been agreed. With a calendar, note pad and your information handy, telephone the airline of your first flight. The staff are patient; they work with computers. Take it stop by stop as it is logged on, making your own notes of the flight number, arrival and departure times, and day of the week as well as the date. One major reason for self-booking is that you can make adjustments to dates as you go along, if that is what flight schedules suggest. If you work through an agent, such branching possibilities are likely to be disregarded. On the involved CP and AWT routes, it can be complicated. Do's and don'ts follow:

- "What days do you fly?"
- Where you can, choose the morning departure.
- Use Saturday or Sunday travel dates for uniformity.
- Fully booked? "What is available, plus or minus a day?"
- Book the second best, with the first choice wait-listed/on stand-by.
- "Is this a non-stop flight?"
- "What day or time is there a non-stop?"
- "Is an aircraft or terminal change involved?"
- "How many flying hours between stops?"
- "Is there seat selection? I need leg room."
- "Window seat(s), please."

- "My frequent flier numbers are…"
- "Cancellation and reconfirmation dates?"
- "Ticket purchase deadline?"
- "Please read back what we have agreed."
- "Log number?"
- "Please send a printout by fax or mail."

All right, you are booked, preferably as far in advance as you could plan. Don't worry about changes. You can alter any part of the plan before the ticket purchase deadline. Dates are easily changed en route without charge, subject to seat availability. *Airlines will require you to reconfirm every 30 days until you pay for the ticket.*

Your dates of flying, in the case of extended travel, are easy to change. If you find a better flight – non-stop or with a more convenient departure time – on Tuesday instead of Sunday, take it. Midnight departures are murderous and there is always a chance of confusion over a 12:10 a.m. departure time, as to which the day is. Losing or gaining days over the International Date Line can be confusing when making hotel reservations.

Going from international to domestic terminals – or even from one end of a mammoth airport to another – for aircraft changes, can cause major problems. Your flight may arrive late, you may have to pick up your luggage, or go twice through immigration procedures, meanwhile getting a jitney to the other terminal. The stress level mounts through frustration over finding a luggage cart, and slow queue lines; and you are tired and irritable from the long flight. So leave reasonable time between flights, and ask specifically whether luggage forwarding is handled by the airlines. If it is the same airline it will usually oblige. Boarding a connecting carrier of a different line normally requires you to transfer your luggage.

☛ **Travel Tip**
When reconfirming flights, if you have an airline change *en route*, make sure the initial airline also reconfirms your connecting flight. You have to ask them; they won't do it ordinarily. Connecting flights are often domestic or feeder airlines not hooked up to major computer programs and with no way of knowing of your arrival.

Actually buying the ticket is easy. Your credit card number is sufficient, whether for a telephone purchase or a visit to the nearest sales office. Local travel agents will be delighted to write the ticket for you; they get a commission even though they do no other work. All they need is the log number (see 'Do's and don'ts' above). Be sure to use an agency which writes the ticket on the premises, and verify all the dates and flight numbers with your own information before you leave the office. A lively or aggressive agent will try to sell you additional services. If they book your hotel, you will have to prepay (see below). Let the buyer beware.

Enrol in frequent-flier clubs when you book your air ticket. Sometimes there is a small fee involved, more often it is free. Even though you may never acquire sufficient credits to get a freebie, there are usually some accommodation and car rental discount privileges.

SELF-BOOKING THE HOTEL

Hotels and resorts love to get direct bookings. They save 15–20% on agency commissions. Fax, telephone and address numbers are easily available for major destinations. Give them the date, arrival time, flight information and credit card number with expiry date. Confirmation commits you to a minimum of one night, though this may be cancelled 48 hours before arrival. Take care about the early morning arrival, which may not be on the day you expect. If 12:10 a.m. Thursday is the arrival time, they will have to hold the room for you on Wednesday night.

Unless you have stayed there before, room styles and location descriptions will mean little to you. 'Deluxe' probably means ordinary; 'Superior', the next level; then the luxury suites. Request Superior, with the bed style you prefer and the best rate available. For example: "Superior, king size, mid-level, non-smoking floor, and a business rate would be much appreciated." The business or commercial rate is a discount offered by most hotels. If you are not in business, create one like 'Fisher Travel Partners'. Many hotels will give you an upgrade or a breakfast coupon instead of a discount, if that is their policy. Whatever advantages you can get are welcome. Don't be shy; you won't embarrass the Reservations Manager.

☛ **Travel Tip**

Ask the name of the person you are talking to. You will refer to this name and its owner's position when you next speak or write to the hotel. Ask them to spell it for you, to make sure you have it right, if you confirm by telephone. On arrival (if not earlier), obtain the names of the General Manager and the Reservations Manager, and include them in your file for the next visit.

Reservations or other requests made to the hotel direct usually put you on a VIP list for extra courtesies on arrival. A personal thank-you letter to the Manager and Staff on leaving is more welcome than filling in the good service form in your room. With modern computer systems, most hotels keep a record of your visit, room style, special services required and your credit card number. When making a reservation for a later visit, always advise them you have been there before.

Many hotel chains have individual club membership systems identifying you as a frequent user. If there is no charge, go ahead and fill out the application. The advantages seem superfluous at first glance, but the major plus is recognition. With a membership card you get reservation preference, often an upgrade and sometimes an extra bowl of fruit and champagne in the room.

Using international reservation numbers is not the same as making a direct reservation. The local international 800 or 008 number connects you with a reservation system operated by the central headquarters of the chain. The hotel actually pays a commission to that exchange, as it does to a travel agent, though with a modified percentage. Contact the hotel direct by phone, fax or letter in order to negotiate a better price.

Most hotel systems – like Shangri-La, Sheraton or Hilton – are hotel management companies. The hotel may be owned by the government, by a private operator or by a consortium hiring the services of the international chain. This gives the owner professional expertise for building and operating the unit, and access to the reservation computer program.

To summarise: treat the system as a fun game. Negotiate prices with a sense of humour and patience. Whatever you save is money in your pocket, allowing you pleasure in another facet of the trip. Make friends wherever you are so that when you return, you are known as a repeat guest. In most instances it will make you feel more comfortable; it might add some unexpected perks; and it could save you some currency.

Independence in travelling is the fifth freedom.

Chapter Six

TRAVEL GUIDES AND HOLIDAY READING

Generally books in a distinctive travel guide series such as *Insight*, *Lonely Planet*, *Fielding*, *Birnbaum*, or *Trav'bug* have a limited shelf-life of one to two years. Check the publication dates before buying. Even those updated and issued every year are about two years old on publication. Basic history and maps do not vary much (except in Russia and some of its neighbours). But accommodation and other facilities are variable as to their service, in real terms and in competition between each other. In aggressive resort areas, new hotels and restaurants continually change anyone's selection of the best places. Old favourites may regress as they age, and be supplanted by newer ones with better facilities and service.

Times Editions' *Culture Shock!* series has a longer shelf-life, since cultures change slowly.

SELECTING A GUIDE BOOK

Guide books have their own market aim. For instance *Lonely Planet* is immensely detailed, published largely for the independent back-packer. These books say much about history, travel systems, accommodation (basic and upward) and street by street detail, but little about fun. *Insight Guide* is much lighter, relegating detail to the end, but well endowed with colour photography. The *Trav'bug* series by Suntree Press is relatively new, and as light and fun-directed as its name implies.

Before purchasing, compare treatments of a single feature. If you are a history buff, you may need more than guides offer. But a casual traveller would find overmuch detail boring, useless and too heavy to carry. Tourist-hungry countries battle each other for cash-flow with new hotels and tour packages. China, in the late seventies, was limited to a handful of historic sites and austere accommodation. Now, there is a broad sweep of hundreds of destinations with comfortable hotels and transport.

Guide books are useful at the start. Some history, culture and map-geography will show where your trail might lead. Arts and crafts are of great interest to the shopoholic. Side trips from major centres are included in the better guides.

A travel guide's function is twofold. For the package-tourist it provides overall information in advance, preparing visitors for the character of the country they hope to enjoy. For Independent Travellers, reading is indispensable. Without it they would not discover, still less be able to select from, all that the world has to offer.

ON-THE-SPOT PUBLICATIONS

Of more immediate use are local books or booklets, bought on arrival. But check the publication dates for the most recent.

STUDY TIME

Many of the guides you might buy are in 800 or more pages of smallish print. One method of studying them is to scan the chapter headings, with an eye on the overall map. Pick out sections to read which deal with the area you might be heading for. There may be a time later for the history and lore. Do not try to read a solid guide as if it were a novel. Like an encyclopaedia, it tells more than any one person could want to know about whichever small corner you will be finding your way about.

You could buy two guides covering the same destination: one with the voluminous detail and the other in a lighter mode, impressive more for its photographs than its larger print. Assuming the cost of your adventure is about US$5,000 for a month's trip, then US$100 for background and foreground material is a very small percentage to invest in print.

Read the fine detail of the area in the guide you have selected. It will often point to you a small, exclusive district or feature not found in the regular tour packages. Travel writers feed their egos with happy finds, off the tourist track. They must whisper the secret somewhere in their pages; and other adventurous souls benefit. Our own scoreboard records eight appearances as first-ever guests. The variety is amusing: the Maharajah's newly-opened tourist rooms in the Shiv Niwas Palace at Udaipur in Rajasthan; Qamea Beach Club off Taveuni, Fiji Islands; and the Pantai Primula new project at Besut, north of Kuala Terengganu on the east coast of West Malaysia – to start with.

Guide books are a help to inexperienced travellers, if used intelligently. Read through and mark the pages you will return to. Use a highlighter to emphasise particular items or paragraphs. Before you set out, do the unthinkable: cut useful pages out and leave the heavy tome at home. (Or, if you are fastidious, duplicate the detail you want to take with you.) Guide books are dated, and of little use a year or two later. Think of your edition as you might of a monthly magazine.

SPEAKING THE LOCAL LANGUAGE

The English language is used throughout the world. Nevertheless, if you plan to spend more than a few days in a country, extract the conversation pages of your guide book or buy a Berlitz-style compact dictionary. Learning how to say hello, thank you, goodbye, plus a few food words, will make your visit more pleasant. The effort will be appreciated by your hosts.

Driving in rural areas may cause some consternation if you have a breakdown or an accident, or if you cannot understand a direction sign. A conversation dictionary can be life-saving then. The third and fourth visits to a country call for some involvement in the culture and the social life. Now it will pay to have more than a smattering of the language and more than a tourist's familiarity with streets, customs and manners.

Once you have become enmeshed you may begin (so long as your interest remains after the novelty has gone) to think in terms of a second home – or even, if the host country permits, permanent settlement.

LITERATURE

There are various levels of book reader. You can pass the time by reading Ludlum's or Clancy's latest spine-tingler. Or you may have been drawn by their fiction to visit the settings of Kipling, Conrad, Hemingway, Maugham or Greene. If so, you are more likely to re-read the books on location, than to pass the time. Hotels now have both semi-advertising and regional history books in their rooms. Newspapers and magazines may provide local colour as well as world events. New novels with (for example) Hong Kong as a background have extra resonance if read while you are in the hyper-city. Bookshops in tourist areas always have a section devoted to local literature.

The point is: read more than 'What's doing in the big city today' while you are in the big city. Historical novels written with local characters are popular. Big coffee-table picture books are too expensive and bulky. Look for paperbacks and Penguin reprints. Prices are modest, but a book you will want to keep is worth half a dozen others.

Literature is the key to a door into greater enjoyment of your travel

Chapter Seven

DESTINATIONS – INTRIGUING, AND ANCESTRAL

There are many ways to choose a travel destination. The easiest is to follow the weekly travel sections of your local newspaper, read the weekend ads and let a target pop out at you. Or perhaps your church group sends a flyer about a specially organised trip to the Falkland Islands; or the local Jockey Club proposes a gourmet tour of France. With this kind of lucky chance you will enjoy a nice trip with friends or family.

Dedicated, innovative, adventurous travellers, eager to see places that have captured their imagination, will do it differently. You may have an overriding urge to photograph every temple and palace; or you may need to climb the highest mountains or sail the longest rivers.

Japan intrigues many travellers. There are strange stories of rituals – and of mixed bathing in hot tubs. Fierce tales, like *Shogun*, relate the frightening experiences of early visitors to the shores of Nippon. Lingering disquiet from the War can inhibit visits to Hiroshima and Nagasaki. Don't let these things deter you; Japan has much to offer the traveller who is free from time restrictions.

China, similarly, remains the tempting culture shock it was to Marco Polo. It is a vast country with so much history that it affects all of us in one way or another. A dozen three- to six-week tours of Old Cathay would barely cover the major scenic and historic wonders.

China and Japan are easily travelled in Independent status, or via one of a host of complex extensive tour packages. Even esoteric countries have made it easy to travel in comfort with or without pre-booked plans. Modern hotels are everywhere; domestic travel agents stand ready to assist with local tours and English-speaking staff. Fears, tremors and trepidations notwithstanding, the adventure is ready for you.

SELECTION

It's a game, and many chapters of this book refer to fun of the sport. Travel is a world board of Monopoly. Roll the dice to decide which part of the globe you will land on first, then second, and so on. Put a good map of the world up on the wall near the breakfast table and contemplate the choices every morning.

The important thing is to obtain as much information as you can about the intended destination. If you plan to travel year after year, start files on the places that intrigue you. Travel is one of the foremost retail industries of our modern world. With few exceptions, distant lands beckon you with open arms, and their districts vie for your business. Write for information, assiduously snip travel articles from newspapers and periodicals, and subscribe to one of the monthly travel magazines. Hotel chains with their links around the world will be delighted to put you on their mailing lists.

THE CONTINENTS

First things first. You have purchased a good traveller's world map such as Bartholomew's, and there it is on the wall. Study the land masses: the Americas, Europe, Africa, Asia – which includes the archipelago of Indonesia with its 17,000 islands – other islands from Australia down to dots like Fiji, Guam, Vanuatu, Samoa, Tahiti and Hawaii.

Start by putting bright-coloured pins in the map at places that intrigue you. Did you see an enticing travel documentary on the television? Put a pin in that area. Or read the Sunday paper with feature articles on the near-fantasy island of Mauritius? Find it on the map and put a pin there. Unless you are a geographer, most of these temptations are merely place-names. The map and pin process connects the names in your vision to their positions on the globe. It becomes clear that when you are in southern India, Sri Lanka and the Maldives aren't too far away. Nepal, Bhutan and Tibet suddenly appear out of nowhere as each others' neighbours – well, almost, because there is no easy highway between them.

The massive island of Australia sits in its own pool of local-name seas between the Indian and Pacific Oceans. New Zealand, looking like separated jigsaw puzzle pieces, becomes part of a path across the Pacific on a line of pins from Sydney to Fiji, Hawaii and Los Angeles. Another line humps over from Los Angeles to Tokyo, curls down through Beijing to Hong Kong, and on to Singapore before it reaches the southern hemisphere with Jakarta and Darwin.

The Circle Pacific air ticket described in Chapter Five makes a sensible pattern as the air route covering the rim destinations of the Pacific Ocean.

FANTASY

According to a fantasy of fiction, an Englishman went 'Around the World in Eighty Days'. Not a bad programme at all, if you keep to it in today's transport. The advantage you have over Phineas Fogg is that you can stay for weeks on each continent during your 80-day odyssey, and enjoy in comfort the distractions of movies and meals while flying on to each new one.

Now, that fantasy can become real. After looking at the world map day after day, you see that no point on the globe is beyond your reach. As each area becomes more familiar, the TV documentaries and Sunday paper travel sections make more sense to you. Clip the latter and save articles in your growing file, first by continent and then by country. As tourist bureaux begin to answer your enquiries, pamphlets and brochures flow in and add to the files. Your bookshelf begins to fill with publications. Assemble travel stories and novels that relate to these areas, near the files, to re-read when you have time. They will maintain the enthusiasm.

The newest sales tool is the video tape. Many advertisers will send a free tape of an area on request. Video rental libraries are starting sections on geography, and publications such as *National Geographic* offer tapes for sale on projects they have published.

You are now changing the fantasy to possibility. Soon the possibility metamorphoses into reality, and the destination daydreams become real plans. Before you know it, the time has come. You have bought your tickets, packed your bags, boarded the aeroplane and flown across the seas. You are about to arrive in what once was the never-never-land of your imagination.

VISITING THE ANCESTORS

Alex Haley, author of the famous novel (and hence of the film) *Roots*, traced his origins with great difficulty and trepidation. They became another written history of the slave trade in North America. No less importantly, the story revealed to the inhabitants of present-day Africa their own roots. Few of us are not tied to a former nationality, race or mix of races.

Fed by old photographs, there is a curiosity in many people to follow that tie back to the land of their ancestors. Immigrant families know where the grandparents once lived. The urge to travel often combines with the instinct to go back to the original soil and to seek out relatives – some heard of, some not.

Welcome?

Do not rely on your welcome in the land of your forefathers. Government attitudes in ancestral nations vary. Foreign-born members of the Chinese race are known in the PRC as Overseas Chinese. A special branch (China Travel Service or CTS) of the travel company, Luxingshe, books them separately from other foreigners (handled by China International Travel Service or CITS). Different hotels and coaches keep local and overseas Chinese from being 'contaminated' by other travellers. This will be explained to you in detail when you apply to any of the Luxingshe International Travel offices.

(We know of a non-Chinese couple who were advised by Chinese friends in Macau to try the CTS office as its tour to Hainan was at half the CITS price. Everything else was the same except that only Cantonese was spoken by the tour party. Our friends enjoyed a week as mascots, cosseted with fragments of Hong Kong English. They recommend Hainan to all who fancy a large tropical island, with huge empty beaches, that is also part of 'Mainland China'. Alas, things may be stricter now.)

Many other countries distinguish between foreign nationals, with and without local family origins. Some authoritarian governments are suspicious or hostile, while others enthusiastically welcome potential 'cash cow' pilgrims. You can find out how the land lies only from 'compatriots' who have recently 'been home'. The written rules may not be the actual state of affairs after you cross the border.

Sometimes the family welcomes you with open arms seeking gifts. In countries under tight government control, there are two special kinds of culture shock: first from officials, and then, perhaps, from the kith and kin. You are seen as Rich Relatives by those who have no freedom of travel or lifestyle. Thus you may be expected to bring a plethora of presents, to spend money entertaining the extended local family at banquets, and to promise monthly stipends thereafter. Unfortunately you, the average person, earn (or used to earn) a modest income – and are probably stretching the budget for the pleasure of meeting them.

No doubt you are rich by comparison of lifestyle, but that does not necessarily provide hundreds of your currency for a banquet. Nor is it always convenient to travel with two or three large cartons of television sets as gifts for expected and unexpected uncles and aunts.

One could write ahead but with no definite dates, to keep the visit uncertain and low key. Or, even less courageously, one can arrive unheralded and decide to move on or not once one has taken a view of the family and its welcome.

The freer the country the more normal the reception of visiting *émigrés* by government and family. The branches of some families will have remained in touch with the tree over the generations, while others have little except a name to trace.

If the trip is largely for the sake of the ancestral visit, you will not need extensive travel plans. Writing ahead to known relatives or to the local tourist information centre should obtain all you need to know. Do not let your travel agent sell you anything besides the transport. This is no time to be saddled with prepaid side trips.

It is necessary, however, to read up your family's history and original geography. If there seems to be no one of your name where there should be, bear in mind that marriages and the hazards of pronunciation may have changed yours. Check back on your forebears long before you go. Remember the stories your mother or grandmother told about your origins. Create a family tree to the best of your knowledge; with luck you will then not be surprised to meet Cousin Wu or Uncle Joseph. If you have a photograph which enables you to guess his name right, he will be delighted. You, of course, will be trading news of the overseas members for what you learn from those who stayed. Indeed you may have been better placed to preserve some of the traditions than they. They may find it harder to picture the land and its ways as they used to be. You, the travellers, may be more, or less, curious about what you do and do not have in common.

Exploring your roots can be an enjoyable and enlightening experience. Take lots of photographs – with you and while there. A small tape recorder is a great help in taking notes and preserving the voices of the current generation, for relatives in either country. Video cameras are better value for both sides than gimmicky polaroids, since replay equipment is in use almost everywhere.

Chapter Eight

MEANS OF TRANSPORT

There is great emphasis today on air travel. We are in a hurry to get there; time limitations, and the major packages offered, point us towards the airport. Air travel is indeed the primary mode, but alternatives should be considered – as adventures in themselves or as useful or pleasant supplements. You are setting out to see the world, but you won't see much from 35,000 feet. Ships, trains, buses, cars, motor boats, canoes, bicycles and feet – all these keep one close to the visible surface of the earth.

BY AIR

The key to air travel is physical comfort. Once you are on board and settled down after take-off, the ride is similar to sitting in an armchair for the next 6 to 12 hours. Which, of course, few people willingly do. Discomfort increases as time passes and the ambience deteriorates. Your clothes become wrinkled, debris accumulates around you, boredom sets in, you are tired of reading and you can't sleep comfortably.

Before boarding, prepare all the articles you might want. Keep handy: reading matter and writing materials, puzzles, a pillow if you use one, your passport (to fill out arrival documents), a headache remedy, and sweets if they help with swallowing or the nerves. It is frustrating to dig out something you need from your luggage, especially when people are waiting to get to their seats. Opening the storage compartment above you in flight is dangerous. If you use a cart for your baggage, detach it before boarding. Take advantage of a toilet in the concourse before you go to the loading bay.

Eat lightly, save the cheese and crackers for a later snack; drink lots of liquid but little, if any, alcohol.

In-flight Exercise

Constant air-travellers have their own routines for limbering up the stiffening muscles. Watch for these rare flying birds. If you see one, get up and copy the performance. (This assumes that you fear discomfort more than the whole process of flying. Otherwise, stay within your seatbelt, as advised in Chapter Three.)

If you do nothing to prevent it, your feet and ankles swell, and your back aches from trying to find a comfortable position (there isn't one). *Conquer Fear of Flying*, a short book written by an Australian pilot, has a good chapter on exercises. The author is indebted to Shanti Gowans, a teacher of yoga, for a series of in-flight toners.

Basically the advice is common sense. Get out of the seat and stretch the arms, do knee bends and torso twists. Meditation, deep breathing, eye-swivelling exercises, and limited isometrics – these are all well-known stress and body relievers. There are pages of detail, none of which will be remembered unless you put them into regular practice for weeks beforehand. Do not despair, though. Merely strolling the aisles does much to ease the strain. And if, nevertheless, you suffer discomfort – well, you will forget it once the plane lands and excitement takes over.

PASSENGER SHIPS

The oceans, seas, rivers and lakes cover much more of the earth's surface than land does. If you can afford it, and you get the chance, consider a voyage on the *QE2* – the liner *Queen Elizabeth the Second*. This, the most majestic ship afloat, crosses the Atlantic between Southampton and New York in a little over four days, usually as part of a longer cruise.

Whichever your ship, instead of being scrunched into a bucket on an aircraft, you will have a cabin of your own, decks on which to amble, walk, jog or run, games to play, fine food and wine, entertainment, and a host of people to serve your every need and whim.

Continent-to-continent passenger ships are becoming rare. Shipping lines or the cruise departments of port authorities are more likely than travel agents to know about them.

CRUISE SHIPS

Luxury cruise ships are floating five-star hotels, in which you both stay, and move – for a few days, a few weeks, or as long as it takes to circle the globe. As you would expect of luxury hotels, they are more expensive than other modes of travel, day for day. However, it is inclusive: you are paying both for your stay and for your passage. You may dine on caviar, foie gras, lobster or quail fondue to your heart's content, and the wine that goes with them is probably included. Other drinks are extra – as are the expected healthy tips. Ports may be explored independently, or you may add organised tours to your accumulating account.

There are levels of market in cruise ships as in other travel modes. You should do your own research, here as elsewhere. Agencies shout the delights of the luxury liners, television commercials depict their romance, and bargain-price ads are common. First, select the time, the area you wish to see, and a level of luxury. These last two sometimes interconnect. Cruising down the Yangtze River is one style, taking a Caribbean or Mediterranean voyage is another. Season is extremely important, as cruises are limited by weather. The same ship will sail the South Seas in January and Norwegian fjords from May to September.

Cost is affected by the luxuriousness and length of travel. Long cruises can be joined and left at intermediate ports. The normal system is to book months in advance on the cruise of your choice, pay the price and enjoy the luxury of the voyage. Air connections are usually included in the quoted price of the package, from and to your home airport. You cannot save money and negotiate prices by booking directly with the company unless, perhaps, you know one of its administrative staff. However, last-minute passages are offered by certain discount operators to fill empty cabins (see pages 73–4).

Take as much luggage as you wish; other than in and out of your car, it will be handled by porters. On the most luxurious liners, dress is formal for dinner, especially if you are invited to dine at the Captain's table on one evening. Other ships require jacket and tie for men and cocktail dresses for women.

☛ Security Caution

Cruise ships are notorious for sophisticated thefts of jewellery and valuables. People become casual, and cabin locks are easy to pick. So use the Purser's lock-up boxes.

Mahjong, poker and bridge games for high stakes with strangers are foolhardy. By all means play the slots and the tables. The *croupiers*, at least, smile when they take your money.

Dining Aboard a Cruise Ship

The normal arrangements are four, eight or twelve people pre-assigned to a table by the *maître d'*. After boarding and before you unpack, go directly to the dining room and identify the head man. If you are travelling as a pair, you might make the following statement after introducing yourself: "We wish to dine in the second seating and will require a deuce for privacy. This is our honeymoon and a romantic corner would be greatly appreciated." The protocol is to accompany this with a US$20 or US$50 bill (depending on the length and luxuriousness of the voyage) folded and visible in the hand. A deuce, in dining room vernacular, is a table for two. Those in the know always dine late, since the first sitting is asked to clear the dining room by a fixed time.

But you may prefer the time and places allotted to you: either because the first session gives more scope for evening activities, or through enjoying the company of like-minded travellers. But, while you will not necessarily choose a table full of your own countrymen, you will want a common language. So you should still find out how you are seated – and if need be, make your wishes known – as soon as you can; but the dollar ritual will not be needed.

On a cruise ship, problems may arise through a combination of close quarters and the engineered social events. The crew assigned to conviviality continually work to get people together and arrange an endless array of entertainment. If you are a single looking for company, or a couple willing to make new friends, the programmes should suit you. Sign up for almost everything. Two people on a special anniversary voyage as a romantic interlude will take a different view, though.

☞ Personal Experience

My wife and I booked a cruise in the Caribbean many years ago. We succeeded in dining alone every night except when invited to the Captain's table. We won a bottle of champagne and a set of eight gold decorated bar glasses for first place in a ballroom dancing contest, with our tribute to Fred Astaire and Ginger Rogers. A friendly chef arranged to share his personal loot of beluga caviar, obtained in barter with a Russian cruise ship tied up next to us in Jamaica. He had to serve with the can concealed under some foliage so that people at the next table would not ask for the same – a rare experience of the furtive habits of the Rich and Famous. Yes, we exchanged a padded handshake on our departure, knowing that we had enjoyed our money's worth.

The Growing Cruise Industry

Increasingly, there are non-luxury cruise ships and ships with sub-luxury classes of accommodation. As some holiday towns are almost taken over at certain times by free-spending workers of this or that nation, so you on a cruise ship may be surrounded by one language and several of its speakers' lifestyles. The expanding industry could not survive on travellers who can afford gracious sailing. It seeks to serve the middle and enterprising other classes, with short cruises (even weekend 'Cruises to Nowhere') while they are still working – and with longer ones later.

Reduced rates are offered by cruise lines surreptitiously through discount vendors. This is their way of filling cabins shortly before sailing, just as airlines fill seats. For you, it provides a last-minute chance to take advantage of a holiday which you would in any case find attractive. Book provisionally, with an agency, one or more cruises during a period when you expect to be free. Make it clear that you will confirm a booking only on being offered a late bargain. The agent will telephone two or three days before a sailing date, offering (say) a second-deck cabin at 40% discount on the good ship *Whatever*, sailing from Hong Kong to Shanghai, Qingdao, Yokohama, Taipei and back to Hong Kong. You answer 'yes' or 'no' on the spot, before the vendor tries the next client on his list. The return air ticket to Hong Kong is also discounted, as part of the package.

Watch for advertisements of these specials in travel journals and weekend newspaper travel sections. If it is not a well-known agency you could verify its credibility with a travel organisation or society, but it is perfectly in order to call a cruise line direct to verify the offer of the agency. But sometimes you might be lucky enough to land a late-offered cruise without going through the nerve-stretching procedure described in the previous paragraph.

FREIGHTERS

A little-known and (so far) seldom used mode of sea travel is the limited passenger accommodation on several of the world's sea-freight lines. Shipping companies have found it profitable to sell cabin space on semi-scheduled and non-scheduled routes. Passengers may book 10-day round trips or 100- to 150-day round-the-world voyages; or go halfway and fly back (or vice versa); or ingeniously take a long sea passage, instead of a flight, before or after a foreign posting. This last may be hampered by ships' tendency to circumnavigate eastwards. Prices per diem are reasonable (US$90–130 in 1994) since the rate varies as to time and distance, and includes services on board. Air passages are not included and may be difficult to secure, though the organisation that arranges your booking may undertake to book a matching flight.

Few travel agents know about freighters. If you do not wish to deal direct with shipping companies or through a coordinator (such as the two mentioned below), you might find a local travel agency willing to explore the options on your behalf. The commission would be 10% or less of a large sum of money. You may wish to tempt your own enterprising agent with a copy of these paragraphs...

Newsletters are available, for the most part mimeographed monthly productions by *aficionados* of the system. More formal information will come from large shipping lines listed in the telephone book and from shipping pages of port-city newspapers. The freight lines will tell you whether they take passengers and where to find details. We offer two addresses: Freighter World Cruises of 180 Lake Street, Suite 335, Pasadena, CA 91101, USA, tel: (818) 449 3106, fax: 449 9537; and The Strand Cruise and Travel Centre, Charing Cross Shopping Concourse, London WC2N 4HZ, UK, tel: 836 6363, fax: 497 0078. Strand deals on behalf of 35 shipping companies which between them take from 2 to 12 passengers on 60 set voyages between Europe, Africa, the Middle and Far East, Australia, New Zealand, the Pacific islands, South and North America, Russia, the Baltic and Iceland.

Freighters provide the ultimate in Independent Travel. You book to sail on a particular ship, from Sydney, say, in the first week of May. The ship will call at New Zealand ports before heading across the Pacific for the Panama Canal. If there is a choice, ask for the largest cabin on the main deck forward, with bow-facing porthole. You pay an advance and you take your chance.

All being well, the shipping line calls you and advises that you should board at 6:00 p.m. on the 3rd of May at Pier #6. The first port of call will be Auckland. Eventually a smiling Captain and First Officer welcome you aboard; you are shown to a roomy cabin and told that dinner will be served in the Officers' Mess as soon as the ship has cleared the harbour. Two couples of different nationalities are already on board; you gather with them on deck below the bridge to watch the departure. One or two months later, you will have visited ports in a dozen countries, read two dozen books, piled up ten rolls of exposed film, written all your letters, and become so completely rested that you are looking ahead for your next adventure. Also you will be watching the intricacies, as the ship enters your last harbour, with something like a seaman's eye.

All the shipping companies impose an upper age limit: some as high as 79 or 80. All require doctors' certificates for passengers over 65, and special insurance cover. The ship provides food and comfort, but you make your own entertainment. Time in port is seldom more than a day; a passenger might set foot in three Australian cities but, unless one is the port of embarkation or disembarkation, will scarcely have seen the country.

Mail is sent and received at each port of call. Passengers may use fax at sea. There are no luggage restrictions; indeed your trunks may go on to your destination, if you complete your journey by air. My publishers are pleased to note three standard voyages which will land passengers in Singapore, but have found none that will take them away.

We hope this section of the book will produce new 'Deluxe Economy' seafarers. And we hope more shipping companies will make that possible by putting spare cabins to good use.

RIVER CRUISES

River cruises are less expensive, since they entail shorter voyages. They are booked as parts of longer itineraries, or are joined as side trips by Independent Travellers as opportunities occur. In China for instance, a Yangtze River voyage takes you through the famous Three Gorges, upriver for five to seven days or down-river for three or four. Some of these cruise ships are operated by the Chinese government, others by joint venture companies. Tickets include food, guides, shore trips, and either a return to the point of embarkation by other means or the next stage of an onward journey.

Adventurous travellers may book on the standard people's passenger and freight ferries for only the price of conveyance. These are much cheaper, and permit breaks of journey for a few hours or days at places of interest. You may start at Chongqing, go ashore at Wuhan, Lushan or Nanjing, stay a few days at each port and continue as far as Shanghai after a fortnight.

One fascinating way to see the northwestern coastal waters of North America is to take the daily car-passenger ferry out of Seattle and sail north for some 750 miles along the coast of Canada. This is more ambitious than a river cruise. Having started amidst islands in the sounds and inlets of Washington State, you may choose to finish in Anchorage, Alaska, via the 150-mile Cook Inlet – overlooked by the Aleutian Range. Luxury cruise ships ply this route less adventurously, but the do-it-yourself traveller may prefer mingling with the back-packers and Alaskan residents in stop-and-stay-awhile ports.

Major rivers offer lengthy water journeys: the Mississippi in the United States, the Murray in Australia, the Mekong between Laos and Myanmar and then between Laos and Thailand and through Cambodia and Vietnam, the Nile in Egypt and the Amazon in South America. You may choose between tourist comfort and the reality of Mekong rice barges.

Slow Long Boats

Canal barges in England and France give homely comfort rather than chrome luxury, soothing rather than dramatic scenery, and all the independence of driving a car. The holiday industry and canal enthusiasts have restored pre-lorry, pre-railway trade routes and the pubs, inns and *auberges* which served them. In some countries 'houseboat' means much the same as 'canal barge'; in others a houseboat is static – a floating residence or, in Kashmir, a floating hotel-chalet. Information on inland waterway travel is easily found in the better travel guides covering the area of interest.

One-Day River Boat Trips

Day trips afloat abound in all countries with water systems. You will uncover many in the guide books and other literature acquired in your research. Some, more esoteric, are discovered when you get there. The Li Chiang River near Guilin in China is historically famous. Joining an armada of 50 other crowded tourist boats is an experience sought by some but shunned by others. Queensland offers an Australian river trip in the Daintree rain forest where you can commune, at a distance, with monstrous crocodiles. The Murray River further south, like the Mississippi, has nostalgic paddle steamers offering one-day or longer trips.

Port cities always offer scenic boat tours of the harbour and adjacent shore line. Auckland, New York, Sydney, San Francisco, Singapore and Hong Kong provide excellent views of the city from the sea. They cost little, often taking only an hour, and give good value.

COASTAL STEAMERS

Coastal steamers are deep-water ships plying coastal routes, as craft have for hundreds of years. They carry passengers and freight cheaply, and are usually ignored by travel agents and package tours. We think highly of this mode of travel and book passages whenever conveniently available. Despite their modest prices, most ships have cabin accommodation, reasonable food (but you may bring your own), and a characteristic ambience. Those stopping at several ports offer a few hours or a day ashore to explore. *Keep within hearing distance of the ship's whistle or siren.*

Travel is leisurely; fellow passengers, predominantly natives of the country, are nearly always friendly. Crew members are helpful to foreign passengers. In most cases you can visit the bridge or engine room on request, listen to the constant jargon on the communication radio, and enjoy moonlit nights at sea.

Examples are: Shanghai to Hong Kong or Shanghai to Qingdao; Seattle to ports of Alaska; Java to Ujung Pandang in Sulawesi to Ambon in the Moluccas and Denpasar in Bali, all in the Indonesian archipelago. Japan offers short voyages between the three major islands: Yokohama to Hokkaido and Kobe to Beppu are unique and enjoyable short voyages in the Sea of Japan.

Booking a coastal steamer follows the train-ticket procedure, with published timetables (see the next page). Most hotels and local travel agencies keep tabs on this mode of travel.

We have had poor food from time to time (in China) but never an uninteresting voyage. Every coastal trip we have taken has been happily memorable. Coastal steamers are the least expensive, while often the least luxurious, mode of 'Economy Deluxe' travel. Always enquire about likely weather and sea conditions. A rough sea trip is no fun.

BY TRAIN

As described by the novelist and travel writer, Paul Theroux, the railway train is a monster, a wonderful experience, a veritable buffet of adventure in many lands. Super-fast bullet trains now exceed 125 mph and go from city centre to city centre in times that equal flight travel. Major stations are in city or town centres, with easy access; boarding takes a minimum amount of time; and trains are even safer than aircraft.

Rail travel is especially suited to the Independent Traveller, as it entails little advance planning – though you would undoubtedly need to organise a journey on the Trans-Siberian Railway or the Orient Express, whether from London to Venice or from Bangkok to Singapore.

A day's notice or two will secure a Pullman compartment (see next page) on an all-day express train. Avoid 'milk runs': trains that start early and stop at every small station become tedious. It is usually possible to reserve seats for journeys of less than 24 hours since extra reservations justify a longer train. For overnight journeys, book sleeping berths unless you won't mind most of the disadvantages of a very long flight.

Cross-country trips are notable successes in some countries. Europe is famous for good train equipment, which supports a traditional means of travel. Eurorail passes are available for modest prices, allowing unlimited travel within a fixed period. South Africa has its Blue Train from Johannesburg to Cape Town. Canada provides a magnificent transcontinental scenic route from Victoria to Montreal. In the United States, Amtrak is improving the cross-country routes; and Mexico has quite interesting trips from the US border southwards. Australia, with vast distances to cross, has modern equipment and good prices, offering an excellent change from hurried flight schedules.

Worldwide, train travel has the easiest booking arrangements. You consult the timetable, buy a ticket at the station, find the right platform, board the train and away you go. A city's tourist office will send details on request, which will highlight scenic routes.

On-the-spot information is available from your hotel or from helpful members of the public. For many people railways are a part of their way of life, and often a source of pride. They will offer advice as to the best routes and times, from personal experience. Only floods or snowstorms are likely to disrupt rail traffic.

Longer routes usually have at least two levels of comfort, First Class and Second Class. At the bottom is the bench car, described in China as 'Hard Seat'. Sleeping berths can be bunks stacked three high, non-reserved. First Class sometimes equates with Chair Car or 'Soft Seat'; but seats in many countries' Second Class are not hard, and can be reserved. First Class is good 'Economy Deluxe', with reserved cushioned seats, and refreshments sold en route and at stops. Special compartments – called Pullman after the originator of sleeper travel – give privacy; they are usually sold on a four-occupant basis.

We recommend reserving a whole compartment for any train trip over eight hours. In some systems you book a compartment as a unit. In others, particularly major train travel areas like China and India, you have to buy all four seats to ensure privacy. Watch out for the porter, whose job it is to convert the seats to bunks, where no bed is visible.

Train travel is hypnotising, with the constant methodical chatter of wheels to rails. For a daytime journey it's very pleasant to stretch out, doze and arrive rested. Sleeping on a train at night is a mixed blessing. The clackety-clack is restful, but the train stopping and starting always wakes me up.

Dining Cars

The walk along the swaying train and the distraction of the meal make an interesting interlude. On a luxury train, the food and the service can be more of a pleasure than an adventure. Down the scale, the reverse is likely. Even so, coffee and cake or a couple of beers and some rice add up to a pleasant diversion. On a high-class train, enquire as soon as you board about table reservations; as you would on a cruise ship, ask for the second sitting. You can then dawdle with a bottle of wine over an extended dinner and leisurely coffee.

☛ **Travel Tip**

Where equipment and facilities are old, or there are doubts about hygiene, think twice about taking a 24-hour journey. Toilets may be even less comfortable than those in aircraft. And it will be better to buy packaged food and fruit at the train stops, and to carry your own swag-bag with snacks.

As against this advice, we should record the testimony of two non-spartan families who travelled by rail at different times in the 1980s from the Pacific Coast to Moscow. They experienced much friendliness and little hardship.

BY COACH OR BUS

'And leave the driving to us' is the famous advertising slogan of the Greyhound Line in the United States. Travelling by bus is a mixed bag of adventure, leisure and comfort; on the other side of the coin it can be miserably confining and boring. There are few general rules to be applied other than the constant: *Do your research, ask the right questions.*

Package Tours by Coach

Generally for seven to 21 days, package tours use modern air-conditioned vehicles, with experienced drivers and a guide. Schedules and scenic routes are well planned, through repetition, and you know approximately what you are in for before you start.

If you can, fly early to the departure destination and spend a couple of days in the city to orient yourself; then join the tour as scheduled. Such a tour is an excellent way to view the land, in a country you haven't visited before. It introduces you to areas that may turn out to be so interesting that you will return the following year, to stay longer in a good spot.

Many tours can be booked on arrival – during your two-day reconnaissance, as it were – allowing your selection to be influenced by weather and a wider range of options. In the high season expect weekly or twice-weekly departures on the popular longer trips.

Advantages of Coach Tours

You know where you must be and when, and where you will be taken. Your luggage will be handled efficiently; hotels and most meals will be of predictable standards, though in unpredictable surroundings; you will have with you a group of like-interest travel companions; and everything that needs to be is pre-booked. The best of local sights are enjoyed without preamble or the business of selecting them.

Since the coach will always pick you up, you lose no time – as you do getting to and waiting at airports. There is ample space to stow your hand-luggage and shopping trophies. A general air of conviviality is felt after the first few hours, when names and home towns are exchanged.

Disadvantages of Coach Tours

The snags include petty annoyances over which seat is best; other passengers who ignore the timetable, constantly holding up the bus; and sometimes a guide who hogs the microphone or deafens with his foreground music.

Shopping stops are too few or too short for you and too many and too long for someone else. Lunch and other pit stops at wayside cafes may range from adequate to various degrees of miserable.

Some older tourists look tired as they leave their coach at the end of the day, exasperated perhaps with queuing up for room keys and restaurant tables; they are rarely seen to smile or laugh. Other members gather in cliques to gossip about the day's events and the morrow's prospects – complaining or enthusing. A whole day of activity is tiring and boring, or exhilarating and memorable, usually as you choose to make it.

If the trip is long and becomes unbearable, cut your losses, rent a car and continue the adventure individually. If you plead health problems, you may be able to get a partial refund.

Crosscountry Public Buses

This is a different story. To see the country and leave the driving to the professionals is a fine way to enjoy exploration, free of pre-booked itinerary – especially if you are adventurous and impulsive. As with train travel, pass tickets may allow you to stop for a day or more and catch an onward bus. As an alternative to a hotel or motel, Bed-and-Breakfast rooms are the vogue in many places, aiming for a family-style house-guest stay. (A 'guest house' is closer to the hotel concept.) Unplanned, a visit to a quaint village or small town is a rare treasure, since the unknown can be more exciting than the expected. The bus depot normally has a public information service to help arrange accommodation.

Japan's standard fixed-route buses are uniformly excellent. Schedules are minute-precise and drivers always stop at scenic views for picture taking. Other passengers are friendly, despite the language barrier. Every lunch place we encountered in Japan was delightful, with a beautiful view and a full meal menu or the alternative of a superior snack. Toilets and washrooms were refreshingly clean.

In some countries, however, I would never buy a ticket for a bus I hadn't seen. Brochures hyped with grandiose pictures of fine equipment, gorgeous scenery and quiet highways may conceal reality: buses which have seen better days, scenery turned urban, crowded and overhung by smog. The bus could fill with chickens, pigs and squalling children. Arrange a chauffeured vehicle or drive yourself, unless the bus is visibly modern and the itinerary specified.

Transport depots in some larger cities are not particularly inviting for the sophisticated traveller, being generally in older, seedier parts of the metropolis. You are wise to watch your purse and valuables while waiting, and be well placed in the queue – for a seat towards the front. Once on the road, the ambience is more pleasant. If in doubt, go to the depot before you buy the ticket and see the general condition of the vehicles. An hour spent in investigation could save you days of discomfort.

Besides North America and Japan, Malaysia and most European countries have good long-distance bus systems. One can take local journeys, anywhere, without thorough investigation, and enjoy the flavour of the country as well as its countryside. In many less developed countries a taxi from town to town is invitingly cheap, if you agree on the fare before you start.

☛ **Travel Tip**
Combine a train and bus trip. For instance, in the US, take the Amtrak from Los Angeles to Chicago, Denver or New Orleans. Then join the Greyhound and explore to the north, the east or the south; and then decide whether to go back by train or bus.

Mini Vans

Mini vans are quite common in Southeast Asia and resort areas elsewhere. They suit uneven road surfaces. With six to eight people in tighter but more informal seating, a sociable spirit quickly develops. This spirit normally includes the driver, who is likely to be affable and informative. It is easier to divert a van than a coach after a road accident or trouble from floods. Enquire at tourist information centres on arrival: by scouting around you may find someone who has recently taken the trip that interests you. First-hand information is always the best way to find out about comfort on such excursions.

Adventurous safari trips explore rain forests, the outback and other happily uncivilised areas with six- to eight-passenger four-wheel drive land cruisers. There are basic hostels, or tent camps are set up at night. This is 'Deluxe Back-packing': you can explore remote areas in some degree of catered comfort.

BY HIRE CAR

Hertz, Avis, Budget and other international names are as familiar as Kodak and Coca Cola in most of the travel world today. Sedans/saloons, mini vans, 4WD rugged vehicles, campers with built-in facilities, topless/convertibles, windowless mokes, motor and pedal cycles, etc. are available for hire. With the proper self-confidence, and a credit card to back up your verve and enthusiasm, rent a vehicle and drive it yourself. International road markings are uniform on major highways; information books are provided for the local 'sign language'. Hire at one end of a country and drop the car off at the other end.

Cruising down a highway or byway in a foreign land with your favourite travelling companion, when it suits you, is the acme of Independent Travel. It is pure freedom to drive through the spring or autumn countryside of Italy, Portugal or Spain, and stop at an ancient hillside walled village. Brush aside the beaded entrance of a roadside cafe, order the house wine, cheese, fruit and a crusty loaf. Sign language and a few words of courtesy will leave both sides smiling. You will remember the sun, the smiles and the taste of the wine and cheese for many years.

FLY AND DRIVE
Major international airlines provide fly-and-drive packages. This is a simple arrangement between the carrier and the car rental agency. Fly to your foreign airport and pick up a reserved car to be used for the period specified, which can be from one day to one month. Some of these arrangements include hotel/motel accommodation along a specified tour route. It is a common practice to buy the combination and not use the rooms unless they suit you. This 'throwaway' package is cheaper than buying the air ticket and car rental separately.

Alternatively, major car rental agencies offer longer international packages at reduced rates, if you book before you leave. The nearest office of the agency will provide the information you need and do the booking for you. Coupon tie-ins for car rental and hotels accompany frequent-flier award certificates.

Members of airline clubs are offered special rates for overseas travel. Ask the car rental agency about membership of their frequent-user or commercial clubs. Don't worry about building up enough mileage credits: you may or may not, but at least they will give you a price advantage in booking.

BUY AND DRIVE

A shrewd traveller will arrange to buy the next Mercedes in Germany, tour in it for weeks or months and then ship it home. This cuts out middlemen, some import fees and the cost of hiring a car during the holiday. Caution: investigate all the rules of the game long before you make a commitment.

HIRE CAR WITH DRIVER

Many countries have strict regulations about foreign drivers. They require an international driver's licence and insurance bonds. In some places, the only foreigners allowed to drive are diplomatic and business residents. An example is China where you book a car and driver, for a short or a long period, through the China International Travel Service.

The good side of this is the safety and pleasure of sightseeing free from the distraction of driving. A day's tour of the city and surrounding countryside is better enjoyed with a driver. Even a week or two on the road with a driver-guide is usually very pleasant, given a congenial driver. Costs are often less than you imagined, as the driver's bed and board are complimentary, in most areas, recognising that he has brought you as paying guests to the domain. Language is seldom a problem as the hire company aims to provide an English-speaking driver. Once in China, and once in Japan, our driver spoke no English. With maps, conversation/translation guides and general goodwill we had no problems of significance. In fact it was pleasant to teach each other bits of our languages.

Furthermore, there would be the strain of driving yourself,

perhaps not on your usual side of the road, through metropolitan traffic of frightening density. Would you really like to drive your own car on the Champs Elysées in Paris, knowing what pictures have shown you of that tooting tangle?

We avoid driving in big cities like London, New York, Paris, Bangkok, Manila or Jakarta. Strangers should be wary of the roads of Sri Lanka, India and Nepal, for example. But, away from huge cities, you should enjoy consistently good roads and well marked motorways in most European countries, Malaysia, North America, Australia and elsewhere.

Advantages of Car Hire

It is nice to have a car handy in a resort area for local travel. The convenience of getting around and the pleasure of wheels immediately available enlarge the scope of the area immensely. You can try to resolve the matter with a cash equation: "How many days will we be using the vehicle, as against bus adventures and taxi fares?" But this may make you miss the real advantage: if you have a car, you will go out more and will therefore see more countryside, eat at more restaurants and have the largely paid-in-advance freedom to go and come on impulse.

TREKKING: THE A, B AND C SPORT

The trick in trekking (or hiking, or walking) is to know thyself and thy limitations. The Chinese call walking the #11 taxi or bus, referring to the two legs. The sport of using one's built-in locomotion is vast, the participants grading themselves into the A, B or C level depending on their physical fitness and expertise.

A's are the past-masters and for the most part will not be reading this text, having their own journals. Their field includes crossing mountain ranges and wildernesses. Cliff scalers and mountain climbers are extreme examples of this group.

B's are very good, primarily using the sport for travel enjoyment; they can endure a three- to five-day crosscountry adventure with little stress. They keep up their physical condition year by year, attuned to many-mile hikes as weekly exercise. Age is rarely a factor, as you can see in Switzerland where octogenarians are commonly found on the longest trails. The B trekkers will seek out walking-tour vacations oriented to their ambitions. They sometimes associate with the A's on lesser mountains for training or to upgrade their ability.

C's include the rest of us. Novices, people who like to walk their five miles a day or swim a few lengths in the pool each morning. If in generally good physical condition most of us, regardless of age, can enjoy organised jungle treks for example. We may lag behind now and then, stopping to rest more often than some, but will wind up at the starting place. Don't try this sort of thing on the first day of your vacation; rest up and take a hike along the beach to get in breathing shape. If you habitually swim, run or row, that will be fine for your general fitness; but you will also need some walking practice. The muscles are not the same.

Your enjoyment is considerably reduced if you do not have physical comfort. Find out exactly the best kind of shoes and clothing to wear. Carry as little as you can, in a light back-pack. Leave your arms free in case you have to grab a branch or tree root for support. If you start panting, as you climb the first tier of 50 steps, stop and settle the heartbeat before continuing. I relate the following experience as the best advice possible for occasional trekkers.

☛ Personal Experience

We were enjoying a Greek tour, booked on a whim one year with a Swiss travel agent. We had no idea what the itinerary was. The ship was a freighter turned cruise ship, our group mixed German and Swiss. We anchored off an island in the morning. The party went ashore to trek across the island and meet the ship in the afternoon on the other side. A Swiss doctor and family befriended us, having long experience of legging it in their native land. Dr Franz noticed my flushed, panting condition (at the age of 50), struggling to keep up with the group ascending a hill. My wife, a perennial walker, had no problems.

"Fritz (he converted my name), walk behind me. We are going to slow the pace – one foot at a time – and not worry about the others." We walked slowly, rarely stopping except when the group halted for *ouzo* at a roadside cafe or a lunch of fresh olives and *feta* cheese. By the end of the day, we were far ahead of the group, my pulse regular; I was breathing normally and felt comfortably tired. What I most needed was the fun of swimming out to the ship instead of joining the really tired trekkers taking the launch.

Pace yourself: the tortoise can beat the hare.

Chapter Nine

COMPANIONSHIP

Travellers vary: families, married couples, unmarried couples, singles including widows and widowers, pensioners, adventurers, workers and career business professionals. Some look for fun and relief from daily business pressures, on their annual holidays. The newly retired are in a change-of-life state, seeking fresh horizons. Itchy footed adventurers and dreamers have been waiting half a lifetime to see a far-off land. With rare exceptions (see Chapter Ten) they have one thought in common: they do not want to travel alone.

COMPANIONABLE SINGLES

Individuals who are uncomfortable with strangers, but reluctant to travel alone, should seek a friend or friends from social groups

91

or the workplace. Or a relative might be asked to travel as a companion, in an adventure of mutual interest. Arrangements of this kind can seldom be worked out and made jointly, as we have recommended to couples. Here, one person completes the research and, before booking, will ask about for a companion who can arrange a holiday at the same time. A friend of many years could be tempted to join the adventure. In the end, three or more may like the idea.

There is a risk in 'tiny group' travel. Two individuals sometimes find it hard to decide what to do for the day, where to dine for the evening or even what to wear. A formula has it that three persons quadruple the problem, while four to six travelling together so magnify the decision processes that a dictator is required.

With or without a dictator, there is the 'disgruntled' factor. One person simply doesn't want to go along with the crowd, which causes annoying confrontations. Thus four good friends who have played poker or whist together for years are now at odds with each other. Think about it and discuss it, well before confirming joint plans. The group must foresee the problem with a sense of humour, and early on devise a system to beat it. One easy solution is similar to a friendly poker game: each player gains status in turn as 'the dealer' who selects the 'hand' to be played. Rotating the decision-making really does make a game out of a problem.

TAKING POT LUCK WITH A SMALL GROUP

Six to eight people can make an ideal tour group. After agreeing on a travel destination, your agent suggests a certain trip, restricted to eight; and they would meet at the airport or boat. Let us say that four are in couples, you and three others are singles, and ages range from 30 to 60.

Travelling in 'double occupancy' means that you will join with one of the other singles to share a room throughout the trip. To some people this is a great opportunity to make a new friend with an interest in the chosen kind of travel. Others fear being 'doubled' with a stranger, even in the interests of economy. What if the new companion has some unfortunate habit?

In another group some members would not like to travel with other people's small children. Couples can take early exception to a hanging-on single, or to another couple who are 'thrilled to be with them'. It is embarrassing constantly to dodge unwanted companions.

Therefore, when undertaking small group travel, it is important to know explicitly who the companions are going to be, in person or by description.

A good travel bureau will arrange a pre-booking plus pairing of singles meeting, ostensibly to discuss destination information, but actually helping the probable group to gel. If the agent doesn't offer, it would be a good idea to suggest such a get-together. One single lady friend of ours always contacts the person she is to be teamed with, face-to-face or by phone – far in advance of the departure date. Tastes, smoking habits and age difference can all make or break the adventure.

Travelling as a couple is less problematical; a single always has some trepidation before meeting the strangers who will be close companions for many days.

☞ Personal Experience

My wife and I booked a seven-day adventure to the tiny Himalayan country of Bhutan. We joined a group of six single ladies, ages 60 to 80, gathered from various directions. A mini van with driver-guide appeared, and the eight passengers spent the next week in very close proximity.

There were annoyances such as the constant shouting to the guide to stop for pictures, bathroom competition and 'when do we eat' distractions. Meal times were exactly

structured which made sure that the party fed together –
though we much prefer dining in private. A mountain-
climbing expedition, partly on horseback, became difficult
because we naturally took responsibility for the ladies
unfamiliar with horses. Whenever we sought privacy we
felt guilty, as if we were sneaking off by ourselves to shop
or whatever.

The most difficult part for us was the constant close-
companionship of the group. It narrowed our perspectives.
We like to meet local people, develop some intimacy with
the guides, and explore villages.

Our chagrin was magnified when we discovered that
group travel had not been necessary. By contacting the
tourist department of Bhutan in Thimbu, we could easily
have arranged an independent trip at no higher cost. Our
great friend, the travel agent, was misinformed or
deliberately misinformed us.

**Lesson and recommendation: extensive research will
reveal alternatives.**

The bright side of small-group travel is that, with the right
mix, the ambience becomes family-like. Waiting for stragglers
happens less. Closeness makes people far more aware of inconvenience to the group. Humour replaces annoyance. Minor
changes of plan are easily agreed upon if weather interferes or a
diverting side trip appears. We would choose a small rather than
a large group whenever possible.

LARGE-GROUP TRAVEL
A sizeable group is necessarily regimented. Shepherding two
score or more people is difficult for the guides; that is, keeping
up to 30 diverse people happy, safe and well fed. Their charges
have paid large sums for the package and expect good value.
Constant counts to ensure that everyone is aboard are annoying;

more so is waiting for the two people who are always late or have to go back for a lost article. Particular seats on the bus are objects of contention. The first row is best for visibility; commandeering it causes resentment. The guide is accused of favouring certain persons to the irritation of others.

Enjoyment of the trip can be clouded by the interplay of social problems generated by a group of strangers vying for recognition. A misunderstanding of arrangements, or a particularly unfortunate occurrence at the breakfast table, can take time away from viewing the scenery. People feel put out instead of uplifted.

More time is spent queuing when a large-group leader must organise his charges long before departure. Mountains of luggage need to be gathered and dispatched. Milling about accelerates annoyance when the weather is too hot, too cold or too wet.

Large groups present their own set of pros and cons. They are more cumbersome to take part in, but have the advantage of anonymity. Singles can pay extra for single rooms or request a switch of roommates; and couples or subgroups can divert themselves without causing attention.

Enough of the possible negatives. Perennial optimists will swear that the usual misfortunes will not happen to them, and I agree. For they keep their sense of humour, pay no attention to the detractors and look on the bright side.

On that bright side, they realise that most large groups are of like-minded people organised by a school, a business or professional association, or some other fraternity. Or they have all been attracted by the tour's special character. Its members will take the opportunity, away from the daily grind, to enjoy relaxed companionship while discussing professional or recreational topics. The interplay extends into exchanges about non-common factors such as each others' professions, skills or talents.

Small circles – or cliques – develop. Sometimes these closer friendships survive to future excursions, and beyond.

SUMMARY

Companionship provides the opportunity to enlarge the scope of personal relationships. Each individual or couple makes of it what they will. It is sensible to conduct relationships to enhance the pleasure of your tour. Don't hesitate to correct any uncomfortable situation from the outset. Group leaders are well attuned to such problems. They will switch your roommate or your seating. In an extreme case they will allow you to detach from the group. You have advanced good money for a rare experience in a congenial ambience. You should insist on good value for your investment.

Chapter Ten

WOMEN TRAVELLING ALONE

The exception to the notion that everyone wants company is the woman who aspires to the exquisite freedom of travelling on her own – of being the quintessential Independent Traveller. This chapter is dedicated to her, and to her accomplishments without tour group or companion.

THE VENTURESOME SPOUSE

Some women, though happily married, prefer to travel alone. Business or professional women, travelling solo on duty, accustom themselves to certain comforts and requirements provided by major hotels. For privacy they use special executive floors, each with a concierge on hand, and there enjoy continental breakfasts plus pre-evening cocktail hours. Articles and books on the subject have long lists of do's and don'ts which the novice pleasure-traveller can learn from.

According to the lore, there are men – gentle and kind husbands or partners – who are horrible to travel with. Leaving home, and spending money in the process, is foreign to their nature. Travel turns them into disgruntled rogues. In a strange environment, they react obstreperously to the change from their home routine. "It's 6:30: why can't we have dinner now instead of 8:00? We always eat at 6:30. This place is awful, I couldn't even get a three-minute egg made right this morning. The maid moved my shaver. It looks like rain today, I think we ought to go home." Trivialities, aggravated by unfamiliar surroundings, destroy the entire sweet aroma of the adventure.

So: leave him at home.

THE ENCAPSULED SINGLE

Many women live independent lives. Never-married women (and men) are accepted and respected in today's world. Professional and business careers encourage single-living amongst achievers. Widowhood and divorces send people back to an individual's lifestyle. Often, however, there are children, still at home and involved in the daily pattern of existence.

Women in these situations may feel encapsuled, caught in the web of career, family, well-meaning friends and the style of life expected of them. To join fellow travellers in a tour group is to transfer from one cage to another. Tour groups invariably have more single women than couples. Being tied to a routine, even in a foreign country, resembles too much the predictable as endured at home. The challenge is to avoid fetters, go off alone, see the grazing lands of the Rich and Famous.

Escapism it may be. But it allows one to recharge the independent batteries, take an overview of one's life, imagine changes, and perhaps use time to reorganise. Treat it more like a holiday than the cure for a malady. What is wrong with wanting to concoct a little fun and toss some new experiences into the salad of travel? Married or single, woman or man, we all get in a rut and can use a new perspective.

By the time this year's escape has prompted next year's programme, no independent woman will need this chapter to tell her how to relax and/or venture overseas. As for details, a knowledgeable concierge will arrange a tour of the city and tickets for the ballet. He will advise about restaurants that cater comfortably for single women, and book a special table.

PHYSICAL SECURITY AND COMFORT

Whatever their age, women worry about being accosted or taken advantage of, especially abroad. Crime is over-publicised almost everywhere. There is anxiety about being charged too much in a taxi, or coerced into an unearned tip, about one's purse being stolen in a busy street – and a hundred greater or lesser disasters. These fears are warranted. The long-planned adventure can be spoiled or ruined, or worse.

This list of do's and don'ts comes from seasoned women business travellers. Take it with you, *and scan the list every morning*, for items which could relate to the day's plan:

- Use inconspicuous luggage, duffels preferably.
- Never bring cases or bags heavier than you can easily lift.
- Two small pieces of luggage are better than one large one.
- Ask for side-row aircraft seating as far forward as possible.
- Put make-up and a change of clothes in the carry-on bag.
- Use a hand trolley for carry-on luggage.
- Carry an ample handbag with a shoulder strap and closed top.
- Wear a minimum of jewellery.
- Put valuables in a safe in the hotel.
- Empty the safe before the final departure.
- Have passport and tickets readily available at the airport.
- Keep a pad and pen handy to make notes during journeys.

- Acquire some (small) local currency before you need it.
- Spend small notes; at the airport exchange any large ones left.
- Never share a taxi.
- When out at night, pre-arrange a return taxi.
- Tell the concierge where you'll be and when to expect you.
- Telephone the concierge if you will return significantly later.
- Re-confirm departure flights and your next hotel arrival time.
- Leave more than ample time for airport departure.
- Dress for physical comfort.
- Never carry anything (however small) for any stranger.

Most of these suggestions appear in one way or another elsewhere in the text. They are concentrated here for the single woman traveller because lone travel is a cause of worry and, often, confusion. Airport check-ins, luggage handling, and customs and immigration procedures are disconcerting. Even the busy crowds are unsettling. You may be tired when you arrive in an unfamiliar country, perhaps later in the small hours than expected. The regulations, the luggage claim, and eventually the strange hotel: taken separately, each can be coped with; it is the cumulative effect that calls for this list and the careful or-ganisation it should ensure. Thus prepared, you should be free from crises.

A note pad in the bag is handy to write down the restaurant a stewardess has recommended or a point of particular interest mentioned in the flight magazine or newspaper. It is invaluable for recording thoughts that surface when you are trying to sleep.

Dress comfortably. Carry a purse with a side pocket reserved for easy-access travel documents and a top that closes. Skirts allow more scrunching-around, and toilet comfort. Shoes that can slip back on when long flights swell the feet, and a sweater to combat the air-conditioning, add to your sense of being smart-cosy. Anticipate the arrival climate in selecting travel garments.

Wear a minimum of jewellery. Costume and *faux* gems have

their place in travelling. Many hotel rooms are equipped with *en suite* safes, and all have a secure lock-box system near the cashier.

Re-pack your luggage and empty the safe the night before your departure, to make leaving less hectic in the morning. Arrange a wake-up call for an early morning check-out; travelling alters waking habits. When you are sure you have everything, look again – under the bed, in drawers, behind the bathroom door, in and on the night table. Leaving a favourite lipstick or undergarment is very annoying, but not worth the effort to recover.

Leave the normal purse or shoulder bag in the hotel for daily excursions or beach visits. Buy a waist pouch for the needs of the day. Passport, tickets and traveller's cheques remain in the safe. You only need your day's cash, a credit card, quick make-up items, handkerchiefs or tissues, and cigarettes if you smoke. Thus you won't have to put a bag down while trying on a new dress or having lunch. Street-wise rip-off characters won't be tempted to grab and run. A bag hanging on the back of a chair in a busy restaurant is a theft invitation. Caution develops routine security habits, which replace constant fear.

Obtain some currency of the country you are visiting, in advance, for arrival tips and taxi fares. Almost all airport concourses have money changers, but arrival processes are confusing enough already.

Never allow anyone you don't know to share a taxi, regardless of the supposed emergency. Similarly, do not accept a ride from a stranger met on the plane. Con artists are often a sweet-looking elderly couple, an efficient-looking executive male with attaché case – or even uniformed, such as airline or military officers. Con men don't look like con men. There are no exceptions to the no-share rule. The taxi driver will support your demand for privacy; if not, get out and take another cab. But don't forget to retrieve your luggage.

Tie a bright-coloured ribbon onto the handle of your luggage, making it easier to identify as it comes round the baggage carousel. If a porter is available, it is well worth a two-buck tip to have him take your luggage and you to the taxi or limousine queue. With a bill in your hand he will wait until you are properly ensconced in the right vehicle. There is no worry or confusion at most airports, but some can be threatening and/or chaotic.

Before leaving the hotel for shopping or other jaunts, ask the concierge to write the destination for the taxi in the local vernacular. Ask the doorman, while you wait for a taxi, to relay this address to the driver. Make sure the driver knows the precise destination. It is both acceptable and advisable to ask the probable cost of the trip.

For single women, it's especially important to travel light. Use the smaller duffel bags that weigh no more than 10 kilos when filled. The normal airline hold-baggage allowance is 20 kilos (44 pounds). When charged, the excess is often steep. What you are permitted to carry on varies – and could be dangerously heavy. It should contain a change of clothes suitable for arrival, and cosmetic requirements in addition to the absolute necessities. A lightweight 'trolley' or 'cart' is very convenient for the long walks down airport wings.

ASSERTING ONESELF

A single woman traveller in a strange city and an impersonal hotel can feel inhibited. Feminists insist the single woman can and should exercise the same prerogatives as a single man. Enter the lounge for a twilight two-for-one cocktail – or a port before retiring – if that is what you would like. You are not looking for company; you want to write some cards, perhaps, or at least get out of the claustrophobic room. Carry a book with you, or an impressive newspaper, to ward off the stares of males who might assume you were looking for company. Starting a conversation with a stranger, male or female, is at your discretion.

Eating alone in one's room is depressing for some. Use the informal coffee shop for plebeian dining amongst the crowd. However, when you would prefer fine dining, wine and formal service, don't deny yourself the pleasure. Inform the *maître d'* that you prefer a semi-private table facing the room, away from any large or noisy groups. A snooty male chauvinist may offer you a table next to the service door or on top of the waiter's section. Look around the room and tell him which place you have in mind. If not satisfied, leave. All hotels have service questionnaires in the rooms, as the staff well know; it is amazing how quickly the sneer turns into a smile and superb service, when you ask for the name and title of an unhelpful employee.

Tipping seems to be part of the male psyche. Men tend to over-tip to impress their female companions and, hopefully, to be recognised next time. Women not used to travelling alone are often uncomfortable with the procedure. When the bill includes a service charge, there is no need to add anything unless you have genuinely enjoyed special attention. Friendly snack shops and cafes, or a porter who takes extra time to show you how to operate all the room gadgets and provides some personal insight to the hotel and city – these have earned a token of your thanks. A taxi driver who drives carefully, talks or doesn't talk as it suits you, and helps with your luggage, deserves extra coinage or the rounding up to a 20-unit note of an 18.60 meter reading.

☛ Travel Tip
If you disagree with the driver over a taxi fare on reaching your hotel, ask the doorman or hotel greeter to sort it out. In other instances of probable rip-off, carefully note down the driver's name and taxi number, plus the date, time and location. Again, this simple act can have a marvellous influence on the perpetrator.

Caution

Among the freedoms of Independent Travel is the freedom to form friendships, probably short-term, with women or men. Different nationalities add to the interest but do not change the rules of the game. If you are a businesswoman, you will know that any opportunity that arises for you to transfer an asset is a sign that the friend is bogus. Men who make their living in this way delight in breaking hearts. They will keep up the pretence, by letter or telephone, when they know they will see no more of the victim or her money.

Chapter Eleven

DE-SHOCKING THE COSTS

Package tour operators make it look easy with the luring advertisement: '21 days in Hawaii, Los Angeles, San Francisco, Denver – including a glorious three days in Las Vegas – for US$2,100.' We have discussed this in Chapter Four. All you have to do is examine the plan, make sure you like it, put down the money, take a few hundred extra for eating and the inevitable at Vegas. When you get home, the shocking overrun on your credit card reveals that you've spent another US$2,100. Where did the money go? Is travelling really worth it?

Costs are always shocking. Even wealthy people fret at the price of a first-class air passage at several hundred dollars per hour of cushy seats and fancy food. We, the great middle income group of society, must guard our dollars from the predators to get the most enjoyment value. The way to make sense out of spending the bundle that, alas, we are going to spend is to estimate a realistic budget and then keep the opportunists away from the wallet. By using some common sense and rules of thumb, we can still have a time that justifies its cost.

TRAVEL BUDGET

To get over any danger of costs stirring up your heart problems, try this travel-budget plan. Package tourists have a basic outlay in the booking agent's price. The 21-day 'United States Fling' on the previous page includes 'all land costs and free American Breakfast'. All you need do is add in the air fare and subtract the total from the maximum you can afford to spend – and divide what remains by the number of whole days (probably 20). The result is your daily average budget for the extras.

Independent Travellers have a more complicated problem. The return air fare for the itinerary is the same, but the land costs must be estimated.

A Package

A couple starts the tabulation with 2 x 2,100 = US$4,200. Wherever you are, Deluxe Economy meal costs depend mainly on your eating and drinking habits. For example, $35 for dinner, $25 for lunch, and $15 for snacks equals $75; but add another $25 if you like a couple of beers during the day and a bottle of wine for dinner, and the amount rounds out to $100. Economisers may skip lunch and the drinks, to shop for souvenirs or enjoy a massage. Rounding up, you can estimate $6,500 for the three-week adventure for two. A similar tour to quieter places nearer home, more Economy than Deluxe, can easily reduce that amount by one third.

Thus, so long as you hold to average daily 'extras' of $100 (or $75), you will know from the outset what the holiday will cost.

The Independent Traveller

The computation is the same as above, except for the basic travel cost. Though the return air fare will not change, you should in either case seek a bargain, as a later chapter will explain. The level of accommodation is controlled by the chosen style of the travelling pair. Large cities have hotel rooms from US$125, while motels can be under $50. A cafe breakfast or lunch is considerably less than a hotel buffet. Splurge for dinner at a fine restaurant, sometimes; have a pizza delivered to the motel room at others. The daily cost of food for two can be regulated up or down between $50 and $150 – giving a high average of $125, say, and a low of $75.

It is the same with the rooms. You will arrive at a similar budget for the 20-night holiday, and a target average overnight bill. Here too you will go for luxury where it beckons, and help the average with a bargain when that offers.

For travel in Asia we lump together the sleeping and eating variables, and budget $150 a day for the pair of us. Journeys within Asia, including side trips, are extra. This is the standard we call Deluxe Economy – using four- or five-star hotels but spending less on food and extra 'extras'. The trick is to buy the least expensive facilities at the finest establishments. If you cannot resist your bottle of Chardonnay with a fancy dinner every night, change the estimate to $200/$250 per day. Our Circle Pacific ticket (see Chapter Five) adds US$5,000 to the total.

Travel Axiom: The Longer You Travel, the Less You Spend

This realistic assumption is justified by the spread of ticket costs over six weeks or two months instead of 21 days. But longer stays in one place can reduce room and food costs per diem, also. The hotel will give you a better room rate; and as you settle in you will tend to eat snacks, in your room or elsewhere, for lunch and/or breakfast; you will also find yourself stepping down to the cheaper colds and salads at buffet dinners, without going hungry.

You now have, for package and Independent Travellers, estimates of the amount necessary to finance the adventure. Add a reserve of 10% for over-spending, and then work out where the money is coming from. Some people keep one credit card exclusively for annual holiday travel. They ignore the bank's requirement of a modicum each month and pay one-twelfth regardless, to clear the debt in time for the next year's odyssey. The guilty feeling lessens if you compare it to the necessity of a rent or mortgage payment on your home or car. The key word is necessity. Enjoying a fine holiday adventure each year is as indispensable to life as owning a residence and an automobile.

Big cities like Singapore, Hong Kong, New York, London and Paris cost more; fine small resorts in (say) Portugal, Malaysia or the Philippines, much less. Back-packing youngsters do it for under US$25 a day, but elders need a little more physical comfort. In northern Europe Deluxe Economy is expensive; in the United States and Australia, middling; and in parts of Asia, very modest. For two, a daily average could range from US$100 to US$500. Initial overseas flights vary with distance and the package you choose.

Chapter Eight has tips on saving money while getting the most out of the system. Consider the money you save as prolonging the adventure. Some of that advice is repeated in the following sections, re-stated for your convenience in this budget context.

Budget for the maximum; never delude yourself with a minimum.

SAVING MONEY
Your dollar stretches when you watch all money transactions.

Changing Currency
This is a mystery to the unwary. Keep in mind that it is a profit-

making business for hotels, money changers, bank exchange services and credit card companies. One per cent is an average handling charge by the banks and major card companies. So be it, as long as the exchange is calculated from the international rates. These are quoted in most national and the bigger local newspapers.

Credit Cards

These provide the best system for spending in foreign countries; the rates are controlled and in order. Conversion is customarily 1% over the published international rate on the day the card company receives the voucher. The system of international cards is so electronically efficient that you may obtain a cash advance almost anywhere in the world in a few minutes. No worry about running out of currency or carrying a lot of cash or traveller's cheques. Transport systems, hotels, restaurants and commercial theatres all readily accept credit cards; large to medium shops do likewise, except in remote areas.

In many countries, travel agents may charge extra for card purchases. You can avoid this, or at least reduce it, by obtaining cash with the credit card.

Traveller's Cheques

This form of flexibility is now little used by the experienced traveller. If you are a worrier and careless with personal effects, you should insure against loss. The issuing company benefits, on a principle opposite to that of the credit card: they have the use of your money until you cash or spend their cheques.

American Express has a great advertising line aimed at keeping unused cheques in your pocket for the next trip. What a way to make money: sell people your cheques, charge them and then tell them not to cash in. Mind you, the customer who prudently buys more than enough of these things would lose in another way through cashing the surplus and then paying another percent to purchase them back from the issuing bank the next year – and at least another 1% off the international rate on cashing them abroad.

Meanwhile the holder must keep track of the cheques used and retain the register list separately. If a loss occurs the company will require to be told which cheques were used where, and the numbers on the remaining block.

Street Money Changers

If you know the international rate beforehand, you will usually find the small-shop (or even open-air) changers very fair as well as convenient. On longer trips, we often change currency with them for the next country on our itinerary.

Hotels and Banks

While they may look more reliable, hotels will take up to 5% more from you than will the man behind the street counter. If you must change money in your hotel, change the minimum. Banks often charge a fee or commission as well. Ask or look for a 'No commission' sign at the changer or in the bank. Hotels and banks post major exchange rates in their lobbies for easy reference: in the former, look for the spread between buying and selling figures.

Airport Money Changers

Perhaps taking advantage of a strategic position, changers in airports usually give less favourable rates than those in shopping streets and malls. So don't change much on the way in or out – but the absence of a commission could influence you the other way.

☛ **Personal Experience**

Sometimes it seems impossible to change money or make purchases at or near the official rate. On a recent visit to the

Philippines, the international rate was almost P29 to US$1, the hotel offered P24, and stores exchanged for P25. One travel agent quoted me P1,400 for a particular side trip, and then asked US$66 for the same service. Even at the high average of P25, he was skimming P250, making it almost 20% off the international rate. It's tough to fight because you are in their country. In such cases, we politely turn down any surcharged service and explain why. Try to pay everything you can with your credit card.

☛ **Travel Tip**

For pocket cash, check with the money changers in one country for the exchange rate of the next. If you know the international rate and are being offered only a point off, get the cash before you leave. If you have money left over at the end of your next stay, use it towards the hotel bill. But keep enough for the taxi and airport departure tax. Also, when the itinerary goes through more than one country, you can change leftover currency to that of the next. This means you only get clipped once on the exchange.

If one of your party has a problem with calculating, make a little card with pre-computed exchange rates both ways for useful denominations of your currency against the local. It makes for easy reference when shopping.

Money exchange and its problems can be annoying and time consuming, and so distract one from enjoying the adventure. Prepare ahead, and there will be no such distraction. Moreover you will be saved from the 'corner clippers', as we call them.

Prepayment

Paying ahead for travel arrangements may make you feel secure, but it means the money comes out of your bank account long before you use the purchased item. Tours often require a major deposit – or all of the price – weeks or months in advance. For our six-month odysseys, we pay as we go except for the basic air ticket. Thus our expenses are paid on our return. If there are interest charges, they mainly begin much later than with full prepayment.

For tours, push the travel agent to hold off until the last possible time of payment. Agents need to collect in advance to make sure of their commission. Independent Travellers should do as little advance paying as possible. The problem is the difficulty of getting a refund if you don't or can't use all you paid for.

To claim a refund, you must apply to the person or company that took your deposit in the first place. That means the agent. If you wish to change hotels, the prepayment is irrecoverable, which is very frustrating. Therefore make reservations yourself by fax or phone, guarantee the first night with your credit card and pay when you leave the hotel. Provided you give 48 hours notice of non-arrival or early departure, neither the hotel nor the credit card company could defend charging for more than the guaranteed period.

There is an interesting phenomenon in hotel bookings. If you reserve for a week, guaranteeing the first night, and leave after two days, no one says a word. The cashier takes your money for the two nights and cheerfully waves you off. Extending your stay is rarely a problem if you're travelling independently. One room in a hotel with 300 or 600 is 'always' available.

Some small and exclusive resorts however will impose their own rules if you want to stay during fully-booked periods. For example: Qamea Beach Club in Fiji, with only 10 *bure*, is soft-hearted and will accept a direct reservation with a credit card guarantee; while the hardened souls at Lizard Island, Great Barrier Reef, want half with the booking and the balance weeks before you get there.

Remember the traveller's axiom: "It is my money, and I'm the customer."

☛ **Travel Tip**
On average, the cheapest way to pay for travel is to charge your credit card and pay within the 'no-service-charge' deadline.

TIPPING

Squander or conserve. You can be a big tipper or save some dollars to spend in a better way. Tipping is an annoyance because customs vary from place to place. Most large hotel chains and restaurants charge '+ +' for a total called 'nett'. This is a 10% (or 15%) service charge (employee benefits supposedly) and a 5% (or 10%) sales tax (government benefit).

When the tip is automatically included and the service is normal we don't add anything. If the bell hop has to struggle with an overload of luggage and renders extra service in settling us in, we do slip him a dollar or so. A helpful taxi driver normally gets the small change left over from the fare.

In some areas – Hong Kong and the US for example – everyone expects to be tipped. Singapore reverses the trend by deliberately requesting no tipping in major hotels (though your credit card chit will thoughtfully leave open the chance to defy that request). Australians consider it demeaning and don't expect it. The same principle should apply universally: tipping is a reward for extra service, not a device to help the employer's payroll.

The new electronic twist to the tipping tail is confusing to some travellers. Automatic processing of credit cards in restaurants uses a form that has a space marked 'tip' on top of (though literally below) the total which includes '+ +'. Don't be browbeaten, ignore it. Whatever you do, avoid giving a percentage of the bill and of the pluses... If a waiter has earned a real thank you, leave a sum in cash on the table. The classic system of making sure the person you want to reward gets the tip, is to conceal it in a goodbye handshake. Old-fashioned but effective.

COMMUNICATION

For Independent Travellers, direct contact with the accommodation at various destinations is very important and easy. Whether
booking with a travel agent or doing it yourself, it is comforting
to have address information and names of staff during planning
and before arrival. Contact and reconfirmation of itinerary while
on the way are important.

There are the usual methods of telephone and mail plus the
newest boon to travellers, facsimile service by telephone wire.
Fax is so prevalent today that all but the most rural of the people
you communicate with are equipped. If you have no office and
your home does not have the facility, local secretarial services
and most post offices make them available. Charges vary, especially for incoming foreign messages, so shop around. In small
communities the local book and office-supplies store usually
offers a fax service.

For long advance planning, mail is sufficient to establish a
contact, get the desired information, and follow up. Fax is better
for more urgent reservations. Date changes are better handled
by phone call with written fax confirmation. A verbal discussion
can resolve differences in time of arrival and temporary fully-
booked problems. (You can dial direct from most hotels, but ask
beforehand about hotel surcharges.)

The same is true of communication with your home whilst
away. Postcards take 10 days to two weeks from the most distant
countries. Fax messages, if you have good points of contact, are
instant though not as personal. Phone calls are often difficult
because of time differences and availability of the other party.
The fax line stands ready 24 hours a day like a good soldier. Send
the family a fax on arrival at each destination, with the hotel
number and the time difference – and whether to add or subtract.

To facilitate telephone calls, we include in the 'arrived' fax
the best time to call calculated in the home zone time. For

instance, we're normally in our room before breakfast and thus available to receive a call if necessary. Most overseas calls are cheaper from home, and contact is readily made. Advise your fax correspondent to be sure to use your name. The Singapore Shangri-La had some difficulty one year delivering a fax addressed to Dear Mom and Dad.

Watch the Costs

Fax and telephone costs vary considerably. It is a profit-making enterprise for most hotels, and they often add from 10% to 40% to the actual charges. Some back-breakers charge by the page, others use a minimum cost plus time used. Be sure to ask for costs before using overseas communication services.

Access to the worldwide AT&T service is unique and low cost. Special facilities (now expanding to other parts of the world) are available for travelling US residents. With the proper card, call a pre-specified number in the foreign country, connecting immediately with an AT&T operator as a collect call. You punch in the number desired and the various card and code numbers. It is billed directly to your own number at local rates. Enquire from your phone service company before you leave, about any special communication services available when out of your country.

The old cliché 'It's a small world' was never more apt than in referring to modern communication systems.

AIR TICKETS

Flight is the major cost reflected in the price of tour packages. The vendor can control hotel portions by the quality and what each hotel will throw into the deal. Thus if you are designing your own package, the first thing to determine is the flight cost. Then you can work in the accommodation and hire car or side trips.

The problem is, prices vary within the same airline and

between booking methods. An intricate web of special dates, times of the year, days of the week, half-fare and frequent-flier arrangements is ultimately confusing.

The choices are:

- Contact the airline direct. Reserve the package; then ask a travel agency to write the ticket.
- Contact the airline and buy the ticket in their office.
- Persuade your agency to shop for the best rate and supply the ticket.
- Shop carefully round discount ticket ('bucket') shops, but with a wary eye on arrangements to deliver the tickets to you.

My favourite system is to call the airline, obtain a quoted rate and flight information, and then see whether travel agencies can produce a better plan.

HIRE CAR

There are special rates for advance booking by international operators like Hertz, Avis, Budget, etc. Local car rental agencies provide a variety of rates depending on limitations and drop-off charges. The international companies are easy to check on. Your hometown office will provide the information. Discover local rental car agencies at your destination by questioning the hotel concierge, reading counter brochures and telephoning Yellow Pages listings on arrival. Hotel personnel get a commission from the rental car vendor if they place the order. Call some of the local people to discover any variation in prices for direct booking.

Competition forces the local companies to offer better prices, sometimes half those of the international ones. As ever, you must check all the details and ask the hotel about reliability. Local companies do not have as many drop-off points, if any, should you want to divest the vehicle at the other end of the trip. There are always two ways to buy the service. One is unlimited mileage, the other is per mile. Go over a map with the clerk to determine the distances you will probably travel. The good companies will compute the cost both ways on your return and charge you the lesser amount. You will also pay for all petrol.

Checklist
- Specific vehicle desired (for uniform comparison of hirers).
- Unlimited mileage, or base charge plus mileage?
- Drop-off charge?
- Drop-off points?
- What if I need repairs or service?
- Extra charges per diem, for insurance or whatever?
- Credit card payment?
- Limits of use, such as unpaved roads, etc.?

TRAVEL INSURANCE

Travel industry people tend to agree that North America, Switzerland, Hong Kong and Japan are notorious for being the most expensive places in which to have an accident or fall ill. However, Thomas Cook's travel agency points out that it can be just as costly in third world countries, despite the likely absence of modern facilities.

Some experienced embassy officers advise that if you can't afford an insurance policy, you can't afford to travel. Some booking agencies offer insurance cover along with an extensive tour, or include it in the total price. Thomas Cook quotes three categories of cover: budget, standard and super plus – ranging in cost from US$175 to US$225 for a family on a 21-day trip.

These policies will include cancellation-of-trip clauses, whether by the traveller or the tour operator. Agencies have gone bankrupt while their clients were in the middle of a tour. Transport and accommodation were therefore unpaid, creating great havoc in the travel plans. Prepaid travel notwithstanding, the travellers were left stranded in a foreign city, and forced to pay (again) for – and make – arrangements to finish the journey and return home.

Each airline will have a policy giving cover for aircraft accidents, but effective only on its leg of the journey. American Express has an automatic accidental death policy purchase system (for 75 US cents) in effect whenever you buy your ticket with their card. Other card companies have similar free or low cost, but often severely restricted, cover.

Health and Accident Policies

Medical/health insurance taken out in your own country will probably not cover expenditure outside territorial limits. You must consider specific travel policies if you want cover abroad. As with any insurance purchase, the customer must evaluate the possible risks and then read the fine print.

A travel policy will cover:
• Trip cancellation.
• Very limited medical services.
• Accidental death or loss of limb.
• Emergency evacuation.
• Repatriation of remains, in case of death.
• Lost or stolen luggage.

A typical 1994 premium would be US$60 for a 31-day family trip. Extended excursions are covered by a surcharge per diem which may make the policy non-cost-effective. Study the exact cover limits and charges before you buy.

Elderly people are susceptible to heart problems, falls and fractures that require hospital treatment and/or expert medical care. Younger persons are prone to sports related accidents like the proverbial broken leg on a ski trip. Scuba divers can buy relevant cover on an annual basis whatever the location, as may racing-car drivers and parachutists.

The important part is the small print, where the exceptions and exclusions appear.

Homeowners' and Worldwide General Policies

Many 'home and effects' (or 'house and contents') policies cover loss worldwide of personal possessions within the limits stated. They can include luggage, jewellery and equipment plus expenses incurred in connection with the loss. Expensive individual items must be specifically listed and appraised, for which you will pay. Look up your policy and check for the exceptions. Take these into consideration when purchasing a travel policy. Double coverage will seldom pay double if you do have a loss. The primary insurer pays first, and the secondary will cover what's left only.

Which insurance company is providing the cover? Make sure it is well known and reputable. This is up to the selling agent to prove to your satisfaction. Insurance policies sold by the big travel companies (Thomas Cook, American Express, etc.) obviously have substantial backing. Unknowns are suspect. If the agent does not satisfy or evades your curiosity, buy a policy direct from a known insurance company.

☛ Observation

Like travel agents, money changers and the many other professionals with whom travellers deal, insurance companies and the vendors of their policies are in business to make profits. You insure your life because, for your dependants, it is irreplaceable. Under much the same compulsion, you insure the house you live in, if you own it. But if you owned 10 houses it would usually be more profitable to stand the risks of damage and destruction than to pay premiums for a company to stand the 10-fold risks. It is simpler, and on average cheaper, not to insure against misfortunes which would cost you – but by no means ruin you. This, you might say, is a near relation of Deluxe Economy.

'Simpler' is an over-simplification, of course. It is true insofar as *laissez-faire* cuts out paper work, which includes the writing of premium cheques. It might still be true when the gamble does not pay off, for whatever you may have to do to restore the position, it won't include making and pursuing a claim. But there will be times when a big organisation will do for you what you cannot easily do yourself, whether the claim relates to travel or domestic disasters.

Checklist

If you haven't already got it, you need to investigate cover for:
- Health care abroad, including accidents to body and limb.
- Medical evacuation to hospital and home.
- Trip cancellation.
- Failure of vendor to complete contract.
- Loss of luggage and personal effects.
- Accidents in vehicles or non-scheduled aircraft.
- Compensation for interruption of journey.
- Extra accidental death cover.

Chapter Twelve

SHOCKING FOODS

Eating a new and unusual gastronomic delight is one of the rare pleasures of life. Enjoyment of a fruit never tasted before is an adventure, though not everyone likes the tropical durian. There must be a taste for excitement in the soul if one is to sample the range of food preparations around the world.

Travellers with simpler tastes will find it easier to enjoy more of their familiar food today than ever before. The prevalence of international food franchises means you can have your fix with a double-whammy burger in Beijing, Moscow or wherever. Local clones of these chains multiply the familiar food menus. You can get fried chicken almost anywhere.

At the other extreme are gourmets who look for fine dining

and rare wines wherever they go. Five-star hotels have fancy dress dining rooms, elegant service, prestige menus, champagne, caviar – and Swiss-trained chefs preparing *haute cuisine*.

Between these two groups are the rest of us: ordinary mortals who like the thrill of new tastes at fair prices, and the fun of variety. As age comes upon us, seven-course dinners are reduced to six, then five and eventually three courses in the interest of better health. We snack more and over-stuff less as physical comfort and good sense overcome greed.

WHERE TO EAT?

Always available in reserve is the average hotel coffee house – not necessarily your hotel's – with a varied menu of soups, salads, pasta, grills, local fare or three-course set dinners. It is easier to use that facility when tired from arrival or after a long day touring. When you have the energy, it is fun to stroll down the fashionable artery of a city like Singapore with an appetite but no set plans for dinner. Look at menus of a dozen different restaurants, peer inside some of them, and then go for what most tempts the palate. Unexpectedly finding a Mövenpick with a Swiss menu of *raclette* and a crisply fresh salad bar, plus a sweet counter from which to take an apple strudel back to the hotel – that is a successful treasure hunt.

In cities with mainly scattered restaurants, consult the telephone book, and ask the concierge and the doorman to recommend eating places. Breakfast away from the hotel is often an interesting and rewarding adventure. Try the central shopping and business district where coffee shops and takeaways abound. Office and retail business people know where to go. Pick the busiest one you can find where you have to queue to get a cappuccino and fresh pastry.

Before an evening dinner, take the trouble to call the suggested restaurant yourself. A few minutes on the phone enquiring about food styles and prices, and gauging the voice-welcome, will tell you what to expect. Try two or three for the most interesting response. When booking, ask the name of the person you are talking to and on arrival try to meet him or her. A compliment on the telephone demeanour may produce instant rapport, because everyone's ego loves to be polished. Now that you are old friends, a nicer table, food suggestions and a positive atmosphere go a long way to make your evening special.

In some of our favourite cities, the dining variety in our hotel is so marvellous that we don't bother to go out. Another factor is the length of sojourn in one location, which brings on a certain contentment with familiar dining. A pleasant dinner, chosen from an excellently varied menu, invites return visits. Staff get to know your tastes, willingly agree to prepare dishes especially to suit, and often suggest unusual items not on the menu. Variety is said to be the spice of life; to enjoy this spice in a continuing comfortable ambience and a contented glow is all the more satisfying. Keep a note in your travel diary of such places and the names of contacts, for the next time you visit.

Your travel guide, local directories and the all encompassing *Yellow Pages* will supply a great range of dining choices. All that's required is some research by phone, and discussion with locals such as your concierge, beauty parlour operator or taxi driver.

STRANGE FOODS

For visitors from afar, the discovery of unique foods is an essential aspect of true adventure. Fresh local fruits tend to symbolise each area, from the start. Fine hotels welcome you with a basket of their best in your room. Northerners rarely see mangosteens with their delicate white puffs, lychees or rambutans – fresh, not out of a can. A mango or a papaya, ripe from the tree, is a rare treat when unfamiliar. Southern Asians visiting the United States have delights in store for them in the superb apples and cherries from Washington State, and shoofly pie from Louisiana.

Knife, fork and spoon are available everywhere, but sometimes local methods are fun to try. Chopsticks, for the initiated, provide a delicate, morsel-enjoying system of eating from a bowl. In India, one can learn to eat with the fingers aided with a bread called *naan* (but be careful to use your right hand, so as not to offend a host). Fried rice, with a different name in each country, is served in infinite variety – and is sometimes eaten with a large spoon.

Southern Chinese and Southeast Asians use chillies with abandon, to enhance the taste of bland foods, thereby burning the mouths of unwary visitors. Experienced travellers learn to ask the degree of enhancement on a scale of "One, two or three chilli-hot?". A temporising waiter's reply, "Very mild," is to be treated with suspicion. In the Chinese province of Sichuan, we soon gathered that the degrees started with very hot, and accelerated to higher magnitudes. We learned preventive tactics, such as washing the morsel in clear soup, unobtrusively, before chewing.

There are eel and squid lovers, as against those of us who are not fond of the slippery and the chewy. The problem is to identify the objects by their local names – when everything is covered with sauces (and names are equally obscure) – unless you speak the language or can have them pointed out in your dictionary. In Italy they call the round, white, edible rubber bands *calamari*.

Various sizes of the other universal seafood are shrimp, prawn and tiger prawn. When these delicacies are served with their shells on, under a hot red sauce, you have to learn a new dimension of eating. The system is to spit out the inedible, indelicate though some might think it. When a whole crab is served so, who could possibly figure out how to pick apart the luscious meat without getting sprayed from chin to lap with chilli-red goo? (So one rolls up one's sleeves, tucks a napkin where it is needed, and sets to.)

☞ Personal Experience

One rare incident, I must share with you. We were dining in a cell-block-like restaurant in a hotel on the Mekong River, at Xishuang Bana, Yunnan. The rice and steamed vegetables were delightful, and side-dish saucers of crunchy titbits were served as requested. Interesting, with a garlic flavour – until we asked what the strange fried whatevers were. "Fried bees," answered our youthful guide, who condescended to finish the lot, with gusto, as we shied off.

Snake restaurants are well known in China; in Japan, poison fish (with a 99% guarantee that the poison has been removed). Vegetarian dishes conjured to look and taste like meat and fish dishes, once the domain of religious sects, are now common. A health restaurant recently opened in Manila, announcing a proper proportion of negative ions in the air to allow all believers in unadulterated and organic growth foods to dine in purity. The Japanese eat their fish raw, tempered with that strong green mustard paste *(wasabi)* in soy sauce; and some of the noodles, like some pasta, are Nile green.

Different names for the same food can be confusing, as in 'papaya' and 'paw paw'.

Australian restaurants in various areas offer buffalo steak or kangaroo, emu and crocodile meat, as alternatives to their ubiquitous barramundi fish fillets. For first-time thrills and something to tell your children about, try some of these. Korean restaurants feature dog meat, something the rest of us (pet lovers or pet haters) have been unable even to think about.

TENDER STOMACHS

For tender stomachs or reluctant palates, we have a few basic recommendations. Ask for vegetables steamed; sauces served on the side, when in doubt; grilled meat, fish and poultry. The char from the flames is less harmful than gooey unknown sauces; besides, the chef can't hide anything that way. Admit readily to finding a taste obnoxious, as in fishy-prawn, and turn it away. Most restaurants will gladly serve something else if you ask.

A major problem arises when you sense that the person serving you doesn't understand your language too well. He will agree to everything you say, and when you get your dinner it will be all wrong. Speak up, don't be shy. Ask for the dining-room manager, compliment him on the wonderful restaurant and request that he or she personally take your order to avoid confusion. My wife hates oil and continually spends time asking for "steam cooked, no oil please". It may sound simple, but we have been surprised by the number of Eastern chefs who find themselves psychologically unable to omit oil completely.

Above all, eating abroad is an adventure: the tastes of new foods and preparation styles are treasures to be garnered. If you happen to be in Lhasa Tibet for the one and only time in your life, taste the offerings anyway. At best you will enjoy them, and at worst you will have a story to tell about how the top of the world has the lowest palatability on earth.

On lengthy stays in a particular location, we often bypass formal dinner and carry something to the room. Lunch is fruit and cheese by the beach or in the comfort of our open-windowed room or private balcony. Most hotels supply, free, the wherewithal to make coffee and tea. Breakfast can be a continental pastry or croissant, and a mango, bought the night before to eat with your tea or coffee on the veranda. A light breakfast has the advantage of creating a hunger for lunch at a friendly street cafe.

A leisurely lunch in a fine restaurant is much less expensive than the same menu in the evening. Most business lunchers eat quickly, leaving the dining room and service to you. Another advantage of eating a siesta-lunch is physical comfort. A heavy meal before you go to bed at night is uncomfortable and un-healthy. A late lunch affords time to walk it off and maybe nap before dinner, when a light meal suffices. It is difficult to get evening reservations at famous restaurants during a short city visit. The concierge will find it much easier to make a luncheon booking for you.

Snacks before retiring can easily be kept in the small refrig-erators that the better hotels provide today. If you don't like the mini-bar prices, stop at a local market and pick up your diet cola and local beer. On longer stays, we request that they take the contents of the mini-bar out to leave room for the fruit and snacks we like to keep handy. Don't be timorous. If they ignore the request, take out the non-perishables and put them nearby. When you are travelling for six weeks, you may not want 126 restaurant breakfasts, lunches and dinners in a row. Saving US$25 a day for six weeks nets over $1,000 – enough to stretch your trip for another week.

☞ Travel Tip
When checking into the hotel, the porter will fuss over getting you settled. At that time, we ask for our usual specials: extra pillows, removal of mini-bar, 'decaf' coffee, daily newspaper, an empty carton to ship home luggage and shopping extras, and turn off the air-conditioning please. A helpful porter, knowing how to please you, will receive a tip then and probably earn a well-deserved gratuity when you leave; meanwhile you will have all the little extra comforts and attention.

BUFFETS
Treat all buffets, *smorgåsbord* and other hyped spreads with great suspicion. Suspicion as to over-pricing, and steam-table dull-ness. Take the time and trouble to review the spread with the same discrimination as you give to a printed menu. Walk through

it and mentally select the dishes that are tempting. Then consult the menu to see which of the two styles is to be the choice of the evening. The opportunity to over-eat at a buffet is there, but the stomach can absorb only so much without severe discomfort – a travel danger which it is very important to avoid.

On the positive side, well designed buffets offer the chance to try small amounts of a variety of local or other superb dishes – and to come back for a little more of what was best. There are often rare delicacies mixed in with row on row of ordinary stuff. Wafer-thin Nova Scotia salmon or Italian *prosciutto*, for instance, may be on the starter table. A resort hotel in the Philippines served a grilled dinner of prawns (two) for P350 with vegetables and rice. A barbecue buffet the next night offered unlimited supplies of the skewered prawns along with fish, chicken, meat, a variety of salads, dessert and coffee for P495. We gorged on the delicious prawns and the grill chef was only too happy to pile our plates.

True gourmet buffet *aficionados* (I consider myself one) will attack interesting buffets with a small plate, and eat in courses, carefully selecting only the finest delicacies, rarest cheeses, tenderest shrimps – and a generous slice from the leg of lamb. Side dishes are chosen for the greenest of pea pods, and hearts of the celery and artichoke. Eat each course slowly; refresh with suitable pauses between courses for conversation, palate-cleansing and perhaps the inexpensive house wine served by the glass. It takes determination and time to enjoy the feast. No one must rush you to go round the table, or look at you with disdain (don't look askance at her plate-piling, either). The culmination is to leave room for at least a thin slice of the tastiest cheesecake and the triple chocolate *Sacher Torte*. Of course, if you are in Vienna, stop at the Sacher Hotel and lunch on their famous *Torte* and chocolate-sprinkled espresso coffee.

Request your tea in a pot: "With the best Orange Pekoe if you please." Pouring from a glass serving pot on a nearby warmer is not for gourmets like yourselves. Coffee drinkers can dawdle for an hour over a favoured espresso, or an Irish coffee.

Now that's how I like a buffet, and I will pay the price if it looks that good. This is part of the system called 'Deluxe Economy'. Get your money's worth in interesting food and good service when you find them.

In summary: food can be shocking, exciting, familiar, enjoyable or distasteful – and sometimes the cause of stomach problems. Look on the bright side. It is Adventure, part and parcel of going to a new country and exploring its character – while adding to your own...

This is no time to be shy or conservative; you may never get another chance to eat fried bees or dine in a negative-ion ambience.

Chapter Thirteen

GOOD HEALTH

It sometimes comes as a shock that other countries besides yours have adequate medical facilities and medicines. Unless you're travelling in a canoe far up the Orinoco, most places in which you will travel are well equipped to handle the usual cold, sniffle and digestion ailments. Broken limbs, heart attacks and more serious problems are frightening; but they do happen, and are efficiently attended to (see Chapter Fourteen).

My doctor in Arizona complained that all his patients came back from China with some respiratory problem. Mostly true, for he handled elderly people who normally took short tours. Beijing is a large air-polluted city. Tourists rise early to get on the bus to climb the Great Wall. If the day is rainy, and there are thousands of locals and visitors around them, then on or off the bus they will have been exposed by the end of the day to every viral element in the world that induces respiratory ailments. Much the same applies in London, Jakarta, New Delhi, Athens, Los Angeles and New York – for example.

COMMON SENSE

The solution is common sense, of course. Even if you're on a scheduled tour, you can opt out and see some sights independently. Hire a taxi or private car, carry a thermos of boiled water or hot tea, and go on a weekday when the locals thin out somewhat. If susceptible to colds and viral infections, wear a nose and mouth mask and don't mind any snide remarks or pointed fingers.

When down with a cold, do the same as you would at home. Rest, aspirin, vitamin C, hot bowls of noodle soup, thermos after thermos of tea, liberally dosed with honey and lemon; and sweat it out. If it hangs on longer, see the local doctor. All hotels have access to medical assistance, many with in-house clinics. You will not be the first tourist to catch a cold in Los Angeles or Kuala Lumpur.

We older folk have misfortunes that at home would be routine. My wife had her dental bridge repaired in Beijing; I've had kidney stone problems in Chiang Mai, north Thailand. Something in the water bit my ankle at Damai Beach in Sarawak. The hotel nurse appeared immediately and applied that rare medicine called vinegar to the wounded place; this allowed me to survive to record the event.

☛ **Family Experience**
Our son-in-law, assigned to a technical project on a joint-venture mission in Beijing, fell while playing badminton. The upper leg was broken into many pieces. Unable to find a flight out for him, a local orthopaedic surgeon did the

repair surgery in an antiquated hospital, fixing the broken pieces to a metal implant. American doctors gave due credit to the surgeon when removing the metal, months later. The patient has no limp or other after-effect. The surgeon was next seen on his way to Florida to address the University Medical School on manipulating bones back into place without surgery, in the ancient Chinese way. We gratefully conclude that, though his primary skill is indeed in traditional Chinese medicine, he was good enough at Western methods to do more than get by in an inadequate hospital.

Carry a sufficient supply of your special medications and a current medical report, if you have physical problems. Most foreign doctors are professionally educated in worldwide methods and systems. It is easy and usual to telephone or fax your home doctor, for consultation in more serious or complex cases. For evacuation, most airlines have stretcher facilities – but they are costly.

By way of milder remedies, we carry Tylenol or Panadol for the usual headaches and colds, Lomotil for diarrhoea; and not much else except elimination pills in case odd foods get our plumbing stopped up. My medi-pack contains band-aids, a thermometer, corn pads, Neosporin for scratches, and lozenges.

Inoculations

Your local government health services are well acquainted with disease problems around the world. Call and ask about the area you are travelling to. For example, the Solomon Islands perennially pose a serious malaria threat. Older nemeses like smallpox, measles and typhoid sometimes recur because the world tends to forget about them. The current worry is far more serious: AIDS.

We take routine gamma globulin (good for three months) before we leave, in case we run into bad drinking water or a new hepatitis area. The theory is that a preventive shot in the butt is worth two cure-alls in the arm.

TROPICAL AILMENTS

People unaccustomed to travelling in the tropics are shocked to discover crotch and foot infections, aggravated by lack of treatment. Insect-bite contamination is often spread by scratching. Careless sunburn can be very painful. Cuts and scrapes from live coral take many days to subside, even when treated promptly. Various types of jellyfish have stingers, some poisonous enough to kill small children. Sea snakes are rarer, but more dangerous.

As always, a gram of prevention is worth a kilo of cure. Simple precautions and wise daily adventure choices go a long way to preserve good health. In humid areas, keep the skin as dry as possible with thorough towelling. Armpit, crotch, between toes, folds of skin, under breast and waist – in both men and women these parts are most susceptible to infection. At the first sign of soreness, apply medicated powders or creams. Get local medical attention immediately if it persists.

These infections spread rapidly, and soaping in the bath is the worst thing you can do. The lye content of most soaps irritates the areas further. Oil-based soaps are better. Medicated powders, such as Johnson's, are sold all over the world.

Insect Protection

The tropics are residential areas for bugs. Mosquitoes, sandflies, gnats, water mites and a million others are out to get you if you don't watch out. Certain people attract them more than others, a rapport that makes you a delicacy to the pesky creatures. Regular travellers have favourite preventives. One expert claims that the Avon product Skin-so-Soft works wonders. Jungle experts use a concoction called Autan Stick. Ask the assistant in the hotel's small-items shop for an appropriate product.

The main ingredient in repellents is diethyl toluamide (DEET). We use an Aerogarde spray and/or cream (yellow container) or Rid cream (maroon container), available in most sophisticated areas in Asia. Creams stick to the skin longer, and so are especially useful on treks, or for sitting on the beach where there may be fearsome sandflies. Apply to exposed areas of ankles, wrists and neck before you venture out. Aerosols are used less, because of their ecological disadvantages. However, they are practical for spraying clothes around those three skin areas, and as a quick refresher when flying creatures become especially irritating. Sandflies and gnats are active in the day; the mosquitoes start flying with the bats at dusk. Before eating alfresco in the evening, coat exposed areas of the ankles and neck well. Food attracts the bugs, too.

When available, use a mosquito-net at night. Even if they fend off just one irksome bug it will be worth it. Many hotels have electrically heated slow-burning, fume-dispensing tablets that kill insects. The green serpentine mosquito coils, which also burn all night, are effective if you can stand the pungent smell. Electronic sound mechanisms are reported to be ineffectual.

Ants are common in all resort areas. Ask the hotel to provide an insect spray for use while you are in residence. Keep all semblances of food in the mini-bar refrigerator out of reach.

Don't get flustered by an occasional cockroach; though nasty looking, they are not particularly dangerous to temporary visitors. But if hunting appeals to you, each cockroach killed without poison will be a small, clean blow in the world's campaign of retaliation against this ancient pest. The tropics have lots of relatives of Leroi the Lizard hanging around as local bug catchers. Thank them for their services when they appear, usually on brief forays from behind pictures or curtains.

Keep in mind that sprays are chemical and can cause skin reactions in people with allergies. Always point the spray away from the eyes and food. Creams on the forehead and near the eyes tend to mix with perspiration and spoil the vision. Use a light hat to cover that area, and put cream below eye level only. Spray the hat rim and it will keep the less persistent buzzers away from the eyes.

What to Wear

Shoes that make your feet sweat, and tight underwear abrading infected areas, are further sources of aggravation. It is better to wear substantial open sandals, like the German Birkenstocks, than sports shoes.

Loose-fitting underwear is more comfortable, as tight garments tend to rub when you walk in humid areas or adjust your position in an aeroplane seat for eight hours.

Spending a full day on the beach? Take an extra swimsuit and change the wet one under a towel so that you won't be chafing. A little practice makes expert changers of us all. Nature-lovers should take advantage of the nudist beaches to be found in many places. It's amazing how fresh air and saltwater, applied to all the nooks and crannies of the body, make them healthier. If you are shy, wear the minimum amount of textile. In either case, apply liberal amounts of sun screen, #15 at the least.

SUNBURN

Sun-induced skin cancer is almost as well publicised as lung cancer. Some doctors advise us to stay out of the sun altogether, or to wear protective hats and clothing. Unfortunately most of us are attuned to a 'tan is healthy' outlook, and we like the bronzing of our skin.

Here are two methods of enjoying the sun without overmuch risk (neither is a medical opinion). One is to use sun screen lotions, at a level no lower than 15. As to the different types, thicker creams stick longer, while watery types and sprays are seldom effective throughout a long day at the beach. Most important, never bask directly in the sun for long stretches of time. Under a palm tree or in a cabana is best. Believe me, you'll tan just as well under filtered sun as in the direct light, while avoiding the lobster-red burn which will soon peel off. Reflected sun, as in a boat on a long day's fishing, is more severe than you imagine. Wear loose shirts and sun hats. Snorkelling exposes the back to direct and reflected sun; therefore wear a tee shirt. Cloudy days simply mean the sun is filtering through, so don't disregard the preventives just because clouds are overhead.

You would think, and are probably saying, that everyone knows all this. Next time you're on the beach, look around. Pale white skins are stretched out in full array, and by dinner that night will be bright red. Remind yourself that physical comfort is the principal way to have an enjoyable vacation. For some, part of 'getting away from routine' is sexual freedom with travelling companions. Severe burns and itchy skin are definitely inhibiting.

MASSAGE AND HEALTH CLUBS

Frequent travellers indulge in body treatments for relaxation, easing of tired muscles and general physical enjoyment. Many hotels have courtesy health clubs where you can begin or continue your aerobics on a planned routine. Depending on your age and physical condition, you should only use the machinery so variously available under professional guidance. A few minutes on a bicycle won't hurt anyone – but if it isn't a sustained programme it won't help much either.

Jacuzzi and sauna are very relaxing if used in moderation. Recommendations for their use are always displayed, and the club attendants will advise you. For those who haven't dipped a toe into these luxuries, a travelling holiday makes a good opportunity to begin. Don't be shy or bashful. Enquire directly at a club, as a novice, for information and assistance. It will become a wonderful way to spend an hour or two during an exhausting tour or extended journey.

Therapeutic massage is a body toner for people not averse to stripping and letting a masseur or masseuse rub down the joints and grind out a knot behind the shoulders. There are various styles, categorised under Sports, Correctional, Relaxation, Chinese, Swedish, Japanese and so on. If you are a first-timer, don't worry; just tell the operator what you want to accomplish. Relax and have your back and buns rubbed down; and your legs, aching from all that mountain climbing. For the most part, therapists advertising publicly are competent – in varying degrees. Some little time after the first session, you will know whether they have helped you or not.

Sensual Massage

A sensual massage is another service altogether. In today's world both male and female customers are solicited – and should be guided by local laws and mores. The worldwide AIDS epidemic has instilled a tremendous amount of caution into the sexual part of the trade, via the operators. Many levels of service are offered by advertisements of 'Full Body Massage'. Operators may be clothed or partly or completely nude, depending on the local customs.

Amongst enlightened customers, eroticism can be a pleasant experience in a clean and welcoming ambience. For others, who wish to maintain the privacy of their bodies, there is no problem. Tell the operators exactly what your limitations are and they will inform you of theirs.

Escorts, male and female, and brothels, male and female, belong to the realm of prostitution. Their customers indulge at their own pleasure and risk. Enough said.

HEALTHY DO'S AND DON'TS

The items on this list are well known as common sense. Put them into practice, for more fun and happiness in your travels:

- On long flights, drink lots of liquid but little alcohol.
- Rest when you're tired.
- Take vitamin C plus an apple a day.
- In remote places, drink only boiled water.
- Avoid street snacks.
- Take a hot shower or bath after a wet or cold adventure.

- Dress for your destination.
- Whether climbing a mountain or wrestling with heavy luggage: don't exert yourself beyond your capacity.
- Wear comfortable broken-in shoes to prevent foot sores.
- Keep toes and feet dry and well aired.
- Wear loose undergarments to prevent chafing.
- Exercise daily – stretch, walk, swim or something.

Good health and the ability to cope with emergencies make travelling more adventurous and more enjoyable.

Chapter Fourteen

WHEN THINGS GO WRONG

Life does have its comeuppances. Statistics say that more accidents occur at or near home than anywhere else. I believe it, because people are most often at or near their homes. But there is always the possibility of you becoming a minority statistic by having a serious problem while travelling. Aircraft, ships, trains and road vehicles can crash. You can fall and dislocate an elbow (it happened to me in Mexico). In the Andes, far above the highest mosquito, you can be struck down by an allergy to the malaria pills you were prescribed for the rest of your Venezuelan holiday. Or, when the ticker elects to go on leave temporarily, you could be in the middle of the Sahara.

In another vein of 'it could only happen to me', passport, credit cards, cash or valuables can be lost or stolen; pre-booked and confirmed hotel reservations can be non-existent on arrival at 2:00 a.m. in a foreign country; a guide may fail to show up in time to get you to the airport for the next leg of the journey.

The essence of this chapter will be to list possible problems and probable solutions, given the likely times and places of an occurrence. The odds against the really serious things happening are equivalent to winning $10 million in a lottery. But someone always does win and, while there is a first time for any problem, you can be fairly sure that the solution to yours has already been found.

In the following discussion we assume there is a victim, and a travelling companion or nearby friend to assist.

DEATH, HEART AND ACCIDENTS

☛ **Death of a travel companion**
Seek out the nearest available embassy or consular official of your country for assistance and advice.

The most serious thing that can happen to you while you are away is to have your travelling companion die. Distress and confusion are compounded by the fact of being in a foreign country. Whether accidental or health-related, the result is the same. Local officials are equipped to handle the emergency. Cause of death will be determined, a certificate issued and your ambassador or consul will be officially notified.

Then the paperwork starts. The country will have its regulations, within which you will have to decide between cremation and repatriation for burial. Fortunately there is great empathy for persons in this saddened state. The hotel you are staying at, the travel agency handling your journey, airlines, consular officials: all will help you find the best way through the two countries' laws and procedures. Matters will be arranged with surprisingly little delay.

Obtain a proper death certificate before you go home. An official from your consulate or embassy must sign as registrar or notary. This formal document will be required in connection with insurance and administration of the estate, and for announcement of the death in a newspaper.

Hospitals and Treatment

For serious bodily injury, heart attack or dangerous illness requiring treatment in hospital, you will need evidence of a travel insurance policy and/or your credit card to show how the costs will be met.

Emergency services will get the patient to a hospital for immediate trauma care. From then on:

- Hospitals and medical personnel worry about how the emergency service and follow-up care are to be paid for. Patient and companion are concerned with survival and remedial care. Diplomatic and consular officials are not authorised to spend embassy funds for this purpose.
- An internationally recognised credit card will overcome any hospital admission problem. Proof of insurance cover will normally suffice thereafter.
- If the patient is in no state to be transported home, the major dilemma does not yet arise; similarly if the treatment available (and affordable) where you are is as good as, or better than, that in your own country. You may have instead the questions of: which local hospital; whether the companion (now hospital visitor) should move to somewhere more convenient or cheaper; and how much recovering to do before going home. (This last could be influenced by your insurer's willingness to accept a medical recommendation in favour of comfort and care in a first-class flight.) You will have to depend on local advice and your own good judgement.

Returning home as a stretcher-patient is an expensive and difficult undertaking unless you are wealthy enough to charter a flight. Most airlines use a row of seats to accommodate a stretcher, but instant booking may be difficult as transoceanic flights are often full. If there is a choice, it is far better to wait until the patient is mobile. Wheelchairs and fork-lifts are common equipment at airports.

To ease your mind, most of the world you will travel in has adequate to fine emergency care, once you have crossed the money line. Hospitals in some countries are not up to modern standards, but emergency heart care will be given until the patient can return home.

Travellers should be well aware of their potential heart or other weaknesses. Such conditions have to be taken into consideration when making travel plans. Broken limbs (which are unforeseeable) present relatively routine repair problems; initial treatment can be improved on later if necessary.

An enigma of modern travel is that the USA, with perhaps the finest health care in the world, can be the worst place in the world in which to fall seriously ill. If, for instance, you break a leg in New York and appear impoverished and without adequate insurance, the ambulance will take you to Bellevue Public Hospital where you will probably be in a queue of 50 or more people awaiting emergency treatment. However, with evidence of guaranteed payment, you would be taken to Cornell University Hospital, one of the world's finest trauma centres. Treatment can cost thousands of dollars a day in America.

Colds, Diarrhoea or General Aches and Pains
Visit local doctors or resort to common remedies. (See Chapter Thirteen.)

LOSS OF PASSPORT, CREDIT CARD OR VALUABLES
Contact your nearest consulate or embassy for passport replacement; make a detailed police report.

Valuables do get stolen, and they can be lost through carelessness. Credit card companies should be notified of card losses as soon as possible. They give certain numbers to be called in the originating country, but any local office of the credit card company will accept a lost card report. A detailed list of cards should be left at home, with the proper number to be notified by someone there as a backup. Card companies have provision for covering fraudulent charges and will not penalise you for other people's misuse of your card. Whether or not you find the card, once its loss is reported it cannot be used again. Though it is convenient for spouses to have cards with the same number, it can be maddening to be denied use of the one that is not lost. You probably won't receive a new pair of cards until you reach home. Couples who travel often should ask for separate numbers/accounts before replacements are due.

Traveller's cheques come complete with instructions for security. Your homeowner's and personal insurance policies cover you for loss of valuables. Report at once to the issuing authority the loss of such documents as air or railway tickets or personal cheques. There is always a chance that your quick reaction will result in apprehension of the thief. Fax is the best method of communication in all these instances, as it provides a quick, written and dated record of your report. But you should send on the hard copy.

Any loss claim on your insurance company must be substantiated by a verified copy of your report to the police.

LOSS OF LUGGAGE

If the loss occurs at an airport or station, report to a lost luggage authority *before you leave the building.*

Independent Travellers are aware of lost luggage as soon as the carousel stops bringing in the load and theirs has not appeared. Lost-luggage counters are nearby with forms to fill in and describe the items. Statistics show 90% recovery within 48 hours, and a further 9% later. International airlines provide small sums (US$200 normally) in cash, to get you through the night.

In the event of permanent loss, airline insurance usually limits claims to US$500 per traveller. This is detailed on your ticket and may vary between airlines. Other compensation must come from personal insurance cover.

Luggage loss when travelling with a tour group presents another problem because the tour staff will be handling your luggage. Even though they agree to collect all the bags (with tour identification tags) for your group, it's safer if you see yours come in and put with the group's pile – or at least verify that the tags are visible. Problems arise when you check in at the hotel and find out then that a case is missing. Frantic backtracking is frustrating and time consuming. If a tag has come off in the handling, the forlorn case sits on the carousel going round and round looking for its owner.

It's fun to shop, but replacing all the favourite items of clothing and nicknacks, plus inspired purchases, is an infuriating subtraction of time from the remains of the holiday. Your vacation will be remembered as the time you lost trying to replicate all your belongings. See Chapter Fifteen on keeping valuables in your hand-baggage.

☞ Personal Experience

Our last luggage loss was at Broome in Australia, where we received our cases in good order from the baggage section and then gave them to the hotel's transfer bus. One duffel was missing when we got to our room. It was late at night; the hotel porter had to find out where the bus driver had parked in town, raid the luggage compartment to find the missing bag, and return that to us two hours later. Don't wait until the next day; insist they follow up immediately.

AIRLINE BUMPING AND DISHONOURED RESERVATIONS

Demand instant satisfaction; don't leave the counter until you have it.
Some travellers are guilty of not showing up for confirmed reservations. The airlines are guilty of overbooking.

These two facts of travel commerce are the root cause, on the rare occasions when genuine passengers are turned away. The immediate cause is that this flight did not produce its quota of 'no-shows'. Getting bumped is especially disconcerting at the beginning of an extensive travel itinerary. The shock waves can cause innumerable changes down the list of reservations on your schedule.

To avoid being a victim, always show up very early for overseas flights. Early arrivals have their boarding passes in hand before anyone knows about no-shows. It is the latecomers who are bumped. If you are refused a passage despite a confirmed reservation, remain at the counter until you are satisfied with arrangements to pacify you. This could be a seat on the next available flight or on another airline flying to the same destination, whichever is the earlier. In addition the airline should offer you monetary or travel-credit compensation, all spelled out in their regulations. Overnight lodging and meal vouchers are issued on the spot for the nearest hotel if there is a next day connection.

If you show sufficient determination, and such space is available, they will upgrade an Economy seat to Business or First Class as their simplest and cheapest solution. You may suddenly find yourself holding a boarding pass for a low seat number compartment without being told. Just get on board and enjoy the extra specials. The more informal your dress, as viewed across the check-in counter, the less likely this privilege.

When You Bump the Airline

Travellers, also, can make mistakes. Our daughter's family was

145

once embarrassed to arrive at the airport with tickets for the previous day, confused by a 12:10 a.m. departure. They thought it was Saturday night they were leaving. Actually it was 12:10 a.m. Saturday, meaning Friday night. After the immediate chaos, passages were available that night and the airline graciously agreed to advise the destination hotel of the confusion and late arrival of their guest. It happens.

FLIGHT DELAYS AND CANCELLATIONS

Cancelled or delayed flights are the airline's problem. Staff will make alternative arrangements to the best of their ability. Be patient, but try using your own initiative to find another airline or means of transport.

Weather is the principal cause of last-minute delays and cancelled flights. A snowstorm comes in just as the plane is about to leave for a sunny climate. (Riots or local disturbances, such as the Los Angeles troubles in May 1992, can cause consternation, but usually have no effect on international flights.)

The airport is chaotic, airline personnel are frantically trying to post bulletins and pacify everyone. You are frustrated, facing disruption of your plans and, until you leave, little prospect of revising them. Severe weather may impound you in the airport, unable to return home or get to a hotel for the night. There is nothing to do but make the best of it and hope to find a comfortable seat, or a table in the restaurant, for the duration.

A delayed flight because of technical problems is a different story. You are free of your ticket obligation and may seek another airline going to the same destination. Your original airline may offer to help you – or attempt to keep you 'on line'. Try to determine how long the delay is expected to last. Minor repairs are usually complete within an hour or two. Defects requiring a replacement aircraft will keep you longer: spare planes are rarely sitting around. The airport concourse flight board will tell you of other aircraft going to or near your destination.

Before the crowd gets the word, go directly to a possible substitute airline's check-in desk and request a transfer to their flight. In most cases they know the situation and will accept your ticket if space is available. The next problem is the luggage. Your original airline must be advised of the new arrangements, to get your cases out of the bin and transfer them to the new airline. This takes time and you will be warned that it may not be possible before departure. Another problem to be faced is security. Some authorities require all luggage to be accompanied by a passenger. Switching carriers is complicated. Decisions, decisions...

Properly tagged luggage, with you in the possession of the claim checks (stapled to your ticket at check-in), will eventually get to you; it does 99 times out of 100. With domestic flying we will accept that risk and jump on the new flight. In overseas flight situations we will back out and await the arrangements of the original airline, even if it means staying overnight. Insist that the airline fax to your next hotel news of the delay, giving you a copy of the fax (or telex). Remember, you have guaranteed or prepaid the first night. Hotels recognise this travel hazard and will adjust if notified properly.

FAILED HOTEL RESERVATIONS

Stand your ground, wave your confirmation advice and demand your rights. Hotel staff are ordinary people and computers sometimes lose information through mistakes of the operators. You arrive in the middle of the night to find the hotel fully booked and your reservation, specifically marked 'late arrival, payment guaranteed', missing from the computer. It is rarely that a hotel cannot scrape up one more room, probably an upgrade suite, until they can match your reservation.

If they can offer only the couch in the lobby, they will try to shift you to another hotel, nearby if possible, and throw in a free breakfast or dinner as appeasement.

Alas you and your companion are weary from the long day's travel; it may be 24 hours since you were in bed. Disgruntled, angry and out of sorts, you can erupt with a cyclone of invective, threaten legal action and swear "never to stay at a Hilton Hotel again, as long as we live." On the other hand, you could think it through creatively and make a deal on the spot. Request some real favours like free rooms and meals or a half-price rate for the duration of your visit. There is always a duty manager on hand, who rules absolutely and can sanction virtually anything to appease you – such as complimentary rooms for your stay, a champagne dinner the next night, and maybe take care of your laundry for a week. Think about that before you give yourself a heart attack by screaming at the desk clerk.

When confronted by an absolute error on the part of an airline or hotel, discretion is the better part of valour. Make a deal: get something tangible for the discomfort you agree to grin and bear. And then be gratefully impressed by such skill in extricating you and the hotel from the unfortunate difficulty.

EMERGENCY, RETURN HOME

If serious illness (say) occurs at home and you have to go back immediately, transport is the first problem. Your travel guides will help if you are on a tour. Hotel concierges are wonderful in emergencies.

Often all you have to do is call the airline, explain the problem and request the earliest available flight. You may have to buy a new flight ticket or fly with a different company. Later, return your unused portion of the old one, for a refund, to the issuing office or travel agent. No problem.

Death or emergency in the family is the most common reason. If a new ticket is required, they will ask details to confirm the emergency and then help with a reduced fare and quick flight confirmation. On a fully-booked aircraft, you will have the first available wait-list seats, which is tantamount to confirmation.

See that the originating airline makes connecting reservations to your home city if you need this service. Thenceforward you are noted as a special passenger who requires assistance. Assigned airline personnel will see that you disembark first, and rush you to the connection. They expect you to be anxious and confused, needing assistance. If this assistance isn't offered, ask for it immediately.

Getting from a remote resort area to the main embarkation point can be more trying, depending on the time of the day, weather problems and boat or intermediate flight availability. Have faith, pack your gear – and don't forget to empty the hotel safe of your valuables. Emergencies compound frustrations into carelessness, chaos and further problems. If things go only semi-smoothly, you will be surprised how much of the globe you can traverse in less than a day.

After the crisis, return tickets or vouchers for all unused parts of prepaid travel to your booking agent, or direct to the carrier if booked that way, along with a complete statement of the emergency. Partial or full refunds will be forthcoming.

RIOT, HIJACKING AND POLITICAL DISTURBANCE

If unrest looks likely before you leave, cancel and go somewhere else. If trapped, keep cool and make the best of the situation.

We never go to an area or country where there is actual or expected trouble. We are not attracted to the 1994 Middle East, the less stable of the former Iron Curtain countries, or much of Africa. Riot-torn areas of New York, Los Angeles or cities in other lands do not appeal to us. There are hundreds of pleasant, peaceful, relaxing and very interesting areas to visit without endangering ourselves or spoiling the fun and adventure of travelling. For instance you can fly into Los Angeles Airport, and immediately fly out to safer and more interesting parts of the continent. North are San Francisco, Colorado and Canada. East are Arizona, Louisiana and the Midwest. South are Mexico and the resorts of Baja California. In Thailand, the same advice leads you to avoid Bangkok. Fly north to Chiang Mai, south to Ko Samui and Hua Hin or west to the resorts of Phuket and Pattaya. Why waste time in the danger/discomfort areas?

When a Riot Occurs

Again, you have lottery odds against being involved in wild or serious local conflicts. The rule of thumb is to remain as cool as possible and think of the best and quickest way to get out. If hijacked, do what comes naturally: tuck your head down and pray. The police and military are equipped and trained to take the risks. If riots erupt around your area, stay in the hotel close to other foreign nationals. Rioters seldom want to harm visitors; there is no benefit in needling foreign governments. Authorities and embassy staff will automatically go all out to protect you and arrange a speedy exit. They too are trained for this.

Whatever happens, don't fret about your luggage. Stow your documents and valuables in your best shoulder bag or waist pouch, ready to leave unencumbered. If there is time, change to the most practical clothes you have. Your main concern is survival. Anything else is secondary.

PSEUDO-GUIDES AND SCAMS

Take particular care when arriving at airports, train stations, ship harbours and scenic sites independently. Many unsophisticated tourist destinations are infiltrated with pseudo-guides or hustlers anxious to latch on to travellers.

The scams are operated by offering guide services to visit, for example, the holy places of Jerusalem or the pyramids of Egypt. After a meagre tour, the unofficial guide demands an exorbitant sum for services rendered. To further intimidate the tourist who protests, loud voice and professed indignation enhance the performance.

When confronted with such a situation, insist the matter must be settled at your hotel or possibly a police station. Thus you can get arbitration assistance. In most instances, the mere threat to do that will settle the situation quickly and fairly. Ignore any aftermath curses; it's all part of the performance.

The recommended procedure is never hire instant guides on the street or in transportation arrival zones. Some countries have official information centres for tourists. In other cases, wait until you have checked into your hotel, then enquire for proper and well-known guides and tours. Heed the advice you give your children, and 'never get into a car with a strange man'.

The same category of hustler or team will offer blackmarket currency exchange with a direct intention to cheat.

In Beijing, for instance, a tourist was offered a much better exchange than the official rate on renminbi (yuan) for dollars. After agreeing to the transaction, the victim handed over his dollars for a thick stack of yuan. While he was counting, another member of the scam team appeared, dressed like an official person, with badge and armband. He demanded an explanation for the illegal transaction. The frightened victim saw the pseudo-official chase the offender away, disappearing himself in the process. The finished count of yuan was far short of even the official exchange rate.

> **Blackmarket money exchange, illegal in most countries, is fraught with problems and sometimes physical danger. It isn't worth it.**

MISADVENTURES

The following incidents happened to us during our first 25 years of foreign travel.

Cabo San Lucas, Baja California

I fell while climbing a hillside and pulled my elbow out of its socket, fainting at the immediate shock. I managed to walk the mile and a half of beach back to the hotel, and was rushed into San Jose del Cabo's small-town clinic. The X-ray was out of commission, but the nurse patched up my skin abrasions and we went nine miles to a doctor's residence in Cabo San Lucas. The pregnant wife of the doctor took the X-ray in her kitchen, and developed it in the bathroom while the doctor shot me up with a painkiller. The three of them pulled the arm back into its socket, strapped up a sling and charged me US$20. On return to the States, my doctor took another X-ray, confirmed that everything had been done properly, and charged me $125.

I recovered completely. My wife, frantic at the time, still worries it may happen again and always warns me to be careful.

Beijing

This time Eileen broke a tooth out of her bridge. We were taken to the hospital; the nice doctor (in China, as elsewhere in the East, dentists are known as doctors) marvelled at the modern contraption. She managed to re-attach the tooth with a metal screw, and charged nothing. We left 20 yuan (US$6) under the tray, and our trip went on. Our home dentist marvelled at the repair in lieu of replacement, re-did the bridge screwlessly, and charged only $150. He did say that the screw would probably have held for ever.

Bangkok
We lost our luggage in transferring overnight from Hong Kong to Singapore. We went on to Singapore, trying to make a list of everything in the three missing cases. Qantas gave us S$200 to cover emergencies. The luggage turned up two days later, delivered to us at the Shangri-La.

Malaysia
A jellyfish attack and insect bites caused severe inflammation. Both were soothed by the hotel nurse. The insect bites persisted and required antibiotics and skin treatment on returning home.

In another incident, we were en route from Kuching in Sarawak, via an aircraft switch at Kuala Lumpur, to Tioman Island. Our flight was delayed, then cancelled, in Kuching. Since all flights from KL to Tioman were fully booked, we flew to Singapore, stayed overnight and took a direct flight to the island of Tioman. Malaysian Airlines refunded our tickets with a credit voucher, but declined to pay overnight compensation.

Korea
We neglected to take passports and valuables from the hotel safe. The mistake was discovered at the airport, where one of us kept a foot (as it were) in the check-in and the other hired a taxi to return to the hotel (30 minutes away) and come back, arriving 10 minutes before flight time. Harassing, but not life-threatening.

Shanghai – 4 June, 1989
The Tiananmen Square massacre in Beijing affected all foreigners. Our problem was getting to the airport through riotous streets in Shanghai. The airport was a mass of humanity, all trying to arrange flights. Customs and immigration personnel were concerned to get the foreigners out. Our previously booked Cathay Pacific flight from Shanghai to Hong Kong took off on schedule, no problem, half full.

☛ Personal Reflection

In our quarter-century of foreign travel, we have had dental and medical assistance many times; and surgery on a cancerous node on my cheek once, in Singapore. We have been treated by hotel clinics countless times after emerging from the wilds with colds, sores, infections and a self-solving case of kidney stones. All of these while covering an estimated quarter-million miles, in some 60 months away from home. By adhering to common sense and good hygiene, we survived and enjoyed the adventures to the fullest extent of our physical and monetary limitations.

Chapter Fifteen

LUGGAGE

One of the biggest bugbears in travelling is to find yourself at a railway station in (say) Japan or China, with a double flight of steps to the tracks and no porter around to tote your luggage. Most fully-packed cases will weigh close to 20 kilos no matter what your good intentions are. Any more than 20 kilos in one bag is risking a heart attack. A couple travelling with two normal duffel bags – and an extra one with books, snacks, shoes, appliances and a supply of optical rinse for their lenses – will carry 40+ kilos.

AVOID HEART SHOCK

Talk about culture shock! Lugging 40 to 50 kilos up two flights of stairs is enough to give your heart a good shock. Now before you get all het up and vow never to go away without all of your necessities, let's get down to brass tacks about what you really need to carry. We concede you may already have luggage with built-in wheels, or a folding luggage trolley, to negotiate the airports. Larger trolleys are available to get you into and out of the concourse with little pain. Hotels do have porters (though not always, in some countries). Given all these facts, you will still have to lift the cases many times to pack, unpack and take them on and off the trolleys at security inspection stations. A month or six weeks of this can cause a lot of backaches, maybe a hernia, and especially an argument with your travelling companion on the theme "how can we need all this?" As in all health recommendations, prevention is far better than cure. It boils down to a nutshell of advice: *travel light.*

CHOOSE WISELY

It is admittedly easier and cheaper to use the same old hard case luggage you've had for years. But with your newfound love of travel we suggest you give it away and invest a modest amount in new cases. Shop carefully: there are bargains, and interesting units that have separate pockets for everything. Others come in glitzy hard plastic, with folding handles and tiny wheels guaranteed to catch on every ripple in the pavement. Some weigh three or four kilograms before you put a toothbrush in them.

We recommend soft-sided duffels, as least subject to handling damage, and with a capacity to swell, if need be, to accommodate extra items. Preferred styles have double zipper tops that can open fully. Thus you can get a tee shirt out of the bottom without having to unpack completely. Two basic requirements override all other advantages:

- *Durable material* such as canvas or a tough synthetic. Canvas is less likely to be pierced by a sharp object, and its durability is evidenced by the long-lasting love for blue jeans originated by Levi Strauss a century ago. Outside zipper compartments use up more room than they provide, with the additional danger of being ripped off. Carry-on and beach duffels on the other hand should provide many useful extra compartments.
- *Support straps* absolutely must go all round the case in one piece and extend to become the carrying handles. No other

arrangement is acceptable, regardless of what the salesperson tells you. With continued use, separately stitched handles and partial bindings will tear off sooner or later. If you don't believe me, peek behind the scenes of the luggage carousel at the airport and watch the muscle men play basketball with your case, flipping it onto the track.

Other things to look for are *removable shoulder straps* that clip on and off easily. Try them in the store before you buy. Remove the strap and tuck it inside before you check the case in at the airport.

Purchase tough *luggage tags* that can strap on securely. Print your name large and bold enough to be seen easily from 10 feet away. Use an office or family/friend's address with telephone and fax number, because you may not be at home when someone wants to tell you that your luggage has been found. Use the airline's cardboard string-tags also, to repeat your name and hotel destination.

Colours should be nondescript but easily recognisable, and the cases should match.

Have *luggage locks* with the same key. Small and efficient locks with matching keys will keep strange fingers out of your case. Moreover, lock the zipper to the ring embedded in the bag, if yours has this facility. Double zipper cases need two locks each, and a few extra in case you lose one or need another for hand luggage. They can be small and inexpensive, and we hide extra keys in a purse or carry-on bag. Our favourite key-holder is in the style of a small Swiss Army pocket knife (with scissors, blade, file, tweezers and toothpick, plus a key loop at one end) carried on the person. It's easy to get to if the customs and immigration people want you to open up.

Stolen luggage is rare; lost luggage, more common. However, 1% of a billion airline passengers per year amounts to 10 million pieces of lost or stolen luggage. Most lost luggage is found and returned within 48 hours. You don't want to be among the 1% – or even be annoyed by the loss and then return of your belongings. Platinum American Express Credit Card replicas for luggage tags are flattering, but they advertise the wealth of their owners. Flashy expensive leather cases also are tempting to an airport or hotel thief.

Tie a bright yellow ribbon on the handle to recognise your own quickly, but always check your name tag. There is a great sameness about much of today's luggage.

For two people on longer trips, we suggest one 36-inch duffel bag for each, and another smaller matching piece for combined extras such as snorkel gear, spare shoes, rain cape, etc. Usually one carry-on is sufficient for two unless you are taking camera equipment or portable computer gear: for you don't want to trust the bouncing around of valuable equipment to check-in luggage systems if you can avoid it.

Carry-on shoulder bags must be within the airline size limit and fit into the sample frame before you board the plane. All luggage stores have those dimensions available. These bags should be of light synthetic fabric, with side pockets for a book, snacks and whatevers. Inside are your cosmetics, change of clothes, and arrival sweater or a very light rain jacket. Cameras, binoculars, jewellery and other valuables are best carried therein.

Carry-ons are with you all the time, and cover immediate needs if your main luggage is lost. They should be light in weight, and have straps that go all the way round to become handles. A cardboard insert for the bottom gives a flat support for the folding trolley.

Carry at least one such small trolley to trundle the hand baggage, because many large airports have long distances to walk to and from the departure and arrival gates. Trolleys are also invaluable when shopping in town or going to the post office with extras to be shipped home. Criteria for a folding trolley are lightness, a good platform and large wheels. An elastic cord helps to hold the load tightly.

PACKING

Lay out everything you absolutely need for the trip and then leave half of it at home.

For some weird psychological reason, we travellers tend to take more clothes than we need, except when the absence will be so long that it is off our scale of reckoning. Women are alleged to be greater offenders than men. Though we have travelled for a quarter of a century, Eileen is guilty of last-minute paranoia, sneaking in that extra pair of shoes, sweater, tee shirt or whatever just as we are leaving. It is a crime punishable by a sigh and a frown from me. The next family will have these roles reversed. Efficient packing is a matter of nesting like items together, folding without wrinkles, and filling each corner with what best fits it.

Where are you going and what will you be doing? The first step is to review the itinerary. Begin with comfortable everyday travel garb in the ratio of one mix-and-match outfit for every three days, up to three sets. Women or men, the same. Thus if you are on a tour bus your neighbours will be amazed to find you have something different on every day for almost a month. Women like to put on the spangles or pretties for dinner at night, if not in a tent camp in the wilds of Nepal. The expected climate will modify the outfits. Except for formal dining in the larger cities, a jacket, shirt and tie at dinner is up to the man. On a cruise ship, they do dress up, and often require formal attire.

That is the basic gamut: from a tee shirt and shorts to tuxedo and long gowns. Not so easy, is it? Frame your selection almost through a day-by-day imagination of what you will be doing, and thus wearing. Believe me, most countries have a good supply of jumpers in case you run into unexpected cold or wet weather. Resorts have stacks of colourful sports wear at modest prices to augment your casual unisex beach or dining room rig. Birkenstocks and Reeboks are now sold by most of the world, in case your old shoes should suddenly deteriorate. Kodak film, Crest toothpaste, Johnson's baby powder and Coca Cola have sold worldwide for decades; there is no need for extra supplies. Tylenol and Panadol are often found on the shelf together with Fisherman's Choice and Ricola throat lozenges.

The big extras that weigh people down are duplicate clothes for an informal travel itinerary that have no possibility of being worn. If your custom is to dress every night for dinner, add a separate mix-and-match set for variety. That is, a man needs a choice of shirts but can survive with one jacket and tie; while a woman requires at least three basic outfits, to be accessorised with scarves and cardigan-style overblouses.

Speedy laundry service is available, making several changes of clothes unnecessary. You will find packets of detergent in our list of necessities; better hotels now supply them along with the body lotion and shampoo. For quick drying, rinse garments well, wring out then wrap in a towel to remove excess moisture before hanging up.

Local tee shirts and casuals are inexpensive and fun to wear. If your light slacks wear out or tear, buy another pair. Eileen gets a great kick out of picking up an inexpensive clever outfit and wearing it that night for dinner. If a cold snap of weather suddenly chills you, add an extra undershirt or two to your outfit, especially if dining *alfresco*.

☛ Personal Experience on Proper Dress

We were in the mountain country of Bhutan on a 10-day small group tour. A friend in Hong Kong suggested we call on the king's relatives in Thimbu as a courtesy to him and a great ego lift to us. Our guide proudly made the connection – the Dorgi family would gladly receive us that evening at six. Our total wardrobe was one duffel with one mix and match each. What to wear for the royal appearance? We donned our cleanest shirt and slacks, with a nylon jacket apiece, and removed the travel dust from our shoes. The royal family cordially received us in their Los Angeles-style suburban home. Three uncles, attired in slacks and tennis shoes, had just finished playing golf. The first and second wives of each uncle wore slacks and tee shirts. Our appearance at court was accepted. Unfortunately King Wangchuk was absent, out hunting tigers.

PLAN AHEAD

The standard procedure is to lay out all the possibilities of clothes, accessories and equipment, days ahead of departure. Re-adjust every time you pass by and look at the pile. After – long after – you have decided, select the necessary luggage.

Use the checklist enclosed or make your own for continued use every year. Would you believe that I actually forgot my camera and binoculars last year? Another trick we use is to store items only used in travel in the small suitcase on our return each year in order to remember them next time. Avoid large cases like the plague for this simple reason, a variant of Parkinson's Law: 'Travellers' luggage expands to fill the space available.' If you exceed the limits of your 36-inch duffel, take two smaller ones, not one larger one. Remember your back and the hundred times you would have to lift the damned thing during the journey.

Inveterate readers should buy paperbacks, and give them away when finished. Hotel staff, guides and other providers of extra friendly service appreciate free books that are not always available to them. In China for instance, a gift of a well-thumbed *Time* or *Newsweek* magazine is treasured. Books are doubly treasured. In tightly controlled countries this can be a problem for the recipient. We get round that by leaving the item (in a bag) where the obvious beneficiary can find or choose not to find it.

Sending a dozen books home costs more than replacing them or buying fresh ones. The 10 best-sellers are sold all over the world today and are seldom worth a permanent place on the shelf. On the other hand, books of local or special interest, bought abroad, become part of my permanent collection.

Get rid of extra weight as you accumulate new clothes or souvenirs. Shipping goods home is covered in Chapter Eighteen: postal services are the chief thread of communication between nations. Prices are relatively uniform (10 kilos sent surface/sea mail averages US$35) and it takes but a few minutes to hump a box to the post office in any city. Post offices sell boxes which they think are more suitable than yours.

CONSERVING SPACE – HINTS FOR PACKING

Women's Wear
Roll or fold each set of the mix-and-match outfits together as a single unit. Pack underwear in one silk or plastic bag.

Men's Wear
Flatten long and short trousers, then fold or roll them together as one. Flatten tees and similar heavier collared shirts, then fold or roll in the same manner. Put shirts on a single hanger, neatly; remove the hanger and fold over once. This is the last item to be packed, giving a soft and protective cover.

General Wear
- Stack shoes vertically along one end, in banded pairs.
- Fill shoes with hose and small articles.
- Make two vertical piles of the clothing pushed to each side.
- Breakables, cosmetic and medical containers, in the middle.
- Sweaters, jackets, little-used things, on the bottom.
- Robe, pyjamas, clean outfit on the top.
- Underwear, swimsuits, other crushables along sides.
- After packing stand the case on end, letting clothes compress.
- New room found at the end takes last-minute items or books.

The basic theory of packing is to fill the spaces neatly and compress the air out of folded clothes. Folds take up space and leave air corners. Rolling forces the air out and compacts the units. The mix-and-match outfits in sets allow you to take one unit out at a time. You can remain semi-packed for short stays with this system. For longer stays, especially in humid climates, unpack completely for airing. *Never use dresser drawers for short stops.* Hang or pile on chairs or shelves. Nine-tenths of left behind items were forgotten in a drawer, and the rest were on hooks in the bathroom. If you pack as suggested, following the same routine at each stop, missing items will be easily noticed.

CHECKLIST
For the record, we list a compendium of normal non-clothing requirements for a 30-day tropical adventure. We have in mind two people, staying at 4- or 5-star resorts and hotels, and using

aeroplanes, trains, coastal steamers, buses and cars. Items for esoteric or special adventures are treated in specialised publications.

- Passport and insurance documents.
- Tickets and itinerary.
- Traveller's cheques and/or cash.
- Credit cards, driving licences and personal identification items.
- Address book or handheld computer with address data.
- Small pocket-size calculator, solar powered.
- Waist pouch for documents.
- Hot rod or hot pot (120-240 volts) for room coffee or tea.
- A set of electrical adaptors and an AC/DC converter.
- Your preferred coffee/tea packets.
- Vitamin C for daily intake to forestall colds.
- Capsules of odourless garlic (for those attuned).
- Lomotil, or similar diarrhoea remedy.
- Prescribed medicines in sufficient quantities for the trip.
- Thermometer and band aids.
- Favourite sunscreen.
- Small packets of detergent to wash your undies.
- Extra folding light nylon duffel to accommodate overload.
- Light plastic rain capes and an umbrella.
- Light nylon lined long jacket for change of temperature.
- Small scissors and nail files along with cosmetics.
- Ziploc bags, rubber bands and a few feet of nylon cord.
- Pocket-size binoculars and camera.
- Shaving kit and toothbrushes (electric or normal).

Hair dryers are common in hotels. If you are going to rough it, you won't need one anyway. If you forget your toothbrush or safety razor, don't fret, the aeroplane and hotel usually have spares to offer, as well as sewing kits. Cosmetics are best carried in lined soft containers. For extra protection use Ziploc bags for the leakables and seepables, inside the main bags.

Waist pouches are handy for documents and immediate cash for day tours or on beaches. The carry-on case should have cosmetics, change of clothing, reading material and snacks. A woman on her own will often use an extra large purse/handbag to avoid two units. Two people travelling together can usually get by with one carry-on between them. All important documents should be on your person for ease in filling out forms, and passing immigration and customs.

CLOTHING LISTS

These are suggested requirements for four to six weeks in the tropics.

Basics for Women:

- Three mix-and-match ensembles:
  a) Three blouses with skirts of various lengths.
  b) Three tee shirts and shorts/culottes/wraparounds.
  c) Three assorted tops and three pairs of slacks.
- Light sweater, decorated for evening wear.
- Cardigan/sweater neutral-colour ensembles for chilly evenings.
- Light nylon rain jacket, lined.
- Swimwear* plus lingerie, hose, kerchiefs.*
- Shoes: beach clogs, walking sandals (dress and casual).
- Make-up tools, not to exceed one small vanity case.
- Hats* to suit personal custom.
- Fine jewellery, but only what you wish to wear.
- Non-precious jewellery, according to taste.

* *You may do better if you buy most of these, plus sarongs and other local outfits, where you find them.*

☛ **Eileen Says:**
Use one neutral basic colour generally throughout the

165

collection. Then match other items to contrast or blend to taste. For instance, dress and casual shoes in the same neutral basic or blend, to avoid carrying extra pairs of different colours. A cardigan of neutral colour can be used over anything. Travel with the minimum, and have fun adding to the collection as you go. With rare exceptions, everything must be washable. Select one combination for all your air travel. Include a long-sleeved, warm shirt with an undershirt for the cold aircraft. Wear sandals or shoes that will take swollen feet, essential on long flights. Make-up, toothbrush and a spare blouse to freshen up before arrival make for a cheery landing.

Basics for Men:
- Three pairs of slacks/jeans, casual and dress.
- Three pairs of shorts, casual and dress.
- Three long-sleeved sports shirts.
- Three short-sleeved sports shirts.
- Three knit/polo tee shirts.
- One neutral-colour sports jacket.
- One neutral-colour tie.
- Sturdy sandals, trainers/walkers, dress loafers/smart slippers.
- Swimwear, underwear and socks.
- Lined rain jacket for outerwear in cool or wet weather.
- Light cotton sweater.

☛ Fred Says:
Everything should be washable except for the dress trousers and sports jacket. Pack non-iron clothes wherever possible: just rinse and hang out to dry. Jacket and tie are optional. Sneak in at least one outfit of well-worn clothes to knock around in on jungle or beach walks. Select your most comfortable combination for air travel. You need deep trouser pockets to prevent your wallet from falling out, and a shirt pocket that will hold your passport temporarily. Long-sleeved

shirts are recommended for the cold aircraft. Feet swell on long flights. My favourite footwear is a velcro-latched pair of Bally loafers that I can still get my feet into on arrival. Track-suit style trousers with elastic waist – loose fitting and wrinkle resistant – reduce the discomfort of long periods in the air.

FINAL NOTE

When packing, make your own checklist in detail of exactly what you are taking. Carry it with your travel documents. It is a useful prompt when repacking – and invaluable for claiming lost luggage. On return, add items you should have taken, drop off those you shouldn't, and put the list in a safe place for the next trip. You are thus ready with your own specifications, updated after each adventure. We keep one duffel in the cupboard with travel items not used at home, so that we don't forget.

Chapter Sixteen

CAMERAS AND PHOTOGRAPHY

TRIGG

We all have our own ideas about taking pictures. I will not try to advise serious photographers because they know what they need. For others: *Think small.* Inexpensive 35 mm cameras abound, with flash enclosed to do all the mechanical thinking for you. A travel analysis once proved that for non-professionals, under good lighting conditions and flash, the inexpensive camera produced results almost identical to those of the finest Nikons and Leicas. Thinking cameras are more efficient than humans in adjusting for light, shadow, distance and focus.

Experience tells us that the easier the camera is to use, the more pictures you will take. Your 36-exposure rolls of 100-, 200- or 400-rated colour print film will net you 38 or 39 usable pictures. Enough to let you throw away the ordinary ones, and enlarge and show off the really good ones. Video cameras and camcorders replace what used to be the vogue for handheld movie cameras. Many of them are relatively small with complex abilities. Competition amongst the manufacturers is fierce, bringing new and interesting models continually to the market. Shop thoroughly, visiting more than one store, for the equipment that meets your needs and ability. After you decide on the model, then you can look for competitive prices.

SELECTING A CAMERA FOR THE AMATEUR

Most homes have a camera or two sitting around that have been in the family for years. Let me urge you to leave them at home and buy a new one. All television, computer, VCR, tape recording and music equipment newly on the market is far in advance of the old. Twelve months and a computer is antiquated. Televisions and VCRs are obsolete in 10 years or less. Cameras have changed radically in the past five years.

For the average non-professional user, the 35 mm cameras currently on the market do everything. They focus, adjust for light, automatically roll the film, flash lights when you can shoot, and snigger when you forget to open the lens.

Recognised brand names are in the price range of US$100 to US$250. Using an average 400-grade colour print film, you will have more than the promised 24 or 36 pictures from each roll, with never a miss.

The next step-up in proficiency is the camera with built-in telephoto and wide-angle adjustments to give longer or wider scope, but still for the average user. Clever built-in electronics date each picture; and there is an option to switch to manual adjustment. Most have timers to set for delayed action, allowing the photographer to jump into the picture. All of this is manageable by anyone interested enough to do a few tricks.

Higher levels are best left to the semi-professionals or hobbyists, who will make their own studies of the equipment on the market. They travel with multiple cameras, multiple lenses, tripods and filters, and are interested in the adventure of travel as seen through the camera lens.

If you haven't used your camera for a year or more, install new batteries whether you need to or not.

Read the instructions, whether the camera is new or old. After a few months, technical details are easily forgotten. Most pamphlets are brief and with diagrams. Long before you leave, expose a whole roll using all the systems and suggestions for use. Pretend you are abroad. Take shots in your local park, at different times of the day (and similarly at night, indoors), with an assortment of subjects. While simple cameras are literally foolproof, there is real skill in framing the scene, and judging distance, background and time of day. Doubly so for the more complex video cameras.

With video cameras, follow the same line of reasoning as above. Handheld camcorders, capturing picture and sound, are down to palm size; the larger shoulder-braced styles are outdated. Remember that they are *movie* cameras. Either the photographer or the subject being recorded has to move. It is important to decide what you are going to take before you press the start button.

There are consumer books to assist selection – necessary if you are going to become involved with the fancier 35 mm's or video camcorders. If you want to build your own library or are interested in travel lecturing, take the time to study the equipment possibilities before you buy. There is sufficient variety on the market to confuse the most knowledgeable photographer.

FILM

The most common film today is 35 mm colour print (Kodacolor, Fujicolor and the like). Actually you are taking still negatives on a strip of movie film. New printing machines process the film mechanically, and produce colour prints. Alternatively, colour-negative film is available where the end product is individually mounted slides that project a finished picture onto a screen. Black-and-white is used by professionals for newspaper and fax reproduction. The speedy develop-and-print, commonly advertised as a one-hour service, is always for 35 mm colour print. Black-and-white or colour-negative film requires laboratory processing.

Film is rated for the speed at which it reacts to light. Ratings of 1000 used by professionals will record images with a minimum amount of light, for instance incandescent bulbs in a dimly lit cave. For the average user, 100, 200 and 400 are suitable, helped by flash for indoor shots. Modern cameras are very intelligent; they interpret the rating when you insert the film. The marking 'DX' on the box indicates that the film will tell the camera what kind it is. The camera will then adjust its sensing equipment to match the right amount of light to the speed of the lens.

400 is recommended for general use inside and outside, especially for parties, people and action. It will 'stop' the motion without blurring. For example, your beloved taking off and descending in a parasail over the ocean at the end of a boat's tether. Or a friend can snap you both dancing romantically in the evening on the veranda in the bright moonlight.

100 is used for general scenery, outdoor shots in bright daylight, or reflected sun in beach and water scenes. This slower reacting film will respond with a finer grain and better detail, for instance on a day's cruise to the Great Barrier Reef for deep water fishing, snorkelling or diving. It is better for recording grand scenery shots – e.g. of the White Cliffs of Dover or the Grand Canyon.

200-speed film is the common choice when you don't know which to use. Frankly, I carry three rolls of 400 and one roll of 100 because most of our photographs are of ourselves and other people in foreign locations. We average photographers take a few shots here and a few shots there, as the mood hits us. We have sometimes left a partly exposed roll in the camera for months, awaiting an opportunity to finish it. If that is you, too, then use a 200-rating film, and you'll never know the difference. And you won't have to remember which film you have in the camera.

Serious but amateur photographers like our friend the album maker, who appears in this chapter's last paragraph, will use 24-exposure rolls of 100 and 400, shooting a whole roll in one episode or day's adventure. He installs a fresh roll especially for the day's events, with the proper rating. The only problem with this approach is money. Developing and printing 20 or 30 rolls can cost a lot, not counting the money to buy the film in the first place.

Don't fret; be yourself, shutter-bug or occasional snapper. Remember that you have brought the camera to serve your holiday purposes. Don't let photography get in the way of your fun. With some help from the pictures, your memory will hold the best record.

BASIC GUIDELINES

Never shoot into the light source; put your back to the sun.

Take a moment to frame the shot for size and suitable background. What you see in the viewfinder is what you get. The viewing lens has built-in guidelines, for you to select the parameters of the shot. The nose should be in the middle of a person's picture. A focal point, such as a tree or rock, can be the centre of a scenery shot.

Scenery and people do not mix well. The result will be too small a subject or a narrowly restricted scenic shot. If you can't see the smile clearly, you are too far from your subject. (But perhaps the scene is the point, and the person merely establishes Nature's grander scale – or proves who was there.)

When the portrait is the picture, your camera has a trick to give you the best of both. The instructions will tell you to focus on the prime subject, allowing the camera to adjust for distance, focus and lighting. Then half-depress the lens button (a light will normally show in the viewfinder), and move the camera slightly to one side to balance the person with the scene. Finish pressing the button. The result should be pleasing, as the subject is well focused; yet you can see the surf pounding in the background. *Take several shots. Film is less expensive than the cost of getting to the scene you are shooting.*

Use the flash where faces are shaded (you have to adjust the gadget on the camera sometimes). Facing a brightly lit area, such as a beach, the subject's face will be dark and unrecognisable. A turn of the face, to catch the best light on the nose and eyes, will capture the moment.

For albums take one shot of the place-name, i.e. hotel entrance, airport arrival building or resort facade. When travelling by car, stop and snap the road sign welcoming you to the area. This is a shot where person and object can share the foreground.

International Friendship

Don't be shy. Line up the camera, then ask someone nearby to press the button after you get into the scene. You need no linguistic skill. Sign language communicates what you desire.

Some people make fun of the 'typical Japanese tourist' with hanging cameras. I have found such fellow travellers especially cordial when asked by gesture to take a picture of us with our camera. I have yet to be refused and we will often take the same shot with their equipment. In this vein, when I see a couple taking pictures of each other, one at a time, I offer to snap them both. Sign language works very well and the smile of appreciation is thanks enough.

Video tapes need editing, with or without voice-overs. More than with a still camera, the tendency is to overdo each scene. If you show it all when you get home, the audience will soon fall asleep. Remember to take shots of place names and moving people and objects, to make a pleasing reminder. There is only one Steven Spielberg: the rest of us are amateurs. But you can learn something from him. Plan your shots ahead and take extra footage; then edit, edit, edit.

Final Hint

Do as the professionals do, take lots of still shots, with different angles and poses. Then – and this hurts – keep the good ones and throw away the others. One friend of ours selects only the very best, has them enlarged into 8 x 10 prints, and makes a special decorated album of each travel odyssey. They include printed memorabilia such as itineraries, menus, playbills, letters and cards from people met. It is a pleasure to look through the couple's recent and past adventures – concise and very interesting.

Chapter Seventeen

PASSPORTS, VISAS AND CUSTOMS REGULATIONS

A passport is a legal identification of citizenship used for travelling outside your country. To the uninitiated, applying for a passport sounds fearsome and complicated. Once you have done all the paperwork and have made the proper application, you are clear for a few years. Most countries issue passports for 5 or 10 years. Be patient and get the job done; then you can relax.

Government passport control offices have the application forms and will normally mail them to you for convenience. They will advise you if a personal appearance is necessary to complete and issue the document. In some countries you can collect blank forms from a post office. Current photographs (of passport size) and evidence of birth/citizenship are required. Passport pictures are easily obtained in any metropolitan area. It's not necessary to get professional portraits. The purpose of the passport picture is to allow the foreign immigration officer to compare the photo with your face to make sure the passport is yours.

Most film developing shops advertise the service. Special polaroid cameras and film are normally used, producing the result in sets of four, while you wait. Automatic photo-booths in train stations and elsewhere will do the job more cheaply but less handsomely. Get extra sets while you are about it, especially if the shop has produced an acceptable likeness; it may be cheaper by the dozen. You could need them for visas or part-time employment applications. The passport is with you for many years so when you pose for the picture, look serious; do not wear a hat – or glasses, unless you travel in them.

In many countries you will need a citizen who has known you for years to vouch that you and your photographs match the particulars in your application. The rest of the process is queuing up one morning to conclude the matter if, indeed, you have to. It's best to obtain the passport long in advance of your planned travel. Last-minute applications are often difficult, an irritation to citizen and bureaucrat alike.

VISAS

That official stamp in your passport authorising you to enter a particular country is obtained either on arrival in that country, or by application to its consulate well before you leave. Whether you need one in advance, and how to get it, can be discovered from many sources: by telephone from the local consulate or tourist office of the country you are going to visit; country-specific travel guides give details of requirements; travel agents booking your itinerary automatically provide the information.

The countries that do require a pre-issued visa need an application with current photographs attached. For nations that do not have local foreign consulates, you must apply to their nearest office. Some require you to go in person to their consulate, make the application and present your passport. Losses in registered mail (or a visa office) do not happen often; in such a case the victim has a real problem to get everything re-issued in time. Travel agents, as well as providing the information, will in some cases handle the applications when you book with them. Handing over passports to a third party is alarming even to experienced travellers. *Always get a receipt with a signature you can read.* Any unusual delay should be followed up assiduously, lest it turn into a holiday-threatening muddle. Your agent, fortunately, is motivated to rescue his reputation and your booking.

Australia and Japan (for instance) require pre-issued visas for many nationals. These authorise a specified period of years with entry entitlement for multiple visits. On a normal tourist visa China allows only one visit within a specified period – i.e. a single entry. Thus if you visit Guangzhou, and decide to go next door to Hong Kong, you have to re-apply before returning to China. Each country has its own system; it behoves you to find out exactly what is required, early in your planning.

On receiving the visa, whether pre-issued or on arrival, *read the time limits carefully* and examine the actual visa stamp before you leave the immigration counter. Thailand allows three weeks, and if you stay on the beach at Phuket a few days longer they will fine you. Malaysia can be confusing because West Malaysia issues one visa; then, if you go on to Sarawak or Sabah, you will need another visa with a different time-span. The Solomon Islands, I'm told, will incarcerate you if you overstay.

Bureaucracy, as the traveller sees it, maintains its territorial rights in every country. The tourist bureau promotes long stays and expects visitors to spend much money. The immigration bureau seems, by propagating paperwork and enforcing restrictions, to hamper tourism. Neither bureau interacts with the other, whether or not they are at cross purposes. Extending a visa, once in the country, means queuing and waiting for papers to pass from desk to desk with frustrating slowness. Arrival immigration officials seldom have authority to extend the standard period allowed.

☞ Personal Experience

The stories of inconvenience are legion. While we were in Hong Kong, awaiting a flight to India, the regulations changed. India suddenly required a pre-issued visa. The Indian consulate in Hong Kong refused to issue a visa in less than ten days even though we held confirmed travel arrangements due to begin shortly. Irritated, we went to Bangkok instead; there we found we could get the visa in an hour and therefore went on to India with no problem. It seems the visa officer in Hong Kong didn't like Americans. We never received the courtesy of a reply when we complained by letter to the proper authorities. We have not returned to India.

Nations allowing you to visit with nothing more than a valid passport require a simple entry form/card to be completed on arrival. All international airlines provide these forms before landing, and explain the routine customs regulations.

☞ Anecdote

Visiting Kenya thirty years ago, a colleague saw that he had to declare his race. He wrote 'Human' on the form. Soon after the aircraft landed a severe-looking official announced that an unfortunate mistake had been found in the arrival documents. Fresh ones were issued, for all to complete. Feeling relieved that the rest of the class did not know whose rash act had kept them all in, my friend wondered what word would be acceptable. He need not have worried. The new form did not ask the question!

CUSTOMS AND EXCISE

There are limits to the alcohol and tobacco each adult may take into a country: usually one litre of spirits and one of wine plus 200 cigarettes. (Between countries of the European Union the allowance is much more fluid.) Australia is very strict about importing anything resembling food, plants or endangered-alligator belts into the country. There are bins on arrival to dispose of the half-eaten cheese sandwich or apple you were saving in case you got hungry. My wallet or belt has never been examined to see if the original crocodile gave its permission.

Be careful about making fun of any country's regulations. They have their serious purpose. We do however sometimes disregard a bold sign requiring one to declare any currency over US$5,000. If I have US5,500, I will not declare it because I don't like to show (or even admit to) a bundle of cash in an airport. It is the money-launderers they are looking for, carrying big bundles, and the regulation does not apply to tourists carrying sensible amounts to be used for internal travel. See Chapter Eleven for information on cash, traveller's cheques and credit cards. (The latter two make 'technical infringements' unlikely.)

Certain countries impose a limit on the amount of cash you may bring in – or take out; the latter figure will sometimes depend on the amount declared on the way in.

HOMECOMING DECLARATIONS

To return with foreign purchases, or to ship some of them home instead, is a question that relates to your country's customs regulations. A phone call to the proper authorities *before you leave* will answer all your points directly. We prefer to get the information from source; never from someone who has been there, or a non-travelling travel agent.

If you are one of those who are only guilty if caught, I have no advice for you. Carriers or sellers of drugs take risks wholly beyond reason. Even stealing a smoke on an aircraft where it is prohibited is a risk defying comprehension – worse, surely, than driving after drinking too much. I report any infraction when I see someone endangering my comfort or life, without compunction. Singapore and Malaysia hang importers of a small quantity of hard drugs or of a medium amount of cannabis; with jail and the cane for minor amounts. Thailand has the death penalty but is less forthright in using it on foreigners.

Your own country is specific about the limits on imported goods – on your overseas purchases brought home. Most have a maximum, with duty charged on any excess. There are prohibitions on, for example, ivory goods when the country has signed the international ban on ivory in defence of the elephant. Plants, animals, foodstuffs and endangered animal products may be banned or closely regulated.

The average tourist is not involved in these matters. Purchases are usually articles of clothing and souvenirs. Items shipped back while you are away are classified as unaccompanied luggage. If sent by mail (see *Shipping It Home* in Chapter Eighteen), contents declared are taxed or not at the whim of the customs. Shipping by commercial carrier is more formal, and in some instances requires payment before the goods can be despatched from the port – or a broker to handle the import. Follow the rules; life is too short to waste time and possible incarceration sneaking around the law of the land.

IN SUMMARY

The paperwork and regulations are inhibiting for first-time travellers. But once you have a passport and the necessary visa, it is plain sailing – and becomes easier every time you travel in the future. Inform yourself, and follow the well-published rules and regulations as a courtesy to the country you are visiting. While you are a welcome visitor helping to improve your hosts' balance of trade, remember that you are also a guest.

Chapter Eighteen

SHOPPING AND COLLECTING

A temple in Sri Lanka where one of the Buddha relics is treasured is a scene you will want to remember. You will take a picture, keep a brochure, buy a postcard and maybe acquire a souvenir model of the site. Adventure memories and memorabilia are inseparable from travel; and then there is the sport of serious shopping. Shopping is what many would call fun and games. The products and markets of the world have tempted travellers since time immemorial. Marco Polo writes of the treasures in China and of the many gifts he took home.

Traders plied the Silk Road for centuries, trekking for months across passes to bring goods to the Middle East and returned home, their camels laden with merchandise. Ship captains sailed the Mediterranean in ancient days seeking to exchange goods between its ports. They were the early wholesalers, establishing bridge-heads and foreign enclaves to consolidate the trade.

Today the traveller has the fun of accumulating 'treasures' of clothing, art, literature and handicraft at source. Like the old traders, you can bargain with vendors for a single item, or for dozens of clever shirts to resell to your friends on return. Fortunately you need not own a camel or a ship today. Huge aircraft take you from one port to the other in hours. Local post offices will send everything home cheaply for you.

Some overseas tours are created for shopping sprees only: Los Angeles to Hong Kong; New York to London; indeed Harrod's in London runs an annual sale for overseas shoppers, subsidising the fare from various airports.

Package tours always have an afternoon free for shopping; the bus takes you to tourism-designated stores. There is a feeling that the tour director or bus driver is getting a commission. In fact a great fuss was made by a group of Singapore merchants recently. Certain Japanese tour guides were directing their clients into specific stores that had paid commissions to them. When their charges wanted to shop elsewhere, they were fobbed off with "no time" or "those stores not approved". These evils of the travel industry will not affect the Independent Traveller. As ever, do your own research and act accordingly.

UP-MARKET AND TOWN-CENTRE SHOPS

Up-market has the connotation of expensive. I prefer to categorise the finer shops, boutiques and department stores as those selling brand-name products at world-level prices. A promotional ploy draws attention to a fabulous designer-garment at an astronomical price. However that same shop will also display the latest styles in clothing at normal prices. There is often a sale-rack with something very special on it, a one-of-a-kind that will be a joy for many years in your wardrobe.

Major department stores are marvellous places to start your shopping in an unfamiliar environment. Classically they are old-line companies with fine reputations for quality and access to finer goods and services. We often book into a city hotel in the central business district (CBD in driver's lexicon) for the convenience of shopping. If one's travelling companion is bored by shopping, one may prowl the CBD alone while he or she enjoys hotel facilities such as health club and massage.

One big problem of shopping in foreign places is allotting time for proper investigation. The serious shopper should set particular days aside for this purpose. Leaving it to unscheduled free time will always lead to frustration. In a large city, a single day hardly allows you to get started, let alone see the major centres. Don't waste the time, be pragmatic. Create a schedule for the up-market places and leave part of a day, or a separate day, for down-market sport.

DOWN-MARKET BAZAARS

A woman will sometimes collect memorabilia by bargaining for a pair of bright coloured loose pants and a mismatched shirt, as in the night market of Chiang Mai. When she wears them to the next neighbourhood get-together on returning home, the acclaim will be heartwarming. Name drop: "I just happened to be at the night market in Chiang Mai and picked up a few things." A green-with-envy look from a friend is ego satisfying.

Her man has always desired an Akubra hat from Australia, after seeing Greg Norman wear one at PGA golf tournaments. Showing the Arizona Cowboys what the Aussie wears when rounding up the cattle is the pride, joy and ego-boost of the international voyager.

The Independent (non-scheduled) Traveller has the time, and therefore the best chance, to ferret out the offbeat markets and bazaars. Some are traditional weekend-only gatherings of the merchants and rural vendors of clothing, food, local handicraft and flea-market type goods. The Chiang Mai market is a nightly affair in a multi-story car park, and there are many like it in Asia. The surrounding streets are filled with the carts of food and trinket hawkers. Inside are four floors of individual stalls, selling everything from high-fashion clothing to crocodile-tooth jewellery. Every Asian city, town and village has a large or small market of this sort with a spread of fascinating goods and services. You can have your fortune told, buy snake-oil medicine, get a 10-minute massage or take a sack of exotic tropical fruit back to the hotel to gorge on. If nothing else, the experience of walking through, smelling the cooking odours and watching and talking with the local people is well worth the time and effort.

The Victoria Sunday Market in Auckland is in a large covered building teeming with people. Stalls are laden with wonderful New Zealand food or piled high with sheepskin and wool products. It has counterparts in Melbourne and Brisbane. Tiny Broome, in Western Australia, has its bazaar on the church lawn every Saturday. Down Under they vary from massive collections of hundreds of vendors to local pockets of a score of open stalls with handicrafts and canned jams and jellies.

In the United States, the version now sweeping the country is called 'swap meets'. Europe has had similar open-air affairs for hundreds of years, once accompanying the battles of knights on the field of honour. In the UK, there are 'car boot sales' where roles are sometimes reversed. Professional vendors stock up selectively from what may or may not be household junk. Rural auctions are another matter, and a treat wherever you come across one.

Eileen loves the game of chase-the-bargains. Interesting clothing is often found in odd lots from international designers fabricating goods locally. Styles are up-to-the-minute, colours and fabrics are exciting. Prices are low, but the challenge is to recognise the better items, and make sure they are first-class merchandise though with prices far below the up-market boutiques. Negotiating prices is fair game for both buyer and seller; if they were too reasonable to start with, the game would be tame and uninteresting.

Part of the joy of foreign travel is getting out amongst the local people, and immersing oneself in their way of life. Language is never an obstacle to a buyer or vendor at any level. While up-market shops and goods are largely intended for high-spending tourists and well-to-do residents, the markets and bazaars with their remnants, and the smells (and sometimes stench) of the city, make for adventure. We have fond memories of eating fresh mangoes at a hawker stand in Kuala Lumpur's Chinatown *pasar malam*. Laughing with young people from an assortment of countries, dripping with the sweet juice, joking with the two women slicing stacks of the golden fruit – what more could the traveller ask?

Eileen has an interesting habit of discussing all of these probable good times with the taxi driver, coming in from the airport. He may want to sell you a morning tour of the city or a day's side trip to the remnants of a ancient temple. What my good wife wants to know is where is the best shopping and when is the big bazaar? There is a problem once in a while over what she means by the market, but diligence and perseverance win through. After all, there are still the porter, the receptionist and various waitresses to advise where the good stuff is.

☞ Shopping Tip

Bring cash to the local markets, for they seldom take credit cards. But don't expect to spend too much as the prices are not painful. Also, beware of pickpockets.

TRICKS OF THE TRADE

Make friends with the waitress at the breakfast table and ask about the best local shops. Men seldom know where to shop and the concierge will usually send you off to places like Double Bay in Sydney – an exclusive shopping area referred to by the natives as Double Pay. Sometimes you can identify local women in the lobby or restaurant wearing a cute something or other. A complimentary "what a lovely blouse, where did you get it?" will result in a quick friendship and local shopping advice.

TRUE COLLECTORS

Art enthusiasts, antique collectors and other special-interest people learn the paths to the galleries and museums in any country, usually armed with advice on people to contact.

My own enthusiasm is for bookshops, a wonderland where I escape from the best-seller lists of multi-million-copy authors. Tales of local history and antique books on pet subjects are treasures to be acquired.

SERIOUS SHOPPING

You will gain greatly from research before you leave home – into exquisitely woven silk carpets from Tianjin or old Wedgwood china in England, for example. Your local stores will provide comparison shopping to make sure you know something of the thread-weave numbers of the carpet. Your library will furnish you with the history of Josiah Wedgwood and his art.

FUN SHOPPING

This is for the rest of us common folk who merely like to buy some characteristic clothes, souvenirs for the family, tee shirts from every resort in the world, or interesting varieties of tea. Stop on impulse at a roadside stand, take in the bazaars and open markets, find out where the locals like best to shop – and look for the bargains. It may take nerve to stop when something catches your eye, disregarding the snide remarks of a companion or tour group. In major cities, don't hesitate to sheer off from the group, have your fun, and take a taxi back to the hotel when you choose.

FINE JEWELLERY

Jewels are a whole world in themselves. My background as a jeweller and Certified Gemologist entitles me to write at some length on this serious subject. Every country has its own source of unusual raw material, and/or talent, for creating jewellery. All have, also, their fine professional purveyors of heirloom jewels, as well as a horde of rip-off vendors concerned only with making a buck.

Beware of the 'Bargain'

Gold, diamonds and rare gems have their stable worldwide value levels. Nightly news broadcasts around the world quote the price of pure gold, within a few cents the same price in every market. Diamond production is tightly controlled at source by the De Beers cartel. Therefore differences in price will stem from manufacturing and marketing the products.

The impulsive purchase of a lovely strand of pearls or a magnificent ruby and diamond ring is a joy forever. Tiffany in America is probably the cheapest place to buy fine jewellery, allowing for variables of quality and value. If you desire such a treasure, seek out first the finest jeweller in the town. Then you can compare other sources. If your treasure costs thousands of dollars, do take the time to shop – and be very wary of the dealer who claims the price to be a third of the average retail value. If so, why is he selling it so cheap?

The words 'manufacturer', 'wholesaler' and 'retailer' are useless to you as level-of-price marketing descriptions. The vendor is a seller and you become a buyer for an agreed price. That price denotes the value of the jewel – what you, a knowing buyer, are willing to pay for it. You are acquiring the treasure because it is beautiful and you love it. The gem has meaning, perhaps as your birthstone or a gift of love, because of its everlasting durability. Never, never buy it because it is a bargain. Never, never take a second choice because that seems a better buy. Horrors!

Fine jewellery has a special meaning and attraction for the possessor. A rare gem with some history – regardless of its price – has beauty and durability as attributes. A royal amethyst of modest value in an antique gold mounting that has been handed down through generations has been loved with more meaning than a new carat-size diamond of considerably more cash value.

SHIPPING IT HOME

Carried away? Bought more than will fit in the extra fold-away duffel bag? Not to worry. Take the lot to the local post office, buy a box plus tape, and pay the postage to ship it home. Some countries are strict. The Philippines may give you a hard time. China wants to look inside the box before you seal it. But in Malaysia the hotel's porter or Business Centre will scrounge up a carton, paper and string, and ship it out for you. We have sent dozens of cartons home from the many countries we have visited. We remember only one box being lost.

Most post offices' package service is limited to specific dimensions and a 10-kilo maximum per parcel. The cost has a fixed plus a weight element. Verify the local system, as they may charge on block weights such as under and over 5 kilos, with anything over 5 charged as 10. Thus if your package weighs 5.1 kilos you will pay the top charge, so you might as well include a few more things. To be safe take the unsealed box to the post office, check the weight and postage, and then seal and address it there.

Check for freight forwarders when you have bulky items to ship home. All bona fide overseas purveyors of carpeting, furniture and large items have the means to ship the goods for you and know the system of export shipping. In some receiving countries, like the United States, it is sensible to enlist the services of a local customs broker or agent to collect the shipment, prepare the customs paperwork, clear the goods and arrange delivery to you. There is a service fee plus whatever duty is payable. *You must have certified copies of your invoice, and declarations of the exact origin and contents of the package.*

☛ **Caution**

Know the incoming customs regulations of your country before you leave it. A phone call or visit to your local customs office will provide the current information. Purchases within the specified limits create no problem. It is when you get carried away, and spend hundreds or thousands of dollars, that the regulations come into play.

SUMMARY

Veteran travellers and adventurers usually acquire a shopping hobby. Inexpensive oddities can be a lot of fun; they set one prowling. One of my daughters collects mugs, another miniatures. For a while in China, Eileen favoured unique pocket knives used mainly for peeling fruit, porcelain spoons and decorative tea cans. I specialised in old-style tales of Chinese lore, printed in English; and colourful posters and calendar prints. Their book-marks and paper-cut artistry are forever tempting: excellent small gifts for friends at home.

In all parts of the inhabited world, there is a never-ending supply of locally produced craft art. Everywhere one finds the inexpensive works of street artists, especially while prowling the night markets after dinner.

We have bought rice paper in China, rough handmade brown pulp paper in Bhutan, and marvellously decorative folding envelopes in Japan. Your stamp-collector friends are ecstatic if you pick out some pretties and send them on the face of a local envelope, cancelled in Lhasa or Kathmandu. My son-in-law requests only a paper-money note from each country we visit. An album of money samples, coins and bills is as interesting to friends as the endless snapshots we've collected over the years.

In Southeast Asia, Hong Kong and Singapore provide notable examples of international imports, international shops and international shoppers. Selling spills out onto most pavements (many of which are covered, cloister-like) and shops and stores are generally open well into the evening. Shopoholics could spend a week in a hotel and adjacent shopping complexes, in either country. Multi-level mall stores are surrounded by five-star hotels. And that doesn't include the special events in the cities.

Whether you are a casual or a dedicated shopper, enjoy the markets of the world. Savour the delight of bargaining for a treasure, whether it be a rare jade carving, a copy of a Dior gown or the newest tight-leg pants and turtle-neck casual combination. With such a collection you will have a small museum, rather than a large album, to enjoy for the rest of your lives – and to pass on. Inherited jewels and works of art will be cherished by generations of your descendants. Go forth on your adventures, and shop to your heart's and your pocket's content.

Chapter Nineteen

TRAVEL TIPS
FOR COMFORT LOVERS

Besides our earlier advice on good health, travelling light and eating sensibly, there are many ways to enhance the physical comfort of long journeys. As we age, petty annoyances bother us more. Sitting for long flights in the narrow confines of an Economy Class seat stiffens the joints. The location of a room in the resort or hotel becomes important when you're staying for weeks instead of days. Special service in the coffee shop is appreciated if, for example, you like a big salad at dinner instead of a meagre bowl. However, creature comforts, expected and important in normal surroundings, are not always available if you're in the 'Tent Camp of Mountain Travel' in the Nepalese jungle.

You acquire information and make plans for months; or you just set out. You investigate hotels before you book locally, and examine the menus that restaurants display; or you choose where to stay or eat, from booklets. Some travellers have a knack of being the Ugly American or Aggressive Taiwanese, with demanding arrogance; others cultivate friendly smiles with an appreciative 'Thank you.' A problem can escalate into heart-threatening aggravation, or be resolved calmly.

All of these pivot points can make your holidays happy, or miserable and memorable in the wrong sense. Properly handled, your investment of thousands of dollars on travel will pay dividends in joy and treasured memories.

BOOKING AIR TICKETS

The subject is very complicated because of the many rules and regulations, and the varieties of choice. Veteran air travellers flying regular routes know how to ask for maximum comfort. Adventure tourists flying once or twice a year are faced with multiple choices of airline, aircraft and price – but are hampered by changing schedules and ignorance of seat configurations.

Sometimes your travel plan gives a choice of airlines. Frequent-flier advantages, reputation and the time of departure and arrival vie for importance. We avoid late night departures because that day-in-waiting always seems to be time wasted. Hotels require midday check-outs, leaving luggage stored and preventing an afternoon siesta and last-minute shower. (But, for the first leg, it could be seen as a bonus day, at or near home, with all chores done and the morrow taken care of – an early start to the holiday, and then a night rather than a precious day given to the tedium of flying.)

Early morning departures are best, except when you have to fly in from a connecting point. Intercontinental flights always generate jet lag to aggravate a bad departure time or a Westbound flight. The correct way to compute time on a long flight, in your own mind, is bed-to-bed elapsed hours. In other words, the time you have to get up on the day of departure until the time you get into your next bed. In this context, waking up at a normal 7 a.m. and departing at midnight puts 18 hours on the clock before you start a long day's travel...

Sometimes you can't avoid it, but try anyway. Airlines often have different schedules according to the day of the week, because the beginnings of a route may vary. On a relaxed schedule you can choose whether to fly on Saturday or Thursday. Competing airlines alternate days with each other on certain routes to provide better commercial services. For instance Qantas flies Sydney – Fiji – Honolulu – Los Angeles. It leaves Sydney at a decent time, but if you pick up the flight in Fiji you depart at midnight. Air New Zealand, flying a similar route from Auckland, picks you up in the early afternoon. Thus you reach Los Angeles earlier without having to fidget for an additional eight hours before take-off.

One more travel tip. If you fly in from a connecting point for the major leg, leave the day before and sleep overnight at a hotel near the connecting airport. This shaves 12 hours off the bed-to-bed stretch.

Don't take the first flight schedule offered as final. If it's inconvenient, look for alternative days or airlines.

SEATING COMFORT

Efficient travel agents will sort all this out for you to the best of their ability. Unfortunately they're not all efficient, nor do many care whether you will spend nine hours cramped in the middle of a five-seat row. The aching-joint generation has a special problem, which most airlines recognise in their seat reservations.

There are two ways to handle this. One, if you are using an agent, is to be very specific. You would like a pair of seats for the two of you preferably in a two-seat row. Most big aircraft are configured two + four/five + two, across the cabin. By asking for windows, you'll seldom get stuck within a long centre row.

Additional leg room is often available in bulkhead- or exit-seats. Many airlines do not allow pre-check-in Economy Class seat reservations; however, if you can claim a physical condition such as arthritis, they will note that on your booking. The person checking you in should seat you accordingly.

One basic precaution helps immeasurably. Arrive at the airport at least two hours before flight time, to be first or early in the check-in queue. Smile nicely at the clerk, make a comment on why you always fly Malaysian because they are so nice, admire the lovely uniforms. Beg politely for a cosy two-seater exit or bulkhead row, with extra leg room next to a window, as far forward as possible. A friendly clerk will read your mind and will so place you that you will get out ahead of the crowd, reach the immigration check-in desk early and be first to the washrooms in the terminal. When you get good seats on an aircraft, note down the details and ask for them next time the same airline flies you in that type of aeroplane.

Eleven hours from Los Angeles to Tokyo nears a limit of 'tolerable endurance', even with the two meals, movies and lights-out sleep time. Even so, the 14-hour non-stop services between London and Singapore are more sought-after than the now old-fashioned, cheaper, stop-on-the-Persian-Gulf alternatives. In either case, break it up with freshening visits to the toilet (just before a film ends and the queues get long). Stretching exercises in the seat are good. Reach for the sky, clasp the hands behind the head and twist 10 or 20 times. When on your feet, go to the space near an exit and do some knee bends and *tai chi chuan* leg and arm stretching. (See Chapter Eight on in-flight exercise.)

Smokers and Non-smokers

Smokers will congregate in the rear of the plane, with or without specified seats. Domestic and short flights are all non-smoking now. Some airlines, weary of the struggle, have no-smoking seats even on long flights. But there remains a danger of the addicted smoker, nervous in the air, sneaking a smoke, thus causing a scene and discomfort to nearby passengers.

It's the smokers now who have seating problems, because the airlines catering for both favour the large majority who don't smoke. They would rather have to displease a smoker than a non-smoker, when fully booked. *Avoid seats near the smoking section.* They are towards the rear, and provide the worst of both worlds; for while you *may* choke on the fumes from the seat behind, you may *not* use tobacco yourself. Discuss seat options thoroughly at the check-in desk, to make sure you have the best available seat for your comfort. *Reminder: arrive early to check in.*

DRINKING AND OTHER DIVERSIONS

Oxygenised air is very dry, therefore you need lots of liquid. Take everything they offer you and ask for refills of juices and plain water. The caffeine in tea and coffee will either calm you or keep you awake – whichever is usual for you.

Alcohol is the worst thing you can drink aloft on long trips because it dehydrates the body. A glass of wine with dinner is about all we ever drink unless on a short flight in a holiday atmosphere. Save a fascinating novel, bring a puzzle book if you're a word-nut; or cards or a chess board for games with your companion. If the newspapers issued are in your language, ask for a different good one each; for once, you will have the time to read them. Films shown may be to your taste, but we seldom watch them. The sound is often poor. With a 'big' screen, you crane your head either up, or round the heads in front.

The worst scenario is a child in the seat behind or in front of you, pounding away by the hour. It's no one's fault. Containing all that energy for more than half a day is more of a problem for a youngster than cramped seating is for older people. An understanding comment to the parents will often help. If the plane isn't too full, the stewards may let you move to other seats, at least for a while.

SHORT FLIGHTS

When booking shorter flights on side trips, always ask for non-stop flights. Many domestic routes have intermediate stops that double travel time. For example, between Darwin and Broome, Ansett has one flight that stops twice and involves a change of planes; another schedule is non-stop. A helpful clerk will tell you of the choice, while another will put you on the first or least-booked flight on the list.

Higher class seats are more comfortable because of their size and special attention by the staff. However, with the Deluxe Economy travel that we suggest, a US$200–300 difference in cost can pay for two more days in a hotel room – a good exchange for the hour or two of luxury. It is on long journeys that higher class travel is worth considering, if you don't mind spending the extra money. We always conclude that those several hundred dollars would be better spent in extending our adventure, perhaps with another three days at a beach resort.

HOTEL ROOM LOCATIONS

We learned early in our travels to Europe that naive guests are usually offered the worst room in the hotel: next to a lift, overlooking an alley, or with a view blocked by another building. Sophisticated travellers always ask to see the room. For one night after a long journey, this is not important – if you can sleep. But on a second morning you want to wake up, throw open the window or step onto a balcony, and enjoy an enticing view. In a city a garden is prettier than a street, and quieter.

Hotel description verbiage is confusing. 'Standard' and 'Deluxe' mean the poorest accommodation, as a rule; 'Superior' is the average room; while the better and more expensive rooms are described as suites with or without further hype. 'Suite' is often a misnomer for an enlarged room with a pair of side chairs and a cocktail table. 'Double' means space for two people, except in China where the older hotels interpret it as two rooms.

You want the most comfortable room at the lowest price – or rather the best compromise between those aims, which we call 'Deluxe Economy'. Don't ask for that (or for 'Economy Deluxe', which relates to it as a half-empty does to a half-full bottle of wine), because hotel people won't know what you mean. Once you have stayed somewhere, write down the room number you want on the next visit, even if you didn't have it this time.

Our favourite hotel in Singapore is rated number one in Asia by certain professional graders. Years ago we used to have a room in the Garden Wing. It was mid-altitude, end of wing, large-balconied, away from the sometimes odorous cooking, and it looked out over the splendid lawns, pool and lagoon.

When the rates accelerated faster than our budget, we switched to the older Tower, with a corner room – a little larger, at half the rate, yet still overlooking the pool and garden. The legendary service prevails there no less, and the room maids even know us by name. They leave a liberal supply of 'decaf' coffee packets for the make-your-own facilities, and the fruit man manages an extra mango or two in the daily fruit basket. The Business Centre arranges my fax communications and always finds both an *Asian Wall Street Journal* and an *International Herald Tribune* for me. The freebies make up for the slightly enhanced cost of a fine hotel.

When reserving at a hotel new to us, we ask for a Superior room with a king-size bed, and a garden or beach view at middle height. On arrival we ask for an exclusive corner, or jokingly a honeymoon suite (for our 46th honeymoon). If they don't offer, we suggest a preview of available rooms. When we book in for a long stay, most hotels will upgrade the room at no extra cost as a courtesy. Chatting with the Reservations or the Duty Manager helps. Ask about the building's history; pay a compliment on the arrival procedures – in other words, make a friend. It works much better than arrogant demands.

Desirable room comforts include spaciousness, a refrigerator, international television, and coffee/tea makings. At resorts, a detached chalet away from the crowd and near the beach, with a porch and screened room for fresh air at night. We do not like to sleep in air-conditioning.

One last thought. 'Fully booked' is often used as a pretext for hotel clerks to place you where it suits them. It usually means they have a group-booking and the weekend is busy. Ask to see the Duty Manager and arrange to be switched to a better room after the crowd leaves on Sunday.

TRAVEL CLOTHES

Unless you are a film star expecting a posse of photographers, dress for comfort, not show. Loose-fitting clothes are the thing. By the time you have wriggled around an airliner seat for hours, tight-belted clothes and Fredericks of Hollywood underwear will have twisted the lower half of your body into excruciating knots. Feet swell, and Economy Class provides no way to prop them up. Wear casual slipper-style shoes that have room to go on and off easily. Sandals like our favourite Birkenstocks are admirable. If you're shy about walking into a posh hotel with 'barefoot sandals', carry a dressier pair at the top of your luggage and switch at the airport before you take a taxi.

Dress for the climate at your *destination*. You can leave Fiji in comfort with a light short-sleeved shirt, shorts and sandals, and find Los Angeles decidedly chilly that winter evening – especially if you walk a half-mile from the international wing to catch a domestic flight. We always travel with a lightly-lined nylon long jacket apiece, that can double as a raincoat or cover-up. They roll up in a small ball in our carry-on, or sit handily on top of the luggage when we arrive. From hot to cold, such as Singapore to Melbourne in the southern winter, you should have a jumper to hand, or wear warmer departure clothes. The airport is air-conditioned, and planes are often kept cold during flights.

SECURITY OF YOUR VALUABLES

Passports, boarding passes, tickets, baggage claim checks and entrance visas are bothersome. Everyone worries about wallets, credit cards and purses being stolen – and it does happen. For travel papers, the current vogue is waist pouches. They are unsightly but handy for the beach or on day tours. Leave the bulk of your valuables in the hotel safe or lock-box.

My system is to wear a shirt or jacket that has an easily accessible pocket to carry passports, entry forms and boarding passes. Everything else can be stored in a carry-on travel case. Women have their invaluable handbags. My side-pocket wallet holds enough currency to change at the airport, and one credit card. Everything else is locked in the carry-on case or money belt. Money belts are old-fashioned but the best possible way to carry extra currency and cards until you reach the hotel. For men, a side-pocket is better than one at the back because it is easy to keep a hand on the wallet in the pocket when walking through crowds.

On reaching the hotel, everything goes into the room safe or a safety deposit box at the reception counter. As for jewellery: wear it or stow it. Jewels in purses/handbags or left in drawers, earrings removed and set temporarily in the bathroom – these are at best cruel temptations to honest staff.

As mentioned in Chapter Eleven, there is now little need to carry large amounts of cash. A credit card gives you the best value for money so long as you don't run up interest charges. It is also an easy and reasonably economical way to draw money in foreign currencies. Traveller's cheques have superficial advantages; but do not buy too many, or cash them in hotels.

Be confident, choose your own travel systems, and follow them – but not so rigidly that they stop you from relaxing, and thus from enjoying the fun.

THE AUTHOR

Frederick and Eileen Fisher have the travel itch to see the faraway places with familiar names in comfort and a style known as Deluxe Economy. They constantly reorganize their lives to accommodate six months of travel pleasure each year. Retired now from the various careers of gemologist, jeweller and Chinese arts and crafts importer, Frederick now claims the career of author. Travel articles, a China travel guide, a novel, *Confucius Jade*, and new works constantly flowing from the laptop computer ensure a steady stream of the pleasure and interest in travel adventure.

Home for the Fishers is the crossroads ranch community of Sonoita, south of Tucson, Arizona, near the Mexican Border.

INDEX

SO-CFJ-363

978 .102 MCA
McArthur, Debra.
The Kansas-Nebraska Act
and "Bleeding Kansas" in
American history /

PALM BEACH COUNTY
LIBRARY SYSTEM
3650 SUMMIT BLVD.
WEST PALM BEACH, FLORIDA 33406

THE KANSAS-NEBRASKA ACT AND "BLEEDING KANSAS" IN AMERICAN HISTORY

Debra McArthur

Enslow Publishers, Inc.

40 Industrial Road   PO Box 38
Box 398   Aldershot
Berkeley Heights, NJ 07922 Hants GU12 6BP
USA   UK

http://www.enslow.com

Copyright © 2003 by Debra McArthur

All rights reserved.

No part of this book may be reproduced by any means
without the written permission of the publisher.

Library of Congress Cataloging-in-Publication Data

McArthur, Debra.
   The Kansas-Nebraska Act and "Bleeding Kansas" in American history /
Debra McArthur.
      p. cm. — (In American history)
   Includes bibliographical references (p.) and index.
   Summary: Describes the violent period of Kansas Territory history,
prior to statehood and the Civil War, when abolitionists and pro-slavery
factions openly murdered in defense of their cause.
   ISBN 0-7660-1988-8
   1. Kansas-Nebraska bill—Juvenile literature. 2. Missouri compromise—
Juvenile literature. 3. Kansas—History—1854-1861—Juvenile literature.
[1. Slavery—History. 2. Kansas—History—1854-1861.] I. Title. II.
Series.
E433.M469 2003
978.1'02—dc21
                                    2002152064

Printed in the United States of America

10 9 8 7 6 5 4 3 2 1

To Our Readers: We have done our best to make sure all Internet Addresses in
this book were active and appropriate when we went to press. However, the
author and the publisher have no control over and assume no liability for the
material available on those Internet sites or on other Web sites they may link to.
Any comments or suggestions can be sent by e-mail to comments@enslow.com or
to the address on the back cover.

Illustration Credits: Courtesy National Archives, Brady Collection, repro-
duced from the *Dictionary of American Portraits*, published by Dover
Publications, Inc., in 1967, p. 64; Daguerreotype by Mathew Brady,
Courtesy Library of Congress, reproduced from the *Dictionary of American
Portraits*, published by Dover Publications, Inc., in 1967, p. 25; Enslow
Publishers, Inc., pp. 4, 17, 21, 42; Kancoll, pp. 8, 58; The Kansas State
Historical Society, Topeka, Kansas, pp. 46, 49, 68, 70, 74, 88, 91, 99, 111;
McAfee Memorial Library, Park University, Parkville, Mo., reproduced with
permission from the Fishburn Archives and Special Collections, p. 52;
Reproduced from the Collections of the Library of Congress, pp. 6, 20, 30,
32, 44, 60, 77.

Cover Illustration: Daguerreotype by Mathew Brady, Courtesy Library of
Congress, reproduced from the *Dictionary of American Portraits*, published by
Dover Publications, Inc., in 1967 (Small vertical photo); Enslow Publishers,
Inc., (Large vertical photo); Kansas State Historical Society, Topeka, Kansas,
(Top and bottom horizontal photos).

★ CONTENTS ★

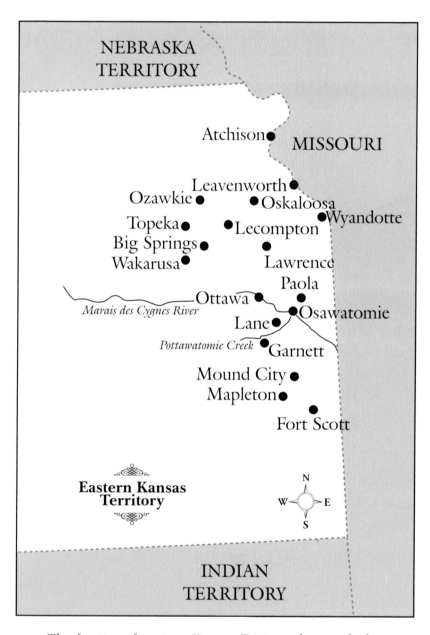

NEBRASKA
TERRITORY

MISSOURI

Atchison

Leavenworth
Ozawkie   Oskaloosa
Topeka   Lecompton   Wyandotte
Big Springs
Wakarusa   Lawrence

Paola
Ottawa
Marais des Cygnes River   Osawatomie
Lane
Pottawatomie Creek   Garnett

Mound City
Mapleton

Fort Scott

**Eastern Kansas
Territory**

N
W — E
S

INDIAN
TERRITORY

*The frontier of eastern Kansas Territory became both a
political and military battleground during the years after
the passage of the Kansas-Nebraska Act. Pictured are some
of the towns and regions that would be affected.*

MASSACRE IN MAY

On May 21, 1856, the men of the Pottawatomie Rifle Company spurred their horses toward the town of Lawrence, in Kansas Territory. Captain John Brown, Jr., commanded the company. They hoped to help protect the settlers in Lawrence. Lawrence was the largest Free-State settlement in the territory. The Free-Staters were against having Kansas become a state where slavery was legal. The proslavery Border Ruffians from Missouri, who wanted legal slavery in Kansas, had threatened Lawrence from the day the settlers arrived. Now the Border Ruffians were attacking the town. Along the road the company met up with the Free-State Osawatomie Rifle Company. Together the two groups continued toward Lawrence.

After riding all night, the soldiers stopped to make camp and prepare breakfast. A rider from Lawrence came with the news that the Border Ruffians had destroyed the town and had arrested several Free-State men. The soldiers continued to Lawrence to see if they could help. They camped that night just south of the town of Palmyra. Through the night the men talked of

John Brown led a night raid against the proslavery men who lived near the Pottawatomie Creek, killing five settlers in one night.

the many threats and attacks the proslavery forces had made against the Free-State settlers. They also heard that some of the proslavery men along the nearby Pottawatomie Creek were threatening to burn the homes of their Free-State neighbors. Captain Brown's father, "Old" John Brown, grew angrier as the night went on.

The Free-State Kansans

The Kansas-Nebraska Act, which had been passed in 1854, provided that the settlers of Kansas and Nebraska, not Congress, would decide whether each territory would be admitted as a slave state or a Free State.

Most of the Lawrence settlers had traveled to Kansas Territory from eastern states. The New England Emigrant Aid Society, an organization formed to help make the new territory of Kansas a Free State instead of a slave state, helped them get started in Kansas. Those involved with the Free-State cause did not want to outlaw slavery in the states where it already existed. They wanted only to keep new slave states from forming. Lawrence's leader, Dr. Charles Robinson, had refused to fight against the Missourians and the proslavery settlers. He knew that many Americans were watching events in Kansas. He did not want the Free-State settlers to be accused of starting a war.

Old John Brown, however, was an abolitionist. He wanted to wipe out slavery wherever he found it.

Dr. Charles Robinson was sent to Kansas Territory by the New England Emigrant Aid Society to be the leader of the new Free-State town of Lawrence.

When Border Ruffians threatened to attack Lawrence the previous December, Robinson had refused the help of John Brown's men. Robinson feared that violence begun by the Free-State settlers would bring more violence on them from the proslavery forces. That time, his strategy worked. The Border Ruffians left without firing a shot. Now, after this attack on Lawrence, the Free-State Hotel and Robinson's home were destroyed. Brown still believed that only force could drive out the Border Ruffians.

A Bloody Plan

About noon on May 23, John Brown announced that he would leave the group to lead a separate expedition. John Brown, Jr., did not want his father to go, but the older man was determined. He gathered four of his sons, Frederick, Owen, Oliver, and Watson; his son-in-law Henry Thompson; and his friend Thomas Winer. They sharpened their double-edged swords on a grindstone and loaded their guns. Since they did not have enough horses, Brown asked James Townsley to take the men in his wagon. As they left the others, John Brown, Jr., warned his father to "do nothing rash."[1]

Old Brown and his men camped that night between the Pottawatomie and Middle creeks in Franklin County. At last Brown told the men the purpose of their expedition: ". . . to sweep the Pottawatomie of all Pro-slavery men living on it."[2] Townsley lived in the area and knew the people there. Brown wanted Townsley to show him where his proslavery neighbors lived so that Brown and his men could kill them. When Townsley refused, Brown angrily asked him, "Why don't you fight your enemies?" Townsley replied, "I have no enemies I can kill in that way."[3] Brown insisted, "It has been ordained by the Almighty God, ordained from eternity, that I should make an example of these men."[4] Brown would find the men he intended to kill, with or without Townsley's help.

Awakened to Death

On May 24, the men spent the day in camp planning their raid. Near midnight, Brown led his company to the home of James P. Doyle. Doyle openly admitted that he was in favor of making Kansas a slave state, but he was not involved in politics. He had come to Kansas to make a claim and raise crops, not to cause trouble with his neighbors. Brown's men knocked on the door. They commanded Doyle and his sons to come out of the house. Doyle's two eldest sons came out with him. Doyle's wife, Mahala, begged the men to spare her youngest son, so they allowed him to stay with her.[5]

Brown's company led Doyle and his two sons into the woods. According to Townsley, "John Brown drew his revolver and shot old man Doyle in the forehead, killing him instantly; and Brown's two youngest sons immediately fell upon the younger Doyles with their two-edged swords."[6] Mahala Doyle heard the shot. The next morning, the Doyles' bodies were found by the side of the road.

Next the group visited the home of Allen Wilkinson, a member of the Kansas Territorial Legislature. After being dragged from his bed, Wilkinson was marched a short distance from his home. One of Brown's sons then killed him with a sword. Wilkinson was also left by the side of the road. There was still one more stop on this bloody night.

At the house of James Harris, Brown and his men hoped to find several proslavers. Harris was dragged out first. In response to Brown's questions, Harris saved his own life by claiming that he did not support the proslavery movement. Next, William Sherman was brought from the house. Brown's two youngest sons led Sherman off toward the creek while Brown's other men stayed to guard Harris. The following morning Harris discovered Sherman's body lying in the creek. Sherman's skull had been split open and his hands cut off.

Conflicting Accounts

Word of the incident in Franklin County spread quickly, but not accurately. The proslavery *Squatter Sovereign* incorrectly reported that eight men were killed, and that the Free-State group consisted of twenty men.[7] The Free-State *Kansas Tribune* said that the proslavery men had been attempting to hang a Free-State settler when they were shot by friends of the threatened man.[8] William Phillips, a reporter for the abolitionist *New York Tribune*, believed that William Sherman was not killed by the Free-State group, but by Comanche Indians. He insisted that Sherman's murder was wrongly linked with the others to place more blame on the Free-State men.[9]

Although newspapers in Kansas covered the incident in great detail, most eastern newspapers barely mentioned it. *The New York Times* carried lengthy stories every day for weeks after the sack of Lawrence, but the Pottawatomie Massacre received no more than a few sentences any day it was mentioned. The *Times* reported the incorrect information of the *Squatter Sovereign* and the proslavery St. Louis *Republican*, that eight proslavery settlers had been killed by Free-State men. It insisted, however, that the story was "quite as improbable as many others that have appeared in that journal and have been proved utterly false."[10] Later, the *Times* published the information sent by the *Kansas Tribune* that the proslavery men were killed during the rescue of a Free-State man threatened with hanging.[11]

The *Times*, whose editors favored the Free-State cause, seemed unwilling to believe that Free-State men could be guilty of such a brutal crime. Although the name of John Brown was not yet well known, the *Times* called him "a man of most desperate courage . . . [W]hen the time comes he will gain for himself much distinction."[12]

Both proslavers and Free-Staters were shocked by the savagery of the murders. Some people, however, thought the killings were justified. They believed the men killed were planning to burn the homes of their Free-State neighbors and force them to leave the territory. William Phillips said the victims ". . . had always been violent, bad men." Although he acknowledged the cruel nature of the crime, he insisted that "the corrupt government and perverted official authority" was to blame.[13]

The Pottawatomie Massacre put enough fear into the proslavery settlers that many of them left the area forever. For that reason, many local residents, and even James Townsley, believed the massacre was important to the Free-State cause. Years later, Townsley recalled John Brown's words that the killing "must be done for the protection of the Free-state settlers, that it was better that a score of bad men should die than that one Free-state man should be driven out."[14]

Revenge Heaped Upon Revenge

The Pottawatomie Massacre did not bring an end to the threats against Free-State settlers. Instead, it seemed to add more fuel to the fiery conflict in Kansas. On June 2, federal troops attempted to capture Brown and his men. The fight turned into a gun battle, later called the Battle of Black Jack. Brown's men fought against proslavery troops in several more battles that summer. They also stole cattle and horses on the Missouri side of the state line. By the end of August, proslavery soldiers were so angry with Brown that they attacked and burned the town of Osawatomie where Brown was living. Brown's son Frederick was killed in that fight.

"Bleeding Kansas" had earned its name.

2

CONFLICT AND COMPROMISE

Americans realized their love for freedom when they felt the lack of it under British rule. Some also recognized that the concept of freedom is not limited to white males. In 1774, the First Continental Congress declared that the thirteen colonies would stop importing slaves and would not have trade relations with any country (including Britain) involved in slave trading. Thomas Jefferson's original version of the Declaration of Independence included a paragraph blaming Britain's King George III for the introduction of slavery to the colonies. Congress later removed this paragraph. Although the final version of the Declaration of Independence made no mention of slavery, some colonists believed slavery violated the spirit of the Declaration of Independence's words "all men are created equal."[1]

In just a few years, the people of the United States were even more clearly divided on the issue of slavery. In the South, plantation owners believed slave labor was necessary for economic survival. With the invention of the cotton gin in 1793, the processing of cotton—the main plantation product—became much easier. Cotton growers took advantage of this by enlarging their plantations—and their profits. As a result, they needed more slaves to harvest the expanded cotton crops.

Most Northerners, however, felt very differently. Some wanted to abolish, or end, all slavery. They were known as abolitionists. Other Northerners did not desire to end slavery in Southern states, but wanted only to stop the spread of slavery. They hoped that the new territories of the United States would not include slavery. These people became known as Free-Soilers.

A Delicate Balance of Political Power

By 1819, less than half of the United States territory had been made into states. Of the twenty-two states established, eleven were Free States and eleven were slave states. In Congress, keeping the number of slave states and Free States equal was important. In the House of Representatives, states are granted representatives according to population. States with more people have more votes. Since Northern states had more people, they had more votes in the House of Representatives than Southern slave states did. In the Senate however, each state is granted two senators, no matter how many residents live in the state. Since the number of Free States was the same as slave states, the two groups had equal power in the Senate.

Because every new bill must be approved by both houses of Congress, the Senate can reject any bill passed by the House of Representatives. Most issues in Congress did not cause conflicts between Free States and slave states. When a new bill caused a conflict based on the issue of slavery, however, the balance of power in the Senate meant that neither Northern nor Southern states had more power.

The Missouri Compromise

When Missourians asked to be granted statehood, Northern senators objected. Missouri had many farmers who owned slaves to work their fields. If Missouri became a slave state, then the slave states would have more votes in the Senate.

Northerners also objected to Missouri as a slave state because of its location. Missouri bordered Iowa and Illinois, both Free States. Slaves who escaped from their masters usually ran toward a Free State to become a free citizen there. If caught there by his or her master or a slave hunter, however, a slave could be arrested and brought back. A person who helped a slave escape or helped him or her to hide from arrest could be sued by the slave's owner and fined five hundred dollars by the court. Conflicts over runaway slaves created many problems in Free States located next to slave states.

About the same time Missouri asked for statehood, Maine, which had previously been a part of Massachusetts, also applied. If Maine were admitted as a Free State along with Missouri as a slave state, then the senatorial balance of Free States and slave states would be preserved.

In February 1820, Senator Jesse B. Thomas of Illinois presented an addition to the statehood bill. His provision would grant admission for Missouri as a slave state, with the agreement that no other slave state could be created north of Missouri's southern border (the imaginary horizontal line of 36 degrees 30 minutes north latitude) from any land that had been part of the Louisiana Purchase. (Under the 1903 Louisiana Purchase, the United States bought a large amount of land from France which nearly doubled the size of the country.) Although Southerners did not like the geographic boundary placed on slavery, they agreed to the compromise. Speaker of the House Henry Clay, of

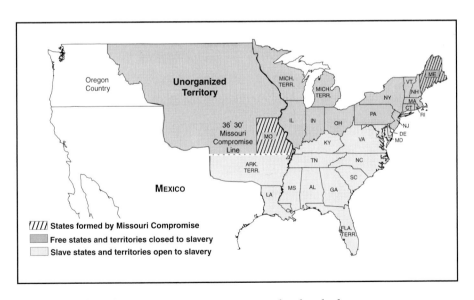

Under the Missouri Compromise, the land that was to become Kansas Territory was part of the Unorganized Territory that was not to allow slavery.

Kentucky, helped win approval of the compromise in the House of Representatives. Missouri and Maine were admitted to the Union.

Another Conflict; Another Compromise

In the years following the Missouri Compromise, the balance of Free States and slave states in the Senate continued. In 1836 and 1837, Arkansas was admitted as a slave state, followed by Michigan as a Free State. Later, Florida and Texas were admitted to the Union as slave states, followed by Iowa and Wisconsin as Free States.

Thirty years after the Missouri Compromise, the slavery issue again divided Congress and the nation. As a result of the gold rush of 1848–1849, enough people had settled in California to ask for statehood. California was free territory. If California were admitted as a Free State without a slave state to balance it, then the South would lose its equal voice in the Senate. The controversy was so intense that Southern states threatened to withdraw, or secede, from the Union over it.

Slavery was also an issue in the Southwest. With the United States's victory in the Mexican War (1846–1848), the country had acquired new land to the west of Texas. Texas claimed that some of this new land was part of its territory. This land west of Texas was mostly south of the line of 36 degrees 30 minutes latitude, within the boundary of slavery as stated in the Missouri Compromise. However, since that land had not been part of the Louisiana Purchase, it did not fall under the rules of the Missouri Compromise.

Slavery had been outlawed in Mexico before the war. If the new territory became part of the slave state of Texas, it would be open to slavery. Northerners did not like the idea of annexing land that had been free and allowing it to permit slavery. Southerners felt that since the land was south of 36 degrees 30 minutes north latitude, it should be slave territory, especially since there was no other new land available south of that line to be made into slave states. If this territory could not allow slavery, then the South would forever lose its equal power in the Senate.

Clay's Compromise

Finally, Henry Clay, now a senator from Kentucky, proposed a compromise. To please Northerners opposed to slavery, California was admitted to the Union as a Free State. Also, Clay included a measure that ended the slave trade in the District of Columbia. To satisfy Southerners whose escaped slaves were being helped by Northern abolitionists, the compromise included the Fugitive Slave Act. This measure increased the punishment for helping a slave escape. It also required all citizens to return escaped slaves to their masters or face a fine of one thousand dollars, additional damages up to one thousand dollars, and up to six months in prison. Under Clay's proposal, Texas would not keep the land to its west, but it would receive a payment of

Senator Henry Clay of Kentucky proposed the Compromise of 1850 which served to preserve the Union by delaying the Civil War for ten years.

$10 million to pay its debt to Mexico from the Mexican War.

Called the Compromise of 1850, Clay's solution organized the territories of New Mexico (which included both present-day states of New Mexico and Arizona) and Utah. Unlike previous territorial bills, the Compromise of 1850 did not specify that the new territories would be free or slaveholding territories. Instead, Congress agreed to let the residents of the territories decide. They would vote on the issue, and then make their decision part of their constitution when they were ready to apply for statehood. This idea was known as popular sovereignty.

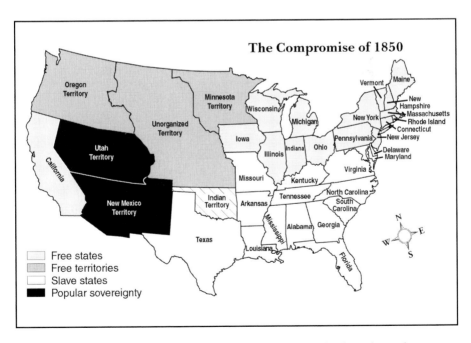

The Compromise of 1850 first introduced the idea of popular sovereignty.

The Compromise of 1850 did not completely satisfy either the North or the South. Northerners did not like the Fugitive Slave Act portion of the bill. Southerners did not like the laws against the slave trade and the imbalance caused by California's admittance as a Free State. Still, both sides recognized that without Clay's Compromise, the United States would be split. After eight months of debate, the bill finally passed both houses of Congress.

Looking Westward

Soon after the Compromise of 1850, Americans were still looking for new land to settle. Just to the west of Iowa and Missouri stretched the great plains of the center of the continent. The land here was good for farming, which appealed to new immigrants from Europe and also to those from the more populous eastern states who wanted to find new homesteads. The industries of the North were also making plans for a transcontinental railroad to extend to California. Acquiring the territory west of Iowa and Missouri would allow the railroad to run a more direct route from Chicago or St. Louis, a route the Northern industries preferred.

The first attempt to organize this new territory came to the House of Representatives on December 13, 1852. A Missouri representative, Willard P. Hall, presented a bill to organize the land known as the Territory of Platte. The bill went to the Committee on Territories, which renamed the area the Territory of

Nebraska in the bill it presented on February 2, 1853. Although Southern representatives objected to it, the bill still passed in the House and went on to the Senate, where it was defeated on March 3. Since the land was all north of the line of 36 degrees 30 minutes north latitude, both the North and the South assumed that any state formed there would be free. The South was not willing to accept any more Free States unless there could be a new slave state as well.[2]

Senator Augustus C. Dodge of Iowa made the next attempt on December 14, 1853. He presented a bill to the Senate proposing to organize the same area as the previous bill. This included land west of Missouri between the lines of 36 degrees 30 minutes north latitude and 43 degrees 30 minutes north latitude. The bill was then sent to the Committee on Territories. The head of that committee was Senator Stephen A. Douglas of Illinois.[3]

Of course, Southern senators still did not like this plan. Therefore, on January 4, 1854, Douglas and his committee presented a revised Nebraska bill. The new bill moved the northern boundary of the territory to 49 degrees north latitude, the northern boundary of the United States. It also included a popular sovereignty provision similar to the wording of the Compromise of 1850. This would allow the residents of the new territory to decide the issue of slavery.

Southern senators were pleased with the new bill, since it offered the possibility that the new territory could become a slave state, even though it seemed unlikely that slavery would extend as far north as the northern boundary of the United States. The senators from the North, however, were very unhappy with the bill. Since the land proposed for Nebraska territory was part of the Louisiana Purchase and was north of 36 degrees 30 minutes north latitude, passage of this bill would contradict the Missouri Compromise. Northerners considered the Missouri Compromise a solemn promise between the North and the South.

Two Territories From One

Senator Douglas and his committee did not give up on the Nebraska bill. On January 23, 1854, the Committee on Territories presented yet another version of the Nebraska bill. The new version divided the land into two separate territories. Nebraska Territory would make up the northern half of it, extending from the line of 40 degrees north latitude to the United States northern border. Kansas Territory would lie next to Missouri, from the line of 40 degrees north latitude to the 37-degree line (this was moved north from 36 degrees 30 minutes to avoid including American Indian tribal land). As in the earlier version, residents in the new territories would decide the issue of slavery.[4]

The most controversial point of the bill, however, was the reference to that portion of the Missouri Compromise that outlawed slavery north of 36 degrees 30 minutes north latitude. The new bill stated that the popular sovereignty wording of the Compromise of

Senator Stephen A. Douglas of Illinois, known in Congress as the "Little Giant," was the head of the Committee on Territories that proposed the Kansas-Nebraska bill on January 23, 1854.

1850 "superseded," or replaced, the Missouri Compromise boundary, and it called that act "inoperative."[5] In other words, the new bill would repeal, or cancel, the prohibition of slavery in certain territories dictated by the Missouri Compromise.

On January 31, Representative William A. Richardson of Illinois introduced a Kansas-Nebraska bill to the House of Representatives that was nearly the same as the bill before the Senate.[6] For the next four months, both houses of Congress would be involved in one of the most bitter struggles ever fought there.

THE KANSAS-NEBRASKA BILL IN CONGRESS

The new bill (often still called by its old name, the Nebraska bill) opened a new round of debate in Congress. Battle lines were drawn between North and South. The angry voices of Northern legislators filled the newspapers. On January 24, the *New York Daily Times* carried "An Address to the People" signed by both senators and two representatives of Ohio. The address called the new Nebraska bill and its repeal of the Missouri Compromise "a gross violation of a sacred pledge," and predicted that, if passed, it would turn the new territory "into a dreary region of despotism [dictatorship], inhabited by masters and slaves."[1] They urged citizens to "protest earnestly and emphatically, by correspondence, through the press, by memorials, by resolutions of public meetings and legislative bodies, and in whatever other mode may seem expedient against this enormous crime."[2]

Stephen Douglas's motives for presenting the

Kansas-Nebraska bill are not clear. One likely reason was business. Many businessmen from Douglas's home state hoped that Chicago would be the starting point for a railroad route through this new territory. A letter from Douglas to a political committee in St. Joseph, Missouri, shows Douglas's commitment to expanding railroads and communication, even at the expense of American Indians, which he calls "hostile savages":

> How are we to develope [sic], cherish and protect our immense interests and possessions on the Pacific, with a vast wilderness fifteen hundred miles in breadth, filled with hostile savages, and cutting off all direct communication. . . . We must therefore have Rail Roads and Telegraphs from the Atlantic to the Pacific, through our own territory. . . . The removal of the Indian barrier and the extension of the laws of the United States in the form of Territorial governments are the first steps toward the accomplishment of each and all of those objects.[3]

Others thought that Douglas's motive was political gain. An unsigned editorial in the *New York Daily Times* said Douglas would "sacrifice any public principle, however valuable, and plunge the country into foreign war or internal dissention, however fatal they might prove, if he could thereby advance himself a single step towards the Presidential chair."[4]

If political gain was Douglas's motive, not everyone thought he was successful. Colonel Thomas Hart Benton, representative from Missouri, remarked to a friend, "Douglas, Sir, is politically dead, Sir. If he fail to carry his bill the South will kick him in the rear, Sir; and if he does carry it the North will beat his brains out, Sir."[5] An editorial in the *Times* agreed: "Two paltry pennies will purchase the political death warrant of the Senator from Illinois."[6] The Kansas-Nebraska bill would need more than just Douglas's enthusiasm to be passed by Congress.

Presidential Support

Douglas asked President Franklin Pierce to give his support to the bill. This placed Pierce in a difficult position. Many citizens of his home state, New Hampshire, were against the spread of slavery. They would be opposed to this bill. But, Pierce was also trying to fill political positions in his administration. If he angered Southern senators, they would not approve his candidates. This would be the first major bill Pierce had supported since he became president. If it were to fail, it would make him look weak. Also, Pierce had to consider the unity of the Democratic party. It was already becoming split between North and South. He dared not provoke Southern Democrats into quitting the party. Pierce decided to support the bill, but he would earn harsh criticism from those who opposed it.

Round One: The Debate in the Senate

From the day it was introduced, the Kansas-Nebraska bill took center stage in the Senate. As the publicity over the bill grew, so did the crowds of spectators who came to observe. When Senator Salmon P. Chase of

President Franklin Pierce, a Democrat wanting the support of the southern Democratic senators, gave strong support to the Kansas-Nebraska bill.

the Free Soil party of Ohio had his chance to speak against the bill on February 3, 1854, he had a full audience. According to the *New York Daily Times*, "The galleries and lobbies were densely crowded an hour before the debates began. . . . The entire audience . . . listened to Mr. Chase's arguments with most profound attention."[7]

Senator Douglas and his strongest ally, the *president pro tempore* of the Senate, David Atchison of Missouri, as well as other supporters of the bill, argued that the Compromise of 1850 had already superceded the slavery provision of the Missouri Compromise. However, Senator Chase insisted that none of the signers of the 1850 bill had believed that. Chase even referred to a speech Mr. Atchison had made in 1853. Atchison had said he would never vote for a Nebraska bill, because, unless the Missouri Compromise was repealed, slavery would not be legal in the territory. At that time, Atchison had said, "But when I came to look into that question, I found that there was no prospect, no hope, of a repeal of the Missouri compromise."[8] Mr. Chase asked why Mr. Atchison now thought the Missouri Compromise could be judged to be superceded, if he had not thought so the year before.

Taking Sides

Most senators from slave states favored the Kansas-Nebraska bill. Since it was clear that Northern congressmen would never admit the new territories as slave territories, popular sovereignty offered the only

President Pro Tempore of the Senate, David Atchison of Missouri, was one of the most outspoken congressmen in favor of the Kansas-Nebraska bill. Later he would play a key role in helping proslavery settlers in Kansas Territory.

chance for a new slave state. With many slaveholders living in western Missouri, it seemed likely that some of them would cross the border, settle in the territory, and vote for slavery.

Of course, that same reasoning worried Northerners about the bill. They had assumed, because of the Missouri Compromise, that this area would never fall into the hands of slaveholders. In order to have a majority of Free State votes, Northern settlers would have to travel through slave state Missouri. How could they get there quickly enough to gain a majority and cast their votes?

Not everyone, however, agreed with these two points of view. Some Northerners, although they did not like the idea of adding a new slave state, did believe that all Americans should have the right to determine the laws under which they lived. One letter to the *New York Daily Times* argued in favor of popular sovereignty, saying that slavery should be an issue decided by the people in each territory. "Congress would only be following the *spirit* of the Constitution by leaving the question of Slavery . . . open to the action of the territorial Legislatures."[9]

Surprisingly, not all Southerners favored popular sovereignty. In his speech before the Senate on February 4, 1854, Senator Archibald Dixon of Kentucky stated his concerns. He said that slaveholders would not want to go to the new territories with their slaves. He reasoned that if they settled there and lost the election, their slaves would be made free by the new territorial government, and they would lose what they considered valuable "property." If slaveholders did not go into the territory, then only Free State settlers would be there to vote, and "that decision could only be made by those who had no interest at all in the subject of slavery but to exclude it."[10]

As public interest grew, many citizens sent petitions to their congressmen. On February 13, senators presented twenty-six different petitions from citizens of Massachusetts, Vermont, Delaware, Ohio, Indiana, and Pennsylvania who voiced their opposition to the Nebraska bill.[11] Other public statements, called memorials, arrived daily from religious groups all across the North. Many daily sessions of the debate in the Senate began with the readings of these memorials.

Not Just North versus South

The geographical boundary between North and South was not the only dividing line separating the legislators. Political party loyalty was also important. Democrats held the majority in both houses of Congress. The other main party, the Whig party, held about 33 percent of the votes in the Senate, and about 30 percent of the votes in the House of Representatives. A third party, the Free Soil party, held two seats in the Senate and four in the House.[12]

Most legislators were loyal to either the proslavery or Free State opinions of their home states, but they also had to consider their loyalty to their party members from other states. Both Northern and Southern states had congressmen belonging to the Whig party. Both Northern and Southern states also had Democratic congressmen. A political party split over the slavery issue could lose many congressional seats in the next election. If the party lost supporters, it would also be difficult to present a successful presidential candidate in the next election. There were many congressional issues besides slavery that a strong party could support. There were few elections that a weak party could win.

Even Democrats from the South did not all agree. Senator Sam Houston of Texas did not want to repeal the Missouri Compromise. He told the Senate, "For more than a third of a century it has given comparative peace and tranquility. . . . It is the principle of truth that should be preserved. The word of one section of the Union should be kept with the other."[13]

However, Houston's fellow Democrat, Senator Andrew P. Butler of South Carolina, disagreed with Houston. He said the Missouri Compromise,

> . . . instead of bringing with it peace and harmony, has brought with it sectional strife . . . [I]nstead of being a healing salve, [it is] a thorn in the side of the southern portion of this Confederacy, and the sooner you extract it, the sooner you will restore harmony and health to the body politic.[14]

Senators from the same state also sometimes disagreed. Senator James Cooper of Pennsylvania argued against the bill, predicting that "its passage will revive all agitation and excitement before experienced on the Slavery question." Like Senator Houston, he argued that "The Missouri Compromise was adopted as the settlement of dangerous and alarming questions, and for that reason ought not to be disturbed."[15]

Senator Richard Brodhead, Jr., another Whig from Pennsylvania, "regretted that he and his colleague . . . could not agree upon this measure." Mr. Brodhead saw no threat to the North because, "Slavery could never go into the Nebraska Kanzas [sic] territories" because the soil and climate would not permit the types of crops that needed slave labor.[16]

The Senate's Decision

The debate intensified at the beginning of March 1854. Senator John M. Clayton of Delaware presented a motion to change the bill by removing a provision that allowed immigrants from other countries to vote in territorial elections. Since immigrants usually did not favor slavery, this would give proslavery voters an advantage in the elections. The motion passed and the amendment was added.

On Friday, March 3, the debate continued, although most of the senators were clearly tired of hearing the same arguments. By evening, tempers were running short. Commenting on this final session of debate, the *New York Daily Times* correspondent described some senators as ill mannered and even drunk: "A glance from the Senate gallery at midnight on Friday revealed the disgraceful fact, that more than one of its members had forgotten in their cups, all of their dignity and not a little of the propriety of a deliberative body."[17] The *Times* correspondent predicted that enough Northern votes would go in favor of the bill to pass it in what he called "a traitorous betrayal of Northern sentiment."[18] The speeches continued until the next morning, as the senators did not want to adjourn until a vote was taken. Although Northern Whigs and Free-Soilers voted unanimously against it, both Whigs and Democrats from the South voted almost unanimously in favor of it. Northern Democrats, however, voted 15 for and 5 against. When the final vote was taken, the Nebraska bill passed 41–17.[19]

Round Two: The Nebraska Bill in the House of Representatives

From the Senate, the bill moved next to the House of Representatives. Representatives made the same arguments over popular sovereignty and the repeal of the Missouri Compromise as their colleagues in the Senate had made. Both North and South understood that this new territory would probably be the last opportunity for slavery to expand. If that effort failed and the territory became a Free State, slavery would probably soon die out when the Senate balance tipped in favor of the Free States.

Those against the bill tried to persuade Southerners that the repeal would violate the honor of the South and those who had supported the Missouri Compromise. It would also lead abolitionists to push even harder to outlaw slavery in all states. They warned

Northerners that passage of the bill meant the extension of slavery into Northern territories and would create a wide belt of slavery between eastern and western states.

Because Stephen Douglas of Illinois led the committee that introduced the bill, Southerners were quick to point out that they did not originate it. Many Northerners did not like the bill and proclaimed that Douglas did not represent them. Neither side would

SOURCE DOCUMENT

STRANGE! HERE IS A MOVEMENT FOR THE IMMENSE EXTENSION OF SLAVERY. OF COURSE, IT IS NOT THE WORK OF THE ANTI-SLAVERY PARTY . . . I TOOK IT FOR GRANTED THAT THE PRO-SLAVERY PARTY DID IT. BUT, IT SEEMS IT DID NOT . . . WELL, IF NEITHER THE ANTI-SLAVERY PARTY, NOR THE PRO-SLAVERY PARTY, DID IT, WHO WAS IT THEN, THAT DID IT? IT FOLLOWS, NECESSARILY, THAT IT MUST BE THE WORK OF THE LORD, OR THE DEVIL. [LAUGHTER.] BUT, IT CANNOT BE THE WORK OF THE LORD—FOR THE GOOD BOOK TELLS US: "WHERE THE SPIRIT OF THE LORD IS, THERE IS LIBERTY"— LIBERTY, NOT SLAVERY. SO THIS NEBRASKA BUSINESS MUST BE THE WORK OF THE DEVIL. [GREAT LAUGHTER.] BUT LOGICAL AS IS THIS CONCLUSION, I AM NEVERTHELESS, TOO POLITE TO PRESS IT. [20]

Gerrit Smith of the Free Soil party of New York, in his speech to the House, used humor to point out the hypocrisy of both sides of the debate over the Kansas-Nebraska bill. This transcript from The Congressional Globe *includes the reaction of the representatives to Smith's speech.*

claim the bill, although legislators from both North and South supported it.

As it had in the Senate, the debate in the House grew louder and angrier as weeks passed. On April 11, Representative William Cullom of Tennessee expressed his impatience with the time spent in debate upon the bill. He called it, "the work of politicians . . . to strangle the legitimate legislation of the country," and added, "I should not be a worthy descendent of my mother State, Kentucky, if I did not here, in my place, denounce this scheme as a plot against the peace and quiet of the country, whether so designed or not."[21]

Representative Phillip Phillips of Alabama spoke on April 24, expressing his support of the bill. He insisted that the South had opposed the Missouri Compromise from the beginning, but had been forced to accept it. Since it was, therefore, not really a compromise at all, Southerners had every reason to support its repeal.[22]

On Monday, May 22, amid much objection and arguing, the representatives voted on the Kansas-Nebraska bill. As in the Senate, Northern Whigs and Free-Soilers in the House voted unanimously against it. Northern Democrats, however, were evenly divided: 44 in favor and 44 against it. Seven Southern Whigs voted against the bill; 21 voted for it. It narrowly passed the House of Representatives by a vote of 115 to 104.[23] The House voted to remove the Clayton amendment, so the bill returned to the Senate for one last vote. This time, a majority of senators voted not to try to add the Clayton amendment again because it would cause the House to reject the bill.

The Challenge

After the Kansas-Nebraska bill's passage, New York senator William Seward addressed the Senate, expressing the intention of abolitionist groups to send settlers to Kansas:

> Come on then, gentlemen of the Slave States. Since there is no escaping your challenge, I accept it in behalf of the cause of freedom. We will engage in competition for the virgin soil of Kansas, and God give the victory to the side which is stronger in numbers as it is in right.[24]

The Kansas-Nebraska bill was signed by President Franklin Pierce on May 30, 1854, and became law. The race for Kansas was on.

THE RACE FOR KANSAS

No more than eight hundred white persons lived in Kansas when the Kansas-Nebraska bill was signed in May 1854. Most of them were soldiers and missionaries.[1] To make land available for settlers, new treaties were drawn with the Indian tribes of the Delaware, Pottawatomie, Kickapoo, Wyandot, Miami, and Shawnee. The tribes gave the United States nearly all the land within two hundred miles of the Missouri border.

Even before the bill was signed, Missourians were preparing to invade Kansas Territory. Without government offices to issue legal titles of ownership to plots of land, a person who wanted a homestead could claim any plot of 160 acres and settle on it. Those who claimed land were called squatters. Some Missourians learned in advance about secret treaties to acquire American Indian tribal land, and rode across the border to claim the best land. They often set some logs out on the land to look like a cabin in the making or simply nailed up a sign threatening anyone who dared to trespass, then returned to their homes in Missouri. Many claimed land in order to vote for slavery in

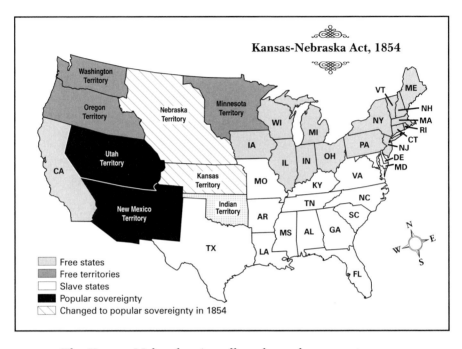

The Kansas-Nebraska Act allowed popular sovereignty to decide whether the new territories of Kansas and Nebraska would be slave states or free states.

Kansas, but few wanted to leave their comfortable Missouri homes.

The New England Emigrant Aid Company

Meanwhile, Eli Thayer, a schoolmaster in Massachusetts, was organizing his own invasion of Kansas. He asked businessmen to help him form a corporation known as the New England Emigrant Aid Society. In April 1854, just before the Kansas-Nebraska bill became law, the company was officially chartered as the Massachusetts Emigrant Aid Company. It would bring parties of Free-State settlers to Kansas at reduced fares for transportation; build boarding houses to hold settlers while they built their own houses; buy the equipment needed to establish a town, such as a mill or steam saw; and begin a newspaper to speak for freedom in Kansas.[2]

In June 1854, Dr. Charles Robinson and Charles H. Branscomb made the first trip to Kansas representing the Emigrant Aid Company. Their mission was to find a suitable place for their first town. After their visit, they went back to Buffalo, New York, to meet their first group of Kansas pioneers.

The New England Emigrants Arrive

On August 1, 1854, Branscomb and the first party of Free-State settlers arrived in Kansas. They called their new town Lawrence, to honor the company's largest financial contributor, Amos A. Lawrence. The group of about thirty men camped on a hill overlooking the town site. They named the hill Mt. Oread, after Eli Thayer's college in Massachusetts. Although some of the pioneers became homesick and left after only a few days, others claimed their future homesteads and began building the town.

First Conflict

The Missourians soon spotted their new Free-State neighbors. About eighty men rode into the area with wagons, horses, shotguns, and a lot of whiskey. They set up camp across the ravine from the Free-State group. That evening, about twenty-five more men

KANSAS.

To those who desire that Kansas should be free.—

Mr. Hoskings, the accredited agent of the Kansas Herald of Freedom, is here for the purpose of procuring subscribers.

That paper is the organ of the Emigrant Aid Company, and if well sustained will be one of the mightiest agencies, in making Kansas a Free State. I am personally acquainted with the editor, G. W. Brown, Esq., and know him to be worthy of his responsible position.

ELI THAYER.

Worcester, Nov. 22, 1854.

———

Shall Kansas be Free?

Let Subscribers Answer.

I am employed to call on such as will subscribe to the Herald, and circulate the first number; all correspondence by mail or otherwise promptly attended to, and such information as I possess cheerfully given.

"I love thee, New England my own native land,
And my spirit exults—I thank God
That the turf where I played in my childhoood's glad morn
By the tyrant may never be trod."

T. H. HOSKINGS,
Canvassing Agent.

A notice from Eli Thayer introducing T. H. Hoskins as agent of the Herald of Freedom, *official newspaper of the Emigrant Aid Society.*

arrived. The Missourians continued to drink and began shooting into the darkness. When several Lawrence men went across the ravine to investigate, the Missourians told them to leave by morning or be prepared for violence. Although worried, the settlers decided they had come too far to back out now.[3]

At daylight, fifty more Missourians arrived. They gave the settlers one more chance to leave, and told them to be gone by ten o'clock. In response, the Lawrence men took out their rifles and began to march in military style around their tent settlement. By eleven o'clock, the Missourians had not made any moves, and Robinson convinced the settlers that they were in no real danger.[4]

Sometime after noon, the Missourians sent another threat. They gave the settlers just ten minutes to leave the territory. The settlers just laughed. Although the proslavers cursed and threatened, none of them rode across the ravine toward the settlers. At dusk, some of the Missourians called their companions cowards and rode off in the direction of Westport, Missouri. The rest of the Missouri party gave up and rode away at sunset.[5] It was the settlers' first encounter with the Border Ruffians, but it would not be their last.

Kansas's First Governor Arrives

Although the settlers of Kansas would soon elect legislators to form a constitution, they would not elect their own governor until they achieved statehood. Congressman Asa Packer, a Democrat from Pennsylvania,

Kansas Territory's first governor, Andrew H. Reeder, was a slavery supporter when he arrived, but he later became committed to making Kansas a free state.

nominated a Pennsylvania lawyer, Andrew H. Reeder, for governor. Reeder had been a supporter of the Kansas-Nebraska bill, so Pierce and the Southern legislators favored him. Reeder arrived in the territory on October 7. Proslavery men were confident that Reeder was in favor of slavery and would help make Kansas a slave state.

Reeder was greeted with a military salute at Fort Leavenworth. The new town of Leavenworth, next to the fort, was a proslavery town. The people expected to hear Reeder support their proslavery views but were disappointed when he spoke only of the right of settlers to decide the issue in a fair election. Governor Reeder toured the territory, then established the election

SOURCE DOCUMENT

BUT ONE GREAT ARGUMENT IN THE SUPPORT OF THE REPEAL OF THE MISSOURI COMPROMISE, IS STILL TO COME. THAT ARGUMENT IS "THE SACRED RIGHT OF SELF GOVERNMENT." . . . WHEN THE WHITE MAN GOVERNS HIMSELF, AND ALSO GOVERNS ANOTHER MAN, THAT IS MORE THAN SELF-GOVERNMENT—THAT IS DESPOTISM. IF THE NEGRO IS A MAN, WHY THEN MY ANCIENT FAITH TEACHES ME THAT "ALL MEN ARE CREATED EQUAL;" AND THAT THERE CAN BE NO MORAL RIGHT IN CONNECTION WITH ONE MAN'S MAKING A SLAVE OF ANOTHER.[6]

In a speech given on October 16, 1854, in Peoria, Illinois, Abraham Lincoln voiced his opposition to repealing the Missouri Compromise.

districts for the territory and announced the date of the first election: November 29, 1854.

Ballot-Box Fraud

The November 1854 election would decide the first delegate to Congress from the Kansas Territory. Three candidates appeared on the ballot: J. W. Whitfield of the Proslavery party, a resident of Jackson County, Missouri; John A. Wakefield of the Free State party, who lived in Kansas Territory; and Robert P. Flenniken, a proslavery Democrat from Pennsylvania and Reeder's friend. Voters cast a total of 2,971 votes that day. Of those, 1,729 were illegally cast by Missourians who rode across the border. Whitfield, the proslavery candidate, was declared the winner with 2,268 votes, over Flenniken's 305 and Wakefield's 249.[7]

The first edition of the *Kansas Free State*, a newspaper published in Lawrence, Kansas, criticized the election. It claimed that proslavers paid people to vote for their cause, and that American Indians voted in the election even though they were not legal voters. It also stated that Free-Soilers voted for Whitfield instead of Wakefield because the names were so similar.[8]

Two weeks later, the Free-State *Herald of Freedom*, also published in Lawrence, included a letter from a citizen of Maryland who had visited Kansas on Election Day. According to his account, the Missourians "threatened and intimidated the judges; crowded out and violently drove off all those who were suspected of being in favor of any other candidate than their own, and put their own votes into the ballot box at the point of the revolver."[9]

Whitfield became the delegate from Kansas Territory, but Governor Reeder was not pleased. Some people believed that Senator David Atchison of St. Joseph, Missouri, was behind the election fraud. Reeder was now convinced that the Border Ruffians were a violent and lawless group that must be stopped.

Governor Reeder wanted to make the next election fair. In February 1855, he sent agents to count the residents of Kansas Territory. The agents were told to do

"Border Ruffians," Missouri residents who wanted to make Kansas a slave state, came across the border by the thousands to vote illegally in Kansas territorial elections.

their work without attracting the attention of Missourians who would surely send riders across the border to be counted. The census was finished in two weeks. Governor Reeder announced that the election for territorial legislature would take place on March 30.

The Election of the Territorial Legislature

As March 30 approached, the race for the polls began. A large group of Free-State settlers from Pennsylvania arrived three days before the election. Hearing of this, the proslavers decided to outnumber the Free-State voters. Thousands of Missourians came across the border on horseback or mule, across the Missouri River on ferryboats, and on foot along the road out of Westport to cast their votes.

While there was no real violence at the polls, there were threats and insults and guns pointed at election judges who did not want to let the Border Ruffians vote. Although the census from February had counted 2,905 legal voters in the territory, over 6,300 votes were cast. Thirty-nine legislators were elected. Three were Free-State candidates, the rest were proslavery.[10]

Even though the election was not fair, most historians believe that, even if the Missourians had not interfered, the Proslavery party would still have won. About two thirds of the legal voters in the territory identified themselves as slavery supporters.[11] Also, the Missourians complained that many eastern emigrants had come into the territory just before the election (one group arrived in Lawrence the day before the election) and had voted. Some of these eastern emigrants left the territory shortly after they voted in the election. Fourteen election districts had been invaded by the Border Ruffians, but only six protested the election results.[12]

Most Missourians were afraid to speak out against the Ruffians. Those who dared to protest them faced severe consequences. Colonel George S. Park, founder of Parkville, Missouri (in Platte County), and owner of the *Parkville Luminary* newspaper, scolded Missourians who rode across the border to vote. In retaliation for Park's boldness, a Platte County mob broke into the newspaper office on April 14. Although Colonel Park was not in the office, his partner, William Patterson, was there when the mob arrived. The mob threatened to kill Patterson, but his wife would not let go of him. The men then carried the *Luminary*'s printing press and the printing type down the hill to the Missouri river and threw them in. The *Squatter Sovereign* of Atchison, Kansas, praised this act, and threatened that "Northern scoundrels. . . . must, for the future, be suppressed—at the cost of their property, if that will accomplish it—at the cost of their lives, when every other remedy fails."[13] Park responded angrily, "An humble individual is in the power of hundreds of armed men; but his death will not destroy the freedom of the AMERICAN PRESS!"[14]

Colonel George S. Park, founder of Parkville, Missouri, and owner of the Parkville Luminary *newspaper dared to speak out against the Border Ruffians and paid dearly.*

Governor Reeder in Trouble

Governor Reeder rejected the election of the seventeen proslavery candidates in the districts that filed objections to the election. He called for new elections in those districts, to be held on May 22. The Missourians were furious. They made threats against the governor's life and complained to President Pierce.

Reeder traveled to Washington to defend his actions regarding the recent elections. Meanwhile, his opponents began a plan to get rid of him. A group of Reeder's friends from Pennsylvania had come to Kansas and settled in the town of Pawnee. Reeder had hinted that Pawnee would likely become the capital city. If so, the land there would increase in value. Reeder's enemies heard these rumors. They accused the governor of buying up plots of land at a low price, influencing the location of the capital, then reselling the land for a profit. It was a serious charge. If true, it could lead to his dismissal from office.

When Reeder arrived in Washington, the president did not help him. Worse, the charges of land speculation had reached the president, and Reeder's job as governor was in trouble. President Pierce said he was concerned for Reeder's safety, and he encouraged Reeder to resign. He urged Reeder not to return to the territory and offered him a position as minister to China. But Reeder felt that resigning his position would be a betrayal of the citizens of Kansas. He was determined to return, hold fair elections, and attend the first meeting of the new legislature.

On May 22, new elections were held in the six districts that had protested the March 30 election. The proslavery Kansans and the Missourians refused to take part in the new elections. Therefore, mostly Free-State voters cast ballots, and Free-State men were elected in five of the six districts.

The "Bogus Legislature" in Action

In the last days of June, the newly elected legislators began their trip to Pawnee, Kansas. Most were unhappy about the governor's choice of the territorial capital, since they were actually residents of Missouri. Pawnee was 125 miles west of the Missouri border. Little was there except the new stone building built to be the house of the legislature, and it was not finished. The legislators carried tents and provisions with them, since there were no hotels in Pawnee.

On the opening day of the session, Governor Reeder addressed the legislature, which had a three-fourths majority of proslavery members. He asked the men to set aside selfish motives and act in the best interest of the citizens. They applauded politely, then began the session by voting to declare the May 22 elections illegal. They expelled the Free-State representatives elected then and replaced them with the proslavery candidates elected on March 30. Next, they voted to move the capital to the Shawnee Manual Labor School. The governor vetoed this action but was overruled by the legislators. The legislature then ended with plans to meet July 16 in the new location.

It now had a completely proslavery membership and had proven that the governor had little if any power over it. Free-State settlers would call this group the "bogus legislature" since they felt it was not elected fairly.

The Bogus Legislature and its Laws

When the legislature met at the Shawnee Mission, it passed the first set of laws for the territory. To guarantee that all officials would support the proslavery legislature, judges, sheriffs, and other government officers would be appointed by the legislature instead of being elected. Many laws were written to protect slavery in the new territory. Chapter 151 was entitled "An act for the protection of slave property." Under this act, any person who stole a slave, helped a slave escape, or even suggested to a slave that he might be able to escape could be hanged. Any person who spoke or wrote against slavery, or brought into the territory any newspaper, pamphlet or magazine that spoke against slavery "shall be deemed guilty of felony, and punished by imprisonment at hard labor for a term of not less than two years." A person who was against slavery would not be allowed to serve on a jury of a person accused under these laws.[15] Under this law, anyone who entered the territory carrying a copy of a Free-State newspaper could be arrested, tried by a jury made up entirely of proslavery men, and sent to prison for two or more years.

The legislature sent a message to President Pierce asking him to dismiss Governor Reeder. By the time the messenger arrived, Governor Reeder had already been fired as governor. Reeder decided to return to the territory, despite the fact that proslavery groups had threatened to hang him. The most violent days of Kansas's history were just beginning.

In the summer of 1855, both proslavers and Free-Soilers knew that their opponents were very hostile. Although violence had been threatened for over a year, the damage was mostly limited to property, such as the destruction of the *Parkville Luminary*'s presses. That was about to change. In territorial Kansas, frontier "justice" would often be delivered at the point of a knife or the loop of a noose.

BLOODY REVENGE

Trouble in Atchison

Proslavers were intent on upholding the new laws and punishing anyone who violated them. Reverend Pardee Butler rode into the town of Atchison, Kansas Territory, on August 15. At the newspaper office of the proslavery *Squatter Sovereign*, he said he would vote to make Kansas a Free State. The next morning, several men dragged Butler from his hotel, held a "trial" before a mob at the edge of the river, and threatened to drown him. Instead, they painted his face black, tied him to a raft, and set him adrift down the Missouri River. They promised to hang him if he ever returned.

The *Squatter Sovereign* praised the treatment of Butler and threatened to hang others who would speak of Kansas as a Free State, saying:

> . . . the same punishment we will be happy to award all Freesoilers, Abolitionists, and their emissaries. . . . We will draw largely on the hemp crops of our Missouri neighbors, for a supply of the article, sufficient to afford every jail-bird in the north, a necklace [noose] twelve feet in length.[1]

The incident made Free-Soilers angry. Could law and order exist in Kansas?

Governor Wilson Shannon arrived September 1, 1855. He had heard stories of violent Free-State men attacking their peaceful proslavery neighbors, and he was instructed to uphold the laws of the bogus legislature. Shannon's first speeches in the territory convinced the Free-State settlers that he would not be sympathetic to them, so they decided to establish their own government.

Governor Wilson Shannon of Kansas sympathized more with the proslavers.

Two Political Parties

On September 4, 1855, over three hundred Free-State settlers met at Big Springs, a town midway between Lawrence and Topeka. They founded the Free State party and refused to submit to the laws of the bogus legislature. Since they knew they could not take part in the proslavery territorial legislature, they established their own legislature, later called the Topeka legislature. They nominated former governor Reeder as their candidate for Congress.

The Free State party adopted a policy of not interfering with any states in which slavery was already established. The Big Springs convention wrote a resolution known as the "Black Law," which prohibited African Americans, free or slave, from settling in Kansas. With the Black Law in place, the Free-Soilers could not be accused of harboring runaway slaves in violation of the Fugitive Slave Law. This Black Law was largely the work of James H. Lane, a former congressman from Indiana. The Big Springs convention also made plans for a state constitution the settlers hoped to submit to Congress for the admission of Kansas to the Union as a Free State.

The Big Springs convention angered the proslavers. In November, a proslavery convention in Leavenworth established the Law and Order party to defend the laws of the territorial legislature. It nominated John Whitfield for Congress. Both parties held elections on separate days, and each claimed victory for its own candidate. Both Reeder and Whitfield arrived in

"UNION IS STRENGTH."

FREE STATE
CONVENTION!

All who are favorable to union

of effort, and a permanent organization of all those who desire to make Kansas a Free State, and who wish to secure, upon the broadest platform, the co-operation of all who agree upon this point, are requested to meet in their respective districts, and appoint **Delegates** who shall meet in general **Convention** at

BIG SPRING, THIRD DISTRICT,

On Wednesday, September 5th,

For the purpose of adopting a Platform upon which all may act harmoniously who prefer Freedom to Slavery.

The nomination of a Delegate to Congress, will also come up before the General Convention.

Every District will be entitled to five Delegates for each Representative apportioned by the Governor previously to the last election.

Let no sectional or party issues distract or prevent the perfect co-operation of Free State men. Union and harmony are absolutely necessary to success. The pro-slavery party are fully and effectually organized. No jars nor minor issues divide them. And to contend against them successfully, we also must be united. Without prudence and harmony of action we are certain to fail.

Let every man then do his duty and we are certain of victory.

All Free State men, without distinction, are earnestly requested to take immediate and effective steps to insure a full and correct representation for every District in the Territory.

The Delegates to represent the First and Second Districts in the Convention, will be chosen on the occasion of the

Mass Meeting

To be held at Lawrence on August 14th. The residents of these **Districts** are requested to attend this meeting.

"United we stand; divided we fall."

By order of the meeting held at Lawrence, **July 17, 1855.**

["Kansas Free State" Print.]

This poster advertises the Free-State convention at Big Springs in Kansas Territory.

Washington to sit in on Congress. Congress recognized Whitfield as the rightfully elected representative. The dispute led to a congressional investigation of affairs in Kansas and a charge of treason against Reeder. Although Reeder was never convicted of treason, he would never again be safe in Kansas.

"Bibles" to the Rescue

As the proslavery towns of Atchison and Leavenworth grew, so did the Free-State communities of Lawrence and Topeka. Claim disputes and fights between settlers were everyday events. Dr. Robinson of Lawrence knew that the Lawrence settlers needed protection from the proslavers. He wrote to Eli Thayer of the Emigrant Aid Society for help. Soon, boxes marked "books" began arriving along with their regular supplies. The crates actually contained Sharps rifles, a new weapon capable of firing faster with greater accuracy than any other rifle available.

Because the church of Reverend Henry Ward Beecher raised the money for the weapons, the rifles became known as "Beecher Bibles." News of the Sharps soon reached the proslavery forces. The so-called "Bibles" made believers of the Border Ruffians, who sent up a howl of dismay that the Free-Soilers were so unfairly armed against them.

A Claim Dispute With a Tragic Ending

Troubles increased during the fall of 1855. Near the settlement of Hickory Point, just south of Lawrence, a

Free-State man named Charles Dow and his proslavery neighbor, Frank Coleman, disagreed about the property line between their claims. The two argued frequently and had several fistfights. On November 21, Coleman shot Dow and left his body in the road.

Dow's friends wanted Coleman arrested, but the sheriff, Samuel Jones, did not respond. Dow's friends threatened Coleman's friends and burned the homes of several proslavery settlers. The sheriff responded by arresting one of the Free-State leaders, Jacob Branson, a friend of Dow. Jones and a posse of about fifteen armed riders arrived at Branson's house in the middle of the night on November 27 to arrest him. As he rode off with his captors, Branson was certain they would kill him.

When Branson's Free-State neighbors learned of the abduction, they gathered about twenty riders who rode toward Lecompton to intercept Jones's men. When confronted by the Free-State men and their Sharps rifles, Jones and his men released Branson. Branson and his rescuers rode to Lawrence for protection.

Jones, insulted by this disrespect for his authority, appealed to the new governor, Wilson Shannon, for aid in fighting the rebellious Free-Staters. Governor Shannon wrote to Major General William P. Richardson, commander of the proslavery militia. He reported, ". . . an armed military force is now in Lawrence and that vicinity in open rebellion against the laws of this Territory." He ordered Richardson to "collect together as large a force as you can. . . . to be used for the sole purpose of aiding the Sheriff in executing the laws. . . ."[2]

The Wakarusa War

By the first of December 1855, both Free-State and proslavery men were ready for battle. In Lawrence, settlers prepared for a fight. A new shipment of Sharps rifles had arrived, along with a howitzer—a type of cannon. The men of Lawrence dug earthen battlements and practiced military drills. The women loaded shells, made bandages, and even practiced shooting. James H. Lane directed the troops. Lane marched the men up and down the streets, inspiring them to action with emotional speeches. Robinson, however, was determined to act only defensively; to fire only if they were fired upon.

Meanwhile, proslavery troops were gathering at Lecompton and Leavenworth. A large group from Missouri was camped along the Wakarusa River, just south of Lawrence. As tempers ran hot, the weather turned cold. The proslavery troops watched the Lawrence men drill with their Sharps rifles. Although convinced they could easily win the war, they were hesitant to advance. They were not afraid, however, to stop those who dared to travel along the road. One Free-State man, Thomas Barber, was shot as he attempted to return home to chop wood for his freezing family.

When the Border Ruffians blocked the Missouri River to Free-State settlers, General James H. Lane led his "Army of the North" across Iowa and Nebraska to enter Kansas.

Governor Shannon Seeks Peace

Governor Shannon rode to Lawrence to negotiate peace. The Border Ruffians would retreat, he said, if Lawrence would surrender the Sharps rifles. Robinson refused to give up the only weapons that were keeping the proslavers from attacking. Meanwhile, a wagonload of armed men rode into town, eager to fight the Ruffians. The fifty-five-year-old man who led them excited his own men and others in Lawrence into an angry mob. It was all Robinson could do to calm the crowd. He still believed they could win this war without ever firing a shot. Unable to convince the Lawrence men to attack, the troops and their leader left. It would not be the last Robinson's men would hear of John Brown and his Pottawatomie Rifle Company.

Governor Shannon returned to the proslavery camp with the news that the settlers would not surrender their weapons. The proslavers wanted to attack, but the Sharps rifles made them hesitate. On December 8, Robinson and Lane visited the Border Ruffians' camp to negotiate. Although the Lawrence settlers still refused to give up their Sharps rifles, they agreed to obey any decisions made by U.S. judges against citizens of Lawrence with respect to the rescue of Branson.

The proslavery leaders accepted that agreement, but the troops were still angry. They had come for a fight, and they intended to have one. Later that evening, however, their enthusiasm cooled as a snowstorm with strong winds blew into the area. Before morning, most of the troops broke camp to go home to their warm fires.

The Wakarusa War was over. Its only casualties were Dow, Barber, and three proslavery soldiers. One proslaver was shot by a soldier from his own camp, one was crushed by a falling tree, and one was killed in a drunken fight. The *Kansas Tribune* gloated, "The conqueror of a country makes the enemy lay down their arms; but we stood to arms until the enemy had left. . . . We have indeed achieved a great victory over an insolent and tyrannical enemy."[3] Most settlers knew, however, that it was only a matter of time before conflict would return.

Sheriff Jones's Wounded Pride

After another attempt in mid-April to arrest the rescuers of Branson, Sheriff Jones and federal troops were camped near Lawrence. One evening, a group of Free-State men gathered near the sheriff's camp. Shots were fired, one of which narrowly missed the sheriff's leg, leaving a hole in his pants. Minutes later, more shots rang out, and a cry went up that Jones was dead.

Actually, Jones was only wounded, but the proslavery newspapers quickly took up a call for revenge. At a meeting of Lawrence residents, a resolution was made, calling the shooting, "a cowardly and atrocious outrage upon Mr. Jones—an insult and injury to the public sentiment and reputation of our town."[4] The Free-State men still wanted to remain free of the accusation of violence, and they worried that the shooting would cause "a desperate attempt . . . to bring against us another murderous horde."[5]

Lawrence Under Attack

A month later, Jones was ready to take his revenge on the Free-State men of Lawrence who had injured and insulted him. On May 21, he rode into town with twenty armed men. He demanded they surrender the howitzer and Sharps rifles, or his troops would destroy the town. General Pomeroy of Lawrence agreed to surrender the howitzer, but insisted that the rifles belonged to individual citizens and were, therefore, not the property of the town. Jones's men captured the howitzer and a few muskets. They left town without any resistance from the citizens and without the Sharps rifles.

Meanwhile, ex-Senator Atchison was giving a drunken speech to the troops assembled at the edge of town. When Jones and his men arrived with the cannon, the proslavery troops marched back into town, where they attacked the newspaper offices of the *Kansas Free State* and the *Herald of Freedom*. They destroyed the offices and printing presses, then dumped the printing type into the Kansas River. Next, the troops attacked the Free-State Hotel. The sturdy building withstood cannon fire and even the explosion of barrels of gunpowder. It was finally destroyed by fire.[6]

Jones dismissed the troops, but they were not finished with their revenge. They looted abandoned houses. Robinson's house on Mt. Oread was burned to the ground. Over the next few days, small bands of Ruffians continued to steal horses and supplies from farmers in the area. Although the Lawrence settlers were frightened, none were killed by the Ruffians. In fact, the only death was a Ruffian killed by a stone which fell from the Free-State Hotel.[7]

News of the attack spread throughout Kansas and farther east. Robinson had directed the people of

After the sack of Lawrence in May 1856, little remained of the Free-State Hotel. The hotel withstood cannon fire and explosions of barrels of gunpowder, but was destroyed by fire.

Lawrence not to fight back against the invaders, so they could continue to be blameless in the public eye. Still, the proslavery newspapers criticized them for their inaction. "We have often denounced [them] . . . as cowards, and the events of the past week go to show that we were right in our conjecture."[8]

A Perilous Escape

Former governor Reeder was staying in a hotel in Kansas City, Missouri, when he heard of the sack of Lawrence. This was no vacation; he was fleeing for his life. Reeder traveled by night out of Kansas Territory and across the Missouri River. He stayed in the hotel two weeks, hidden in an upstairs room. The hotel was surrounded by proslavers, and Reeder knew if he was discovered they might murder him.

One evening, he borrowed overalls, a large hat, an old shirt, and an axe from the hotel owner. He walked out onto the hotel porch, pretending to be a woodcutter looking for work. He walked up the street toward the Missouri River, where he met a friend with a small boat. The two floated downstream to a landing, and Reeder boarded a steamboat bound for St. Louis, Missouri.

A proslaver on the steamer recognized Reeder. The man got off the boat, planning to take a train to St. Louis and have Missouri authorities arrest Reeder there. Reeder realized he was in danger and got off the boat at St. Charles, Missouri, a few miles northwest of St. Louis. From there he walked to the Mississippi River,

With threats against his life, Andrew Reeder had to flee Missouri dressed as a woodcutter.

where he paid a man with a boat to row him across the river to Illinois. Once there, he got passage to Chicago, then back home to Pennsylvania.[9] Kansas's first governor was fortunate to make it safely out of the territory. He would not be the last Kansas governor to flee for his life.

6

PRAIRIE POLITICS

After the sacking of Lawrence, the situation looked bleak for the Free-Soilers. President Pierce declared the proslavery territorial legislature the only legal governing body in Kansas Territory. Federal troops, under the command of Colonel Edwin Sumner were sent to break up the July 4, 1856, meeting of the Topeka legislature. Sumner rode into Topeka with two hundred soldiers and several cannons. The Free-State legislators left without a fight.[1]

Proslavers in Kansas decided the best way to have peace was to drive out the Free-State settlers and keep any others from entering the territory. Border Ruffians stopped all boats on the Missouri River and searched them for Free-State settlers. Ruffians threatened passengers at gunpoint. Those judged to be Free-State settlers were not allowed to set foot in Kansas Territory. The boats were sent back to river ports east of Missouri. Free-State emigrants would have to find another route into Kansas.

Lane's "Army of the North"

Meanwhile, James H. Lane began a campaign in the East to raise money and troops to fight the proslavers in Kansas. He traveled from town to town, rallying citizens to his cause. He was a powerful speaker and drew large enthusiastic crowds. In Chicago, he raised fifteen thousand at a single rally. According to historian Craig Miner, "He would close his teeth together and talk through them with a hissing sound that would make the flesh crawl, only to speak a moment later in mellow manner that would bring tears."[2] As Lane traveled, his army of recruits grew.

In August, the rumor came to Kansas that Lane and his "army of the North" were coming across Iowa and Nebraska into Kansas to fight the Ruffians. John Brown's company joined Lane's men. They first attacked the town of Franklin, where they captured a cannon. They continued on to a proslavery fort at Washington Creek. After that, the army rode to the Lecompton home of Henry Titus, who had helped lead the attack against Lawrence. They burned the cabin and took Titus and several others prisoner. Shannon negotiated the release of the prisoners but wrote his resignation the following day. Like Reeder, Shannon fled the territory with threats against his life.

Geary to the Rescue

On September 1, 1856, Kansas's third governor arrived, John W. Geary of Pennsylvania. His mission from the president was simple: Restore order in Kansas. The proslavery *Kansas Weekly Herald* was optimistic about the new governor. "Thank heaven we have now for our distracted Territory a Governor who has shown his competency and ability to bring order out of confusion and restore peace and harmony."[3] Accomplishing that mission, however, would not be simple.

When Geary arrived, the first situation he faced was a threatened attack on Lawrence by the "Kansas Militia," a military group made up mostly of Missourians. Geary ordered the militia to go back to Missouri, but they ignored him. Geary then called in U.S. troops to protect Lawrence. Again he ordered the

Members of John Brown's "Free-State Battery" went to Lawrence in September 1856. Pictured here are (from left to right) James Redpath, August Bondi, Augustus Wattles, Tauy Jones, George B. Gill, and Owen Brown, with the cannon they captured at Franklin.

militia to disband. This time they obeyed him, although they caused much damage on their way home.

Geary next sent federal troops to the Kansas-Nebraska border to intercept a group from Lane's Free-Soiler army. An armed group of 130 men was arrested at the border. They were later freed by Geary when they convinced him they were settlers armed only for self-protection. Next, Geary ordered the Ruffians to stop interfering with Free-State settlers and supplies on the Missouri River. Angry that Geary would side with Free-Staters, the Ruffians vowed to rid Kansas of this threat to their authority.

A Change of Presidents

Meanwhile, politics in Washington, D.C., had changed as well. The Northern and Southern Democrats argued bitterly about Pierce's handling of the Kansas situation. The party did not nominate him for reelection. Although James Buchanan came from the North, he was loyal to the Democratic party and sympathetic to the South. He had been on political business out of the country during the time when arguments over Kansas affairs had threatened to split the party, so he had not made enemies on either side. Buchanan won the Democratic nomination.

At the time of the presidential election, Geary had disbanded the Missouri militia and intercepted Lane's army of settlers at the border. Things were temporarily quiet in Kansas, and Buchanan won by a narrow margin. By the time Buchanan took his presidential oath, the situation was not so stable.

In the territorial election of October 1856, the proslavery Law and Order party claimed victory and made plans to create a state constitution for the admission of Kansas as a slave state. On January 12, the proslavery territorial legislature met at Lecompton. The Law and Order party now renamed itself the National Democratic party of Kansas. Because of their anger at Geary, the legislators determined that they would veto anything Geary presented.

Geary Steps Down; Stanton Steps Up

The Lecompton legislature proposed a June election for delegates to a constitutional convention. Their count of eligible voters was judged to be false. Geary vetoed the census, but the legislature passed it over Geary's veto. The proslavers began plotting to kill Geary. In March 1857, Geary fled Kansas as the two previous governors had.

Secretary of Kansas Territory Frederick P. Stanton became acting governor when Geary left. The new governor favored slavery and was determined to squash all Free-State resistance to the recognized proslavery government. He angered the Free-Soilers with a speech in which he threatened, "war to the knife, and the knife to the hilt," to those who refused to obey the laws of the legislature.[4] His position was only temporary until a new governor could be found.

Help Wanted: Governor

The vacant position left by Geary was not easy to fill. Buchanan offered the job to Robert J. Walker of Pennsylvania, but he declined. He already had a successful political career and had served as secretary of the treasury under President James K. Polk. He at first felt his reputation could only be hurt by involvement in Kansas affairs. Finally, Buchanan, along with Stephen Douglas, convinced Walker to take the office. Buchanan gave Walker two directives: (1) Enforce the laws of the proslavery legislature, and (2) Oversee the formation of a constitution under which Kansas could be admitted to the Union as a state. Walker arrived in May 1857, prepared to accomplish those goals.

In June, the Topeka legislature met again and decided to make Topeka the state capital. They set an election day in August to elect state officers for their legislature. Instead of forbidding them to

Governor Robert J. Walker lost his job as Kansas governor after he encouraged the Free-State men to vote in the territorial elections and they won control of the territorial legislature.

meet, as Shannon had, Governor Walker attended the meeting himself and urged the Free-State men to take part in the upcoming territorial election scheduled for October. In that way they could make their voices heard in an election that would be recognized by Congress and the president.

The proslavery territorial legislature, however, was still up to its old tricks. At their constitutional convention in June, they elected only delegates from proslavery towns. This would ensure that the new constitution would include slavery. If the Free-State men refused to participate in the territorial elections, the proslavers would continue to win and pass their own laws. That August, however, the Free-State men decided to vote in the October territorial election.

The Turning Point

The October 1857 election brought surprising results. Despite some Border-Ruffian voting, the Free-State party won a majority of the seats in the legislature. Walker rejected fraudulent returns from two precincts, and so won the trust of the Free-State men of Kansas. Historian William Connelley called this the turning point for the Free-State movement. "They had gained control of the Territorial Legislature, the law-making power recognized by the Federal Government, and legal self-government was now for the first time within their reach."[5] It was also a turning point in Robert Walker's political career. Instead of supporting the proslavery legislature, he had allowed the Free-State men to gain control of the legislature. President Buchanan and his Cabinet wanted to remove Walker.

Buchanan was determined to make Kansas a slave state. Under instructions from Washington, the proslavery constitutional convention (a separate group from the legislature) met at Lecompton and wrote a constitution to submit to Congress for Kansas statehood. Buchanan insisted that the new constitution be submitted to a full vote of the people. To prevent interference from Governor Walker, the president placed John Calhoun, the surveyor general of Kansas Territory and a known supporter of slavery, in charge of the election.

The Lecompton constitutional convention still had one more trick up its sleeve. Because Free-State voters now held a majority, as shown by the October election, it was clear that the voters would never approve a proslavery constitution. Instead of calling for a vote to either approve or reject the Lecompton constitution, the ballot was worded to allow voters to choose either "Accept the constitution with slavery" or "Accept the constitution without slavery." Either way, the constitution would be accepted, because rejecting the constitution was not a choice on the ballot.

If it were accepted "with slavery," then Kansas would become a slave state like any other in the South. If it were accepted "without slavery," no new slaves could be brought into the state, but current slaveholders would not be required to free their slaves. The new constitution would allow slaveholders to keep their human property through the slaves' lives and even to continue to own their slaves' children.[6] In this way, Kansas could be admitted as a state without slavery, even with legal slaveholders as citizens. With Calhoun in charge of the election, Walker was powerless. He submitted his resignation and left the territory in November 1857.

An Unexpected Free-State Ally

With Walker gone and no one to take his place, Secretary of Kansas Territory Frederick P. Stanton was again named acting governor. Since his previous term after Geary's departure, however, Stanton had seen the true nature of affairs in Kansas. He now realized that most of the people in the territory opposed the Lecompton constitution and recognized the trick the convention was using to force the constitution on the citizens. Although his term would be short, he would play a vital role in Kansas's political future.

Many people in Kansas were alarmed by the Lecompton constitution and the upcoming election. On December 7, Stanton called a special session of the legislature to find a way to stop the election. The legislature overturned the act passed the previous June that had authorized the formation of a constitution. Next, they passed an act to submit the Lecompton constitution to a vote for either acceptance or rejection by voters. Third, they wrote to Congress asking that Kansas not be admitted to the Union under the Lecompton constitution regardless of the outcome of the election, and that it instead be admitted under the constitution written by the Topeka legislature. The final act of Stanton's special legislative session was to repeal the laws that punished rebellion against the laws of the bogus legislature. Buchanan was so angry at this turn of events that he removed Stanton from office less than one month after his appointment.

Lecompton Wins, Then Loses

On Election Day, December 21, 1857, James W. Denver became both secretary of the territory and acting governor. He was working as the commissioner of Indian Affairs in the territory when Stanton was fired. The vote on the Lecompton constitution went forward as scheduled. John Calhoun was in charge of the election, so he had control of receiving the returns and certifying their validity.

Since Free-State citizens could not support the Lecompton constitution because it would allow slavery either way, few of them voted. Calhoun's report certified about six thousand votes for the constitution "with slavery," and fewer than six hundred for the constitution "without slavery." A later investigation proved that more than half the proslavery votes were cast illegally. [7] The three thousand legal votes cast represented only about one third of Kansas voters.

Clearly, the majority of the people of Kansas Territory did not support the Lecompton constitution. A letter printed by the Free-State *Geary City Era* declared, "The Lecompton Constitution may be accepted by Congress, but the people of Kansas will never submit to it."[8] Legally, however, the constitution had been approved. Next, Congress would have to decide whether to admit Kansas as a state under the Lecompton constitution. There was a battle to come in Congress, but Governor Denver needed to deal with battles closer to home.

On December 21, 1857, James Denver's first day as governor, southeastern Kansas was ready for war. In the summer and fall of 1856, proslavery settlers and Border Ruffians, alarmed by the events at Pottawatomie and the rumors of Lane's "army of the North," had begun a campaign to drive out Free-State settlers. Pro-slavery riders went to the homes of Free-State set-

MORE TROUBLE IN KANSAS TERRITORY

tlers with reports that Lane's army was coming to kill everyone in the area. The settlers were ordered to ride to proslavery Fort Scott, the largest town in the area, to help protect it. Once there, the settlers were ordered to leave their rifles for the defense of the fort and go home. On the road, the unarmed men were then robbed of their horses and told to leave the territory.

Squatters' Court

George W. Clarke and a group of raiders attacked many Free-State settlers. The raiders burned homes, stole cattle, and destroyed crops. Although the settlers complained to the courts about Clarke's raiders, the proslavery judges refused to punish Clarke and his men. Many Free-State settlers left the area in the fall of 1856. Those who returned the next spring found that proslavery settlers had moved into their homes.

The government had not yet set up a land office in southeast Kansas, so most claims had not been legally registered. In a dispute, the Free-State settlers had to make their claims to the same proslavery judges who had refused to help them before. In March 1857, the government finally opened a land office in the area. The settlers were dismayed to discover that William H. Doak, the register of the new land office, was actually G. W. Clarke, using a false name.[1]

The Free-State settlers could not obtain justice in the proslavery court. They formed their own court in Bourbon County for delivering justice in the territory, the "squatters' court." At first, most of the cases involved property crimes against Free-State settlers. Later, proslavery men from the area were arrested by the squatters' court for more violent crimes.

In December 1857, during Governor Stanton's brief term as acting governor, violence reached a new level. After a claim dispute between a proslaver and a Free-Soiler, a proslavery "vigilance committee" in Fort Scott sent a message to Governor Stanton charging the squatters' court with violating the Rebellion Act of the bogus legislature. The committee asked for federal troops to help break up the squatters' court and enforce the territorial laws.

On the snowy day that Governor Denver took office, he got his first taste of Kansas conflict. About two hundred armed men sent by James H. Lane to protect the squatters' court marched into the area of Sugar Mound, near Fort Scott. About the same time, the federal troops requested by Fort Scott arrived. With armed troops on both sides, there could be no real advantage for either group. Governor Denver ordered both regiments to disband, and so peace was restored, for the moment.[2]

New Election; Different Results

Tension still ran high, even after the troops had dispersed. On January 5, 1858, the territorial legislature held a second election on the Lecompton constitution. This time voters had three choices: reject the entire constitution, accept it with slavery, or accept it without slavery. With the option to reject the constitution on the ballot, the Free-State men could finally vote on the Lecompton constitution. Over ten thousand votes were cast against it; less than two hundred in favor of it.[3]

Acting Governor Denver informed President Buchanan of the voters' rejection of the constitution. Denver asked that Buchanan not submit the constitution for congressional approval. If Congress approved the constitution, Kansas would be admitted as a state under it. Despite Denver's request, the president sent

SOURCE DOCUMENT

IF THE PEOPLE OF KANSAS WANT A SLAVEHOLDING STATE, LET THEM HAVE IT, AND IF THEY WANT A FREE STATE THEY HAVE A RIGHT TO IT, AND IT IS NOT FOR THE PEOPLE OF ILLINOIS, OR MISSOURI, OR NEW YORK, OR KENTUCKY, TO COMPLAIN, WHATEVER THE DECISION OF THE PEOPLE OF KANSAS MAY BE UPON THAT POINT.[4]

Senator Stephen A. Douglas spoke these words in a political debate with Abraham Lincoln during the senatorial campaign of 1858.

the constitution to Congress on February 2, 1858. He blamed the Free-State settlers for the troubles in Kansas, and asked Congress to accept the December 21 election results as proof that Kansans had approved their constitution. Denver could not stop Buchanan's push for the constitution. He also had more immediate concerns in southeastern Kansas to deal with.

Montgomery's Jayhawkers

Even though Denver had disbanded the troops on December 21, Lane had left James Montgomery in command of a group of armed men to protect the Free-State settlers from further abuse by their proslavery enemies. Montgomery championed the Free-State cause by hunting down the most vicious proslavery men who threatened the lives and property of the Free-State settlers.

At first, the Free-State settlers and newspapers thought of him as a Free-State "Robin Hood" who would protect them. By spring 1858, however, Montgomery's band of men, known as "Jayhawkers," had become more violent. The Jayhawkers used their Free-State cause as an excuse to rob anyone they came across on the roads. The settlers and even the Free-State newspapers began to mistrust Montgomery. An editorial in the *Herald of Freedom* described many offenses by the Jayhawkers and concluded, "We are frank to confess that we have no love for these things. They must be stopped, and immediately, else civil war must follow. Life nor property is safe!"[5]

Hamilton and the Border Ruffians

Charles Hamilton led the proslavery settlers in Linn County. He, too, had been accused of highway robbery and other crimes against his Free-State neighbors. Although many of his followers were Kansas settlers like himself, he also had many Border Ruffians in his group.

According to author William Phillips, after the defeat of the Lecompton constitution, Hamilton had proclaimed, "If slaveholders cannot live in Kansas and hold slaves, Abolitionists should not live there either."[6] He reportedly made a list of Free-State settlers he intended to kill.

Montgomery heard about Hamilton's list and decided that Linn County would not be safe for Free-State settlers while Hamilton and his followers remained there. He gathered a large group of riders, threatened to kill the proslavers if they refused to leave

James Montgomery and his Jayhawkers were both applauded and feared in Kansas Territory. Although they claimed to protect the Free-State settlers, they were known to rob travelers along the back roads of Kansas with little regard to the politics of their victims.

or if they ever returned, and burned their houses and crops. Hamilton and his followers rode to Missouri for safety. He sent a message back to other proslavery settlers in Linn County to "come out of the territory at once, as we are coming up there to kill snakes, and will treat all we find there as snakes."[7]

The state militia was sent to Linn County to guard against a raid by Hamilton's men. Since no raid had taken place after a week's time, the troops left the area on May 17. Hamilton's friends were watching the movements of the troops. They rode across the state line with word that the militia was gone.

Checking Off the List

The customers at Choteau's Trading Post the morning of May 19, 1858, never heard the clatter of hooves on the road outside. Hamilton and about twenty-five men got off their horses, went into the store, took the customers' guns, and tied their hands. Hamilton's men helped themselves to the merchandise they wanted and took several men with them as prisoners, including John F. Campbell, the storekeeper.[8]

As Hamilton's group traveled northeast with their prisoners walking single file, Hamilton called out the names of Free-State settlers he wanted to capture. The group continued along the road, capturing other men and robbing them of anything of value they had in their possession, including their horses. As the group traveled along, Hamilton released some of the prisoners but kept their horses.

About eight o'clock that morning, Hamilton and his men arrived at a farm where several men were working. Here Reverend Benjamin Reed and two of his neighbors were captured and taken at gunpoint. Hamilton's men then searched the house and returned with some guns. They caught three horses from the farm and also took Reed's horse.[9]

Another mile down the road, they came to William Hargrove's farm. There they captured both William and his brother Asa. At the next farm, Free-Soilers Charles Snyder and Michael Robinson spotted Hamilton and his men and headed for the house to take up their guns. Robinson wanted to fight them, but Snyder thought it would be better to go quietly. Since they knew the men in Hamilton's group, Snyder was convinced the proslavers would not harm them. They fell into line with the other prisoners and the group continued marching northeast along the road. One more prisoner, Austin Hall, was captured as they walked.[10]

When Hamilton arrived at the blacksmith shop of Eli Snyder, he encountered more of a fight than he expected. He left the prisoners and most of the group nearby, taking a few men with him to confront Snyder. The shop was on a hill, and Snyder saw Hamilton coming. Snyder fired his shotgun at Hamilton, and hit Hamilton's horse in the neck. Snyder then fired at Hamilton's men and crouched behind a stone wall. Snyder's son Elias joined him, and together they fought off the riders until Hamilton retreated and rejoined the rest of the group.[11]

The Bloody Conclusion

The riders then marched their captives to a deep ravine near the Marais des Cygnes River. The prisoners were forced to stand in a line in the ravine while the riders lined up opposite them. Hamilton ordered his men to draw their weapons and aim, but some refused. One Missourian lowered his gun and said, "I'll have nothing to do with such a piece of business as this." Hamilton swore at them and repeated his order. Prepared for death, John Campbell told his captors, "Gentlemen, if you are going to shoot, take good aim."[12] At the call to fire, shots rang out and all the prisoners dropped to the ground. Some were dead, and those who still lived pretended to be dead. Hamilton's

The Marais Des Cygnes massacre was one of the deadliest and most publicized events in Bleeding Kansas.

men searched the pockets of the victims before they rode away. Five men were dead, five wounded, and one was unharmed.

Differing Viewpoints

As usual, the territorial newspapers carried different versions of the "truth." Although the Free-State newspapers considered Hamilton's motive at Marais des Cygnes to be revenge, the proslavery viewpoint was very different. The *Kansas Weekly Herald* reported, "It appears that about twenty-five of the citizens of Linn and Bourbon Counties who had been forced to flee to Missouri for protection, with their families, determined to return to their homes to secure their stock etc."[13] While the victims who survived the assault insisted they were occupied with preparing to plant corn on May 19, the proslavery papers insisted the settlers were gathering for a fight they expected. The shootout at Eli Snyder's blacksmith shop supported this claim. Hamilton was never prosecuted for the massacre.

Placing Blame

News of the Marais des Cygnes massacre spread quickly to the eastern states. Everyone wanted to place blame on someone else. Northerners blamed Hamilton and the Border Ruffians. President Buchanan and Southerners blamed Free-State radicals like John Brown, Lane, and Montgomery for the violence. The newly formed Republican party blamed the Democrats for passing the Kansas-Nebraska Act with its popular sovereignty provision. Democrats blamed the "Black Republicans" for their abolitionist views.

Governor Denver became a target for blame from all sides, for his apparent failure to control the violence. One writer to *The New York Times*, identifying himself as a resident of Kansas, asserted, "On him [Denver], then, and not on the people, or the Free State party, must rest the infamy and the crime of not sooner instituting peace in Kansas. That he had the power, no one can doubt; that it was his duty, his own assumptions prove."[14] Days later, a second letter writer, also a resident of Kansas, defended Governor Denver, calling him, "the most liberal-minded, honest, and conscientious governor ever sent to Kansas." That writer concluded his letter with the question, "Who, then, is responsible? . . . Let the future record of Kansas answer."[15]

constitution; they had already done so in the election just two months before.

The English Bill: Bargain or Bribe?

The only way to get Kansas admitted as a slave state would be to convince the people to accept the Lecompton constitution. A conference committee headed by William H. English of Indiana presented a bill that would allow Kansans to again vote on the Lecompton constitution, but with some added incentives to accept it.

The English bill contained three main provisions. First, Kansas would be guaranteed admission if a majority of voters accepted the Lecompton constitution. Second, on admission, Kansas would receive 5.5 million more acres of public land than had been provided in the previous constitution. And third, if the voters refused to accept the Lecompton constitution, they could not write a new constitution or ask for statehood until they could prove they had at least 93,560 residents living in the territory, enough to hold a seat in the House of Representatives. At the time, fewer than sixty thousand people lived in Kansas. Although the vote was close, the English bill passed both houses of Congress. The Lecompton constitution would go back to the voters in Kansas.

Few Kansans liked the English bill. *The New York Times* carried a letter from Thomas Ewing, a Free-State conservative from Kansas. He referred to the bill as the "English Bribe," and seemed insulted that people would think the voters of Kansas foolish enough to accept it. "The proffered bribe," he insisted, "will get no hearing before the people, but will be rejected with indignation and scorn."[2]

Ewing proved correct: More than eleven thousand voters rejected the English bill on August 2, 1858; less than two thousand accepted it. The Lecompton constitution was finally laid to rest. The gamble of the English bill had not paid off for Buchanan. A congressional investigation two years later proved that Buchanan had used "the open employment of money" (bribery) to help pass the English bill through Congress, paid "enormous sums" of money to people to convince others to vote for the bill, and had spoken out against Democrats who refused to support the bill.[3]

Denver Resigns

After the final vote on the constitution, a period of calm settled over Kansas. In June, Denver had called together representatives from both Free-State and proslavery factions in southeastern Kansas and persuaded them to agree to a truce. The rest of the summer was mostly peaceful. By fall, however, the two sides were battling again.

Finally, James Denver was tired of it. On October 10, he submitted his resignation as governor of the Kansas Territory. In his final address to the people, he charged them to remember "that the continuance of peace and quiet depends henceforward more on the people themselves, than on the Executive of the Territory." In a parting shot at Lane and Montgomery, he also warned the people against, "the tricks and machinations of designing demagogues [agitators] who prefer turmoil and strife to peace and prosperity, for it is only at such times that they can bring themselves into notice."[4]

He did not know how prophetic his words would be. By December of that year, Montgomery's men had again raided Fort Scott, this time burning personal property, robbing stores and citizens, and leaving a man dead. Days later, John Brown invaded Missouri. He and his men attacked several farms, robbing the occupants of cash and stealing their slaves. One Missourian was killed in the raid, and eleven slaves were taken. After hiding in Osawatomie for a time, Brown took the slaves to Canada and left Kansas for good.

A New Governor; a New Era

When Samuel Medary took office in December 1858, after the departure of Denver, most of the hardest battles had already been fought and won. The territorial legislature was in Free-State control, the Lecompton constitution was dead and buried, John Brown's reign of terror in Kansas was over, and except for in Linn and Bourbon counties, the violence that marked Kansas's early days was over. According to the *Kansas Weekly Herald*, "Kansas is made up of men from all portions of our great confederacy, and being thrown in

Samuel Medary was the last governor of the Kansas Territory. During his term, the Topeka constitution was formed and approved and Kansas achieved statehood.

close connection, they are beginning to know and appreciate each other."[5]

The territorial legislature of January 1859 met in Lawrence and voted to repeal all laws of the bogus legislature, and to pardon all prisoners charged under the Rebellion Act of that legislature. Governor Medary approved the bill. After the session, the old laws were taken into the street and burned.

Even though the defeat of the English bill forbade the forming of a new Kansas constitution until the population increased, in February 1859, the territorial legislature passed a law providing for a constitutional convention to be held at Lawrence the following summer. The proslavery *Kansas National Democrat* was outraged by this. "As the law is in gross violation of a law of Congress, it is a nullity, and we have no doubt the Court will so decide. . . ."[6] Despite such objections, Governor Medary called an election for March 28 to authorize the convention. Kansans cast 5,306 votes in favor of a new constitution, and 1,425 against.[7]

The Wyandotte Constitution

On May 18, 1859, the Kansas Republican party was organized at a meeting in Osawatomie. It would replace the former Free State party, which had been dissolved at the last convention at Big Springs on May 12. On July 5, the fifty-two delegates elected in June, now classified as "Democrats" and "Republicans," met at Wyandotte for the new constitutional convention. They used the constitution of the state of Ohio as a model for their new document. The new constitution abolished slavery in Kansas, established Topeka as the state capital, and defined the boundaries of the state. By July 29, the constitution was complete.

On October 4, 1859, the citizens of Kansas accepted the Wyandotte constitution, with 10,421 votes in favor and 5,530 against.[8] On December 6, an election was held for state officers under the Wyandotte constitution. In this election, Charles Robinson defeated Samuel Medary for the office of governor, to take office when Kansas was granted statehood under the new constitution.

New Census

When the territorial legislature next met in January 1860, it addressed the matter of the population of the territory. The latest count showed a total of 71,770 people living in Kansas Territory. This was far below the number needed for presentation of the new constitution to Congress. A new count was ordered. The new census of 1860 reported that the total population in the territory was 143,643. Although that total was large enough to be considered for statehood, it could not be reported to Congress. The count included about 34,200 people who lived in the region of Pike's Peak, where gold had been discovered. That region was not included in the boundary of Kansas as defined in the Wyandotte constitution. When the Pike's Peak residents were subtracted from the count, the total was 109,401, still enough to elect a representative to the

House and to be considered for statehood.[9] But the battle for Kansas statehood was not yet won.

Battle of Wills in the Senate

On February 10, 1860, the Wyandotte constitution was presented to the House of Representatives as part of the bill to grant statehood to Kansas. On April 11, the vote was called, and the bill passed, 134 yeas to 73 nays. The Senate, however, was not so easy to please.

When William Seward presented the bill on February 29, it was met with violent opposition from Stephen Douglas and other Democrats. Although Douglas had argued insistently on the "rights of the people" when the Lecompton constitution had been considered, now, when the will of the people was quite clear, he opposed the approval of the new Free-State constitution. More important to Southern Democrats, however, was the fact that, as long as Kansas remained a territory with no approved constitution, slaveholders could continue to legally own slaves there.

To make matters worse, Kansas was suffering from the worst drought in its short history. Since June of the previous year, very little rain had fallen. People were starving in Kansas. Many states were sending aid, and some senators used this as evidence that Kansas would be a burden to the United States if admitted. Also, settlers were leaving the territory by the thousands, making the last census questionable. Despite angry debate, the Democrats in the Senate refused to consider the bill. It was never called to a vote before the Senate adjourned on June 7.

Secession and Statehood

When the 36th Congress opened its second session in December 1860, everything had changed. President-elect Abraham Lincoln would take office in a few months. With the victory of the Republican party, the slaveholding states lost all hope of keeping their power in the houses of Congress. The only obstacle to Kansas statehood was the Democratic majority in the Senate.

Because Lincoln was antislavery and had won the election, South Carolina seceded, or withdrew, from the Union on December 20, 1860. Other Southern states would also secede in the weeks ahead. On January 21, 1861, the question of the Kansas state-hood bill was again called. Before discussion could begin, however, Senator David L. Yulee of Florida took the floor and announced his resignation from the Senate because his state had seceded from the Union. His pronouncement was followed by similar state-ments from the senators of Alabama, South Carolina, and Mississippi. After the Southern senators left, William Seward called the vote on Kansas, and it passed, 36–16.[10] A week later it passed in the House, as it had the previous April. Accepting his defeat, President Buchanan signed the bill on January 29, a day still known and celebrated as Kansas Day. Samuel Medary had already resigned his position as governor.

Charles Robinson would be the first governor of the new state of Kansas.

The days of territorial elections and ballot-box fraud were over. The will of the people had prevailed to make Kansas a Free State. Still, the days of Bleeding Kansas were not over. Kansas still had much blood to shed in the Civil War that was about to begin.

The Kansas-Nebraska Act marked a turning point in the course of American history. As with all significant events of history, it was a product of its past, and a reflection of its present. It would also make an enormous impact on the geographic, cultural, and political future of the United States.

Old Resentments Renewed

The hostilities surrounding the introduction, debate, and passage of the Kansas-Nebraska Act were old ones. The national division on the slavery issue had flared several times in American history, but had previously been settled, at least temporarily. Proposing the Kansas-Nebraska Act with its repeal of the Missouri Compromise revived the same controversy that had already threatened to split the Union.

Both North and South had felt cheated in some ways with the previous agreements, and each side felt that the Kansas-Nebraska Act offered its opponent an

9

LOOKING BACK ON THE KANSAS-NEBRASKA ACT

opportunity to gain a political advantage. Both North and South played the role of victim in the conflict. Henry Wilson, a Republican senator from Massachusetts, called the repeal of the Missouri Compromise, "a deliberate and direct assault upon freedom," committed by the South.[1] On the other side, Jefferson Davis of Mississippi accused the North of a "systematic and persistent struggle to deprive the Southern States of equality in the Union."[2] This resentment would be the leading cause of the conflict to come.

Political Battles; Personal Bloodshed

The Kansas-Nebraska Act was a product of the uncertain political climate of 1854. Congress was unable to take a firm stand on the issue of slavery. The popular sovereignty provision of the Kansas-Nebraska Act allowed Congress to avoid making a difficult decision by forcing the people to make that decision, no matter what the cost or the outcome.

The political events that shaped the 1850s took a tragic toll on the lives of many innocent people. Homesteading was an American tradition. As civilization moved west, so did settlers in search of new land. The territories of Kansas and Nebraska offered this same promise. The concept of popular sovereignty, however, gave a new angle to homesteading: the quest for political advantage.

Despite the deliberate campaigns of both Northern and Southern emigrant aid societies, the majority of the people who settled in Kansas did not do so for political reasons. According to historian Thomas Goodrich, "For most of these immigrants the opening of the territory was viewed not as an opportunity to either end or extend slavery, but as a chance to better themselves."[3]

The violence that sprang up in the territory was mostly at the hand of outsiders. Radicals like David Atchison, James Lane, and John Brown cared more about their own political positions and their ability to carry out their own violent schemes than they cared

SOURCE DOCUMENT

ABOUT TWELVE O'CLOCK THE BUSH WHACKERS CAME . . . THEY ENTERED THE HOUSE AND THE LEADER SAID TO FATHER, "YOU ARE MY PRISONER." FATHER SAID, "LET ME GET MY HAT AND COAT." THE MAN SAID, "YOU DON'T NEED ANY." FATHER PUT ON HIS SHOES AND STARTED OFF WITH THEM . . . I HEARD A SHOT FIRED AND I SAID, "OH THEY HAVE KILLED MY FATHER." . . . WE SLEPT NO MORE THAT NIGHT. MOTHER SPENT THE NIGHT WEEPING . . . EARLY THE NEXT MORNING I RAN TO THE WIDOW'S HOUSE TO SEE IF SHE WERE DEAD OR ALIVE. THEN I RAN ON DOWN THE MAIN TRAVELED ROAD AND FOUND MY FATHER LYING DEAD ON THE GROUND ABOUT ONE HALF MILE FROM THE WIDOW LADY'S HOUSE. HIS RIGHT HAND LAY ACROSS HIS HEART AND HIS LEFT HAND HUNG AT HIS SIDE. I PUT MY HAND ON HIS AND FOUND IT ICY COLD.[4]

Mary F. Beeson's family moved to the Kansas Territory when she was a child, and settled near the Shawnee Mission. Her account of the above incident illustrates the tragedy that so many families suffered during the years before and during the Civil War.

about the wishes of the people of Kansas. The result was financial ruin for families whose property was destroyed and stolen, and grief for many who lost loved ones to the swords and bullets of anger and revenge.

Clash of Cultures

The expansion of the United States to the west also brought about another important change: the relocation of American Indian tribes. Many of the tribes displaced by settlers as a result of the Kansas-Nebraska Act had already been relocated from Ohio and other eastern states. Each time they were moved, the tribes were promised that their new home would be theirs forever—that they would never be moved again. Each move brought more resentment and distrust from tribal leaders.

Additionally, the white men, particularly missionaries, worked hard to change the American Indians' culture to more closely resemble the white man's. They schooled the tribal children in religion and other subjects while they taught them farming and other trades. They also educated them in another custom of the white man: slavery. Although the Northerners were determined that slavery never be introduced into Kansas, most did not know it was already an established institution there. In fact, Methodist missionary Thomas Johnson had brought slaves with him to work at the Shawnee Mission as early as 1832.[5] By 1845, even members of the Wyandot tribe held slaves.[6]

Changing the Landscape of America

Of course, the two new territories made the political boundaries of the United States larger, but in some ways, the changes brought about by this addition made America seem smaller. Vacant plains became dotted with houses and crisscrossed with roads. As more people moved west, the need for transportation grew, and Douglas's vision of connecting Pacific to Atlantic was realized. The railroad companies were among the first to take advantage of the acquisition of the new land, although the transcontinental railroad would not be completed until after the Civil War. In 1859, the need for better communication brought the Pony Express route through Kansas Territory, but it was soon replaced by telegraph, which allowed almost instantaneous communication.

Cultural Changes

Although it would be several years before the Thirteenth Amendment to the Constitution would free the slaves, and a century before the Civil Rights movement would advocate equal rights for people of all races, the ideas behind those events were visible in Kansas. The Leavenworth constitution of 1858, although never adopted, was a groundbreaking document with its guarantee of voting rights for "every male citizen" and education for "every child" without the word "white" in those phrases. It was a step forward especially from the Free-State constitution formed at Big Springs. Its Black Law made Kansas a Free State only because it prohibited any African Americans, free or slave, from living in Kansas. The accepted Wyandotte constitution gave the right to vote to only white men, though. It would be many years before voting rights would be extended to all people. In just a few years, however, Kansas would be the home of the first Union regiment of African-American soldiers in the Civil War.

Another group denied the vote but allowed a hearing before the Wyandotte constitutional convention, was women. Clarina J. H. Nichols was present for each of the twenty-four days the convention was in session. She requested that women receive the right to vote. Although she failed on that issue, she did succeed in gaining equal rights for girls' education and equal rights for married women with regard to property and children in the new constitution. These rights for women were not granted by most other states at the time.[7]

Harper's Ferry

On October 17, 1859, John Brown and eighteen other men captured the arsenal at Harper's Ferry, Virginia (now in West Virginia). Brown hoped to use the weapons in an invasion of the South. However, he was captured the next day, convicted, and hanged on December 2.

Clarina Nichols attended every session of the forming of the Topeka constitution and helped make the Kansas constitution a leading voice for women's rights.

Political Changes

The controversy in Congress during the years between the passage of the Kansas-Nebraska Act and the Civil War saw important changes in the political party system in the United States. Even though the Free-Soil party was never a strong voice in Congress, it was a voice to be heard. The slavery issue forced many people to redefine their ideas of "freedom." The Whig party dissolved as northern Whigs, along with the Free-Soilers, joined the new Republican party. Republicans argued that slavery would destroy the free labor system of industry in the North, if allowed to spread.

The debates over the Kansas-Nebraska Act caused a serious split in the Democratic party. Northern Democrats lost their political strength because of the proslavery views of their Southern brothers. Northern and Southern loyalties became as important as party loyalties. This split in the Democratic party cost it the election of 1860. In just a few short years since its formation, the new Republican party had gained enough strength to elect a president, Abraham Lincoln.

The Kansas-Nebraska Act and the Civil War

The withdrawal of the Southern states from the Union had been threatened before 1861. The controversy over the admission of Missouri in 1820 had been serious enough to require the compromise act. It also began the practice of admitting states in pairs to preserve the Senate's balance of Free States and slave states. In 1850, the Southern states threatened to secede over the admission of California, New Mexico, and Utah. It seems likely that the slavery issue would have eventually divided the nation, even without the Kansas-Nebraska Act.

Still, it is possible that the Kansas-Nebraska Act and the resulting events in Kansas influenced politics enough to bring about the Civil War sooner. Harriet Beecher Stowe's *Uncle Tom's Cabin* had already aroused intense feelings against slavery in the North. In the South, it brought equally intense resentment against abolitionists. Newspapers on both sides of the controversy had eager audiences to read the daily arguments on the subject of slavery. The highly publicized violence in Kansas Territory intensified those emotions.

The violence acted out in Kansas was also a preview of the guerilla warfare that would become so common in the Civil War. James Montgomery's Jayhawkers would distinguish themselves in battle for the Union during the Civil War. Many of their raids, however, used principally the same tricks and tactics they had learned in territorial days while they robbed their neighbors and terrorized their enemies.

A young man named Charles Hart was known as a loafer and petty thief on both sides of the Missouri/Kansas state line before the Civil War. In Kansas, he claimed to be a Free-State man; on the Missouri side, he called himself proslavery.[8] During the Civil War he would go by his real name, William Quantrill, and fight for the Confederacy. In 1863,

Quantrill and his men led a raid on Lawrence even more deadly and destructive than the first sack of Lawrence in 1856.

Triumph of the Kansas-Nebraska Act

Despite the tragic effects of the border warfare and the Civil War, the Kansas-Nebraska Act had at least one positive outcome: it proved the power of the American vote. Despite the influence of outsiders, ballot-box fraud, congressional opposition, and presidential interference, the will of the majority of Kansans was eventually accomplished. Even though the Civil War would ultimately make all states free, Kansas proved to the nation that it would choose to be free.

★ TIMELINE ★

1820—Missouri Compromise passed, with a provision that no new slave states will be formed north of the line of 36 degrees 30 minutes north latitude from any land that was part of the Louisiana Purchase.

1850—Compromise of 1850 passed, offering the residents of the new territories of New Mexico and Utah popular sovereignty, the opportunity to vote on the issue of slavery in their states.

1852 –1853—Several bills to organize the "Territory of Platte," later called Nebraska, are introduced; All fail to gain support of the Senate.

1854—*January 23*: Kansas-Nebraska bill presented in Senate; The bill includes two territories instead of one, and offers popular sovereignty to new residents of the territories.

March 4: Kansas-Nebraska bill is passed in the Senate.

May 22: Kansas-Nebraska bill is passed by the House of Representatives.

May 30: Kansas-Nebraska bill is signed by President Franklin Pierce; proslavery settlers from Missouri are already beginning to stake claims in Kansas Territory.

August 1: First Free-State settlers sponsored by the New England Emigrant Aid Society arrive in Kansas Territory and establish the town of Lawrence.

November 29: First territorial election held; proslavery candidate is elected to represent Kansas Territory in Congress.

1855—*March 30*: Election of territorial legislature. Illegal voting by Border Ruffians results in nearly unanimous election of proslavery men to legislature.

May 22: New elections held in six districts where results of first election were protested; Free-State candidates elected in five of the six districts.

July 2: First meeting of territorial legislature: May 22 election declared invalid; all Free-State delegates expelled; The territorial legislature is now called "bogus legislature" by Free-State men.

July 16: Bogus legislature meets again, adopts territorial laws.

September 4: Free-State convention at Big Springs; Free-State Topeka legislature formed.

November 21: Free-State settler Frank Dow killed by proslavery settler Charles Coleman.

December 1–8: Proslavery troops threaten to destroy Lawrence in Wakarusa War, but a fierce winter storm sends them home without a fight.

1856—*May 21*: Sack of Lawrence by proslavery troops led by Sheriff Samuel Jones.

May 25: John Brown leads abolitionist raiders in Pottawatomie Massacre; Months of violence follow.

July 4: Governor Shannon sends troops to break up the Free-State Topeka legislature.

November: President Buchanan elected.

1857—*June*: Election held for delegates to constitutional convention; Only proslavery men are elected; Governor Robert J. Walker encourages Free-State men to vote in upcoming territorial legislature election.

October: Free-State men win majority in territorial legislature.

December 21: First election on Lecompton constitution; Voters accept it "with slavery," but were not allowed to vote to reject it; Free-State men boycott election.

1858—*January 5*: Second election on Lecompton constitution; Voters reject it by an overwhelming majority.

February 2: President Buchanan submits Lecompton constitution to Congress, despite results of second election, and over Governor Denver's objection.

March: Constitutional convention at Leavenworth, Kansas Territory.

May 19: Marais des Cygnes Massacre in Linn County, Kansas Territory.

August 2: Kansas voters again consider Lecompton constitution, this time with English bill; Voters again reject it.

1859—*January*: New legislature repeals all laws of the bogus legislature.

July 5: New constitutional convention meets at Wyandotte.

October 4: Voters accept Wyandotte constitution.

1860—*January*: New census shows enough people in Kansas Territory to petition for statehood.

February 10: House of Representatives approves Wyandotte constitution.

June 7: Senate adjourns without voting on Wyandotte constitution.

1861—*January 21*: Southern senators resign from the Senate, new vote taken on Wyandotte constitution; Senate approves constitution, and grants statehood to Kansas.

January 29: President Buchanan approves Kansas statehood under the Wyandotte constitution.

★ Chapter Notes ★

Chapter 1. Massacre in May

1. William G. Cutler, "The Pottawatomie Murders," *History of the State of Kansas*, n.d. (originally published in 1883), <http://www.ukans.edu/carrie/kancoll/books/cutler/terrhist/terrhist-p33.html#THE_POTTAWATOMIE_MURDERS> (August 11, 2002).

2. William G. Cutler, "Franklin County, Part 3: The Pottawatomie Massacre," *History of the State of Kansas*, n.d. (originally published in 1883), <http://www.ukans.edu/carrie/kancoll/books/cutler/franklin/franklin-co-p3.html#THE_ POTTAWATOMIE_MASSACRE> (August 11, 2002).

3. Ibid.

4. Alice Nichols, *Bleeding Kansas* (New York: Oxford University Press, 1954), p. 113.

5. Thomas Goodrich, *War to the Knife: Bleeding Kansas, 1854–1861* (Mechanicsburg, Pa.: Stackpole Books, 1998), pp. 125–126.

6. Cutler, "Franklin County, Part 3: The Pottawatomie Massacre."

7. "War! War!" *Squatter Sovereign*, June 10, 1856, p. 2.

8. "Our Troubles," *Kansas Tribune*, June 6, 1856, p. 2.

9. William Phillips, *The Conquest of Kansas by Missouri and Her Allies* (Boston: Phillips, Sampson, and Co., 1856), p. 317.

10. "Latest News from Kansas," *New York Daily Times*, May 31, 1856, p. 4.

11. "News from Kansas: Property Destroyed at Lawrence—The Fight at Osawatomie," *New York Daily Times*, June 4, 1856, p. 1.

12. "Later from Kansas," *New York Daily Times*, June 6, 1856, p. 2.

13. Phillips, p. 317.

14. Territorial Kansas Heritage Alliance, *John Brown and Bleeding Kansas: Prelude to the Civil War* (Territorial Kansas Heritage Alliance, 2001), p. 6.

Chapter 2. Conflict and Compromise

1. Don E. Fehrenbacher, *The Slaveholding Republic* (New York: Oxford University Press, 2001), pp. 16–17.

2. William G. Cutler, "Territorial Organization of Kansas, 1853–54," *History of the State of Kansas*, n.d. (originally published in 1883), <http://www.ukans.edu/carrie/kancoll/books/cutler/deschist/prehist-p3.html> (September 5, 2002).

3. Robert R. Russell, "The Issues in the Congressional Struggle Over the Kansas-Nebraska Bill, 1854," *Journal of Southern American History*, Vol. 29, No. 2, May 1963, p. 192.

4. Ibid., p. 196.

5. "Latest Intelligence from Washington: Proceedings of Congress," *New York Daily Times*, January 24, 1854, p. 1.

6. Russell, p. 198.

Chapter 3. The Kansas-Nebraska Bill in Congress

1. "Slavery Extension: The Nebraska Bill in Congress," *New York Daily Times*, January 24, 1854, p. 2.

2. Ibid.

3. Stephen Douglas. Letter to J. H. Crane, D. M. Johnson, and L. J. Eastin, December 17, 1853. Robert W. Johannsen, ed., *The Letters of Stephen A. Douglas* (Urbana, Ill.: University of Illinois Press, 1961), pp. 270–271.

4. "Renewal of Slavery Agitation—The Nebraska Bill," *New York Daily Times,* January 24, 1854, p. 4.

5. "Latest Intelligence from Washington: Prospects of the Nebraska Bill," *New York Daily Times*, February 3, 1854, p. 1.

6. "Northern Sentiment on the Little Giant and his Nebraska Bill," *New York Daily Times*, February 18, 1854, p. 4.

7. "Latest Intelligence from Washington: Debate on the Nebraska Bill," *New York Daily Times*, February 6, 1854, p. 1.

8. Salmon P. Chase, speech before the Senate, *Appendix to The Congressional Globe*, February 3, 1854, p. 134.

9. J.W.R., "The Repeal of the Missouri Compromise," *New York Daily Times*, January 27, 1854, p. 2.

10. Archibald Dixon, speech before the Senate, *Appendix to The Congressional Globe*, February 4, 1854, pp. 140–141.

11. "Latest Intelligence from Washington: Prospects of the Nebraska Bill," *New York Daily Times*, February 14, 1854, p. 1.

12. "Thirty-Third Congress: First Session," *Congressional Globe*, December 7, 1853, pp. 1–2.

13. Sam Houston, speech before the Senate, *Appendix to The Congressional Globe*, February 15, 1854, p. 206.

14. Andrew P. Butler, speech before the Senate, *Appendix to The Congressional Globe*, February 24, 1854, p. 232.

15. "Latest Intelligence from Washington: Prospects of the Nebraska Bill," *New York Daily Times*, February 28, 1854, p. 1.

16. "Latest Intelligence from Washington: Prospects of the Nebraska Bill," *New York Daily Times*, March 1, 1854, p. 1.

17. "Latest Intelligence from Washington: Prospects of the Nebraska Bill," *New York Daily Times*, March 7, 1854, p. 1.

18. Ibid.

19. Robert R. Russell, "The Issues in the Congressional Struggle Over the Kansas-Nebraska Bill, 1854," *Journal of Southern American History*, Vol. 29, No. 2, May 1963, p. 208.

20. Gerrit Smith, speech before the House of Representatives, *Appendix to The Congressional Globe*, April 6, 1854, p. 520.

21. William Cullom, speech before the House of Representatives, *Appendix to The Congressional Globe*, April 11, 1854, p. 538.

22. "From Washington: Nebraska Movement," *New York Daily Times*, April 25, 1854, p. 1.

23. Russell, p. 209.

24. "Speech of Senator Seward: The Constitution and Compromises," *New York Daily Times,* May 27, 1854, p. 1.

Chapter 4. The Race for Kansas

1. William Elsey Connelly, *Kansas Territorial Governors* (Topeka, Kans.: Crane and Company Publishers, 1900), p. 11.

2. Kansas State Historical Society, "New England Emigrant Aid Company Papers," n.d. <http://www.kshs.org/ms/neweng.htm#bio> (September 5, 2002).

3. William Phillips, *The Conquest of Kansas, by Missouri and her Allies* (Boston: Phillips, Sampson, and Co., 1856), pp. 30–31.

4. Ibid., pp. 31–32.

5. Ibid., pp. 32–33.

6. Abraham Lincoln, "Repeal of the Missouri Compromise: The Right of Self-Government" [A speech given at Peoria, Illinois, October 16, 1854]. Ida M. Tarbell, Ed. *Selections from the Letters, Speeches, and State Papers of Abraham Lincoln*. (Boston: Ginn and Co., 1911), pp. 18–19.

7. Phillips, p. 42.

8. "Late Election in Kansas," *Kansas Free State*, January 3, 1855, p. 1.

9. "Letter From a Southerner," *Herald of Freedom*, January 20, 1855, p. 1.

10. Alice Nichols, *Bleeding Kansas* (New York: Oxford University Press, 1954), p. 28.

11. Ibid., p. 29.

12. Ibid.

13. "Wetting down the Dog Star," *Squatter Sovereign*, May 1, 1855, p. 2.

14. George S. Park, Letter to the Editor, *Herald of Freedom*, May 5, 1855, p. 2.

15. Phillips, pp. 102–106.

Chapter 5. Bloody Revenge

1. "Great Excitement in Atchison—An Abolitionist Preacher Shipped on a Raft," *Sovereign Squatter*, August 21, 1855, p. 2.

2. "The Kansas War," *Sovereign Squatter*, December 12, 1855, p. 1.

3. "The Invasion of Kansas," *Kansas Tribune*, December 10, 1855, p. 2.

4. "Arrests—U.S. Troops—Sheriff Jones Shot," *Kansas Free State*, April 23, 1856, p. 2.

5. Ibid.

6. Thomas Goodrich, *War to the Knife: Bleeding Kansas, 1854–1861* (Mechanicsburg, Pa.: Stackpole Books, 1998), pp. 114–117.

7. Ibid., p. 117.

8. "Bravery of the Yankees," *Squatter Sovereign*, May 27, 1856, p. 2.

9. Tom and Carolyn Ward, "Andrew H. Reeder," *KSGenWeb Project, 1998*, <http://skyways.lib.ks.us/genweb/archives/1918ks/bior/reederah.html> (January 26, 2002).

Chapter 6. Prairie Politics

1. Alice Nichols, *Bleeding Kansas* (New York: Oxford University Press, 1954), pp. 131–132.

2. Craig Miner, "Lane and Lincoln: A Mysterious Connection," *Kansas History*, Vol. 24, No. 3, Autumn 2001, p. 192.

3. "Governor Geary," *Kansas Weekly Herald*, October 11, 1856, p. 2.

4. William Elsey Connelley, *Kansas Territorial Governors* (Topeka, Kans.: Crane and Company, 1900), p. 113.

5. Connelley, p. 105.

6. Nichols, p. 202.

7. Kenneth M. Stampp, *America in 1857* (New York: Oxford University Press, 1990), p. 320.

8. "Correspondence of the Era," *Geary City Era*, January 2, 1858, p. 2.

Chapter 7. More Trouble in Kansas Territory

1. G. Murlin Welch, *Border Warfare in Southeastern Kansas, 1856–1859* (Pleasanton, Kans.: Linn County Publishers, 1977), p. 37.

2. Ibid., pp. 41–47.

3. William G. Cutler, "Territorial History, Part 52: The Vote on the Lecompton Constitution," *History of the State of Kansas*, n.d. (originally published in 1883), <http://www.ukans.edu/carrie/kancoll/books/cutler/terrhist/terrhist-p52.html#THE_VOTE_ON_THE_LECOMPTON-CONSTITUTION> (August 23, 2002).

4. Kenneth M. Stampp, Ed. *The Causes of the Civil War*. (New York: Simon and Schuster, 1991), p. 108.

5. "Robbers," *Herald of Freedom*, May 22, 1858, p. 2.

6. Cutler, "Linn County, Part 4: The Marais des Cygne Massacre," *History of the State of Kansas*, n.d. (originally

published in 1883), <http://www.ku.edu/carrie/kancoll/ books/ cutler/linn/linn-co-p4.html#THE_MARAIS_DES_ CYGNES_MASSACRE> (August 23, 2002).

7. Kansas State Historical Society, "History of Marais des Cygnes Massacre State Historical Site," 1999, <http:// www.kshs.org/places/marahist.htm> (August 23, 2002).

8. "Horrible Tragedy!—Cold Blooded Murder," *Herald of Freedom*, May 29, 1858, p. 2.

9. Welch, pp. 98–99.

10. Ibid., pp. 99–100.

11. Welch, pp. 100–101.

12. James Monaghan, *Civil War on the Western Border 1854–1865* (Boston: Little, Brown, and Co., 1955), pp. 103–104.

13. "Fort Scott Difficulties," *Kansas Weekly Herald*, June 5, 1858, p. 2.

14. "Views of a Citizen of Kansas on the Late Disturbances," *New York Daily Times*, June 4, 1858, p. 3.

15. "Captain Montgomery and his Proceedings in Kansas—Who is Responsible?" *New York Daily Times*, June 8, 1858, p. 2.

Chapter 8. The Road to Statehood

1. "Leavenworth Constitution," *Kansas Weekly Herald*, April 17, 1858, p. 2.

2. Thomas Ewing, Jr., "Kansas Politics," *New York Times*, May 28, 1858, p. 3.

3. William G. Cutler, "Territorial History, Part 55," *History of the State of Kansas*, n.d. (originally published in 1883), <http://www.ukans.edu/carrie/kancoll/books/cutler/ terrhist/terrhist-p55.html#KANSAS_AFFAIRS_ AT_WASHINGTON> (August 25, 2002).

4. J. W. Denver, "Address to the People of Kansas Territory," *Kansas Weekly Herald*, October 16, 1858, p. 2.

5. "The Dawn of a New Era in Kansas," *Kansas Weekly Herald*, November 13, 1858, p. 1.

6. "Another Farce," *Kansas National Democrat*, February 17, 1959, p. 2.

7. William G. Cutler, "Territorial History, Part 57," *History of the State of Kansas*, n.d. (originally published in 1883), <http://www.ukans.edu/carrie/kancoll/books/cutler/terrhist/terrhist-p57.html> (January 26, 2002).

8. Noble L. Prentis, *A History of Kansas* (Winfield, Kans.: E. P. Greer, 1899), p. 79.

9. William G. Cutler, "Territorial History, Part 60," *History of the State of Kansas*, n.d. (originally published in 1883), <http://www.ukans.edu/carrie/kancoll/books/cutler/terrhist/terrhist-p60.html> (January 26, 2002).

10. Proceedings in the Senate, January 21, 1861, *Congressional Globe: Thirty-Sixth Congress, Second Session*, January 22, 1861, pp. 483–489.

Chapter 9. Looking Back on the Kansas-Nebraska Act

1. Henry Wilson, "The Record of the Slave Power," *Causes of the Civil War*, 3rd ed., ed. Kenneth Stampp (New York: Simon and Schuster, 1991), p. 31.

2. Jefferson Davis, "The Injured South," *Causes of the Civil War*, 3rd ed., ed. Kenneth Stampp (New York: Simon and Schuster, 1991), p. 49.

3. Thomas Goodrich, *War to the Knife: Bleeding Kansas, 1854–1861* (Mechanicsburg, Pa.: Stackpole Books, 1998), p. 13.

4. Mary F. Beeson, "Autobiography of Mary F. Beeson," *KanColl: The Kansas Collection* n.d. <http://www.ukans.edu/carrie/kancoll/articles/beeson.htm> (August 31, 2002).

5. Kevin Abing, "Before Bleeding Kansas: Christian Missionaries, Slavery, and the Shawnee Indians in Pre-Territorial Kansas, 1844–1854," *Kansas History*, Spring 2001, Vol. 24, No. 1, pp. 57–58.

6. C. E. Cory, "Slavery in Kansas," *Transactions of the Kansas State Historical Society, 1901–1902* (Topeka, Kans.: W. Y. Morgan, 1902), p. 239.

7. Bliss Isely and W. M. Richards, *Four Centuries in Kansas* (Wichita, Kans.: The McCormick-Mathers Co., 1936), p. 162.

8. Jay Monaghan, *Civil War on the Western Border 1854–1865* (Boston: Little, Brown and Co., 1955), p. 122.

★ FURTHER READING ★

Arnold, James A., and Roberta Wiener. *Divided in Two: The Road to Civil War, 1861.* Minneapolis: The Lerner Publishing Group, 2001.

Bonner, Mike. *Stephen A. Douglas: Champion of the Union.* Broomhall, Pa.: Chelsea House Publishers, 2001.

Brackett, Virginia. *John Brown: Abolitionist.* Broomhall, Pa.: Chelsea House Publishers, 2001.

Brewer, Paul. *The American Civil War.* Orlando: Raintree Steck-Vaughn Publishers, 1999.

Naden, Corinne J., and Rose Blue. *Why Fight?: The Causes of the American Civil War.* Orlando: Raintree Steck-Vaughn Publishers, 1999.

Robinson-Masters, Nancy. *Kansas.* Danbury, Conn.: Children's Press, 1999.

Zeinert, Karen. *Tragic Prelude: Bleeding Kansas.* North Haven, Conn.: Shoe String Press, 2001.

★ INTERNET ADDRESSES ★

"Topics in Kansas History: War 'Bleeding Kansas.'" *Kansas State Historical Society.* 2003. <http://www.kshs.org/research/topics/war/bleeding.htm>.

"Bleeding Kansas Gallery." *Kansas Collection.* n.d. <http://www.kancoll.org/galbks.htm>.

Cutler, William G. "*History of the State of Kansas.*" *Kansas Collection Books.* April 1999. (originally published in 1883). <http://www.kancoll.org/books/cutler/>.

★ INDEX ★